CRITICAL RACE THEORY IN TEACHER EDUCATION

CRITICAL RACE THEORY IN TEACHER EDUCATION

INFORMING CLASSROOM CULTURE AND PRACTICE

EDITED BY

Keonghee Tao Han
Judson Laughter

Foreword by Tyrone C. Howard

TEACHERS COLLEGE PRESS
TEACHERS COLLEGE | COLUMBIA UNIVERSITY
NEW YORK AND LONDON

Published by Teachers College Press, 1234 Amsterdam Avenue, New York, NY 10027

Copyright © 2019 by Teachers College, Columbia University

Cover art courtesy of Emilie Leger (top) and Enchantedgal-Stock / Kimberly Crick (bottom).

Library of Congress Cataloging-in-Publication Data is available at loc.gov

Names: Han, Keonghee Tao, editor.
Title: Critical race theory in teacher education : informing classroom
 culture and practice / edited by Tao Han, Judson Laughter.
Description: First edition. | New York : Teachers College Press, [2019] |
 Includes bibliographical references and index. |
Identifiers: LCCN 2018059842 (print) | LCCN 2019013539 (ebook) |
 ISBN   9780807777756 (ebook)
 ISBN   9780807761373 (pbk. : alk. paper)
Subjects: LCSH: Teachers—Training of—Social aspects—United States. |
 Teaching—Social aspects—United States. | Multicultural education—United
 States. | Minorities—Education—United States. | Culturally relevant
 pedagogy—United States. | Critical pedagogy—United States.
Classification: LCC LB1715 (ebook) | LCC LB1715 .C733 2019 (print) |
DDC   370.71/1—dc23
LC record available at https://lccn.loc.gov/2018059842

ISBN 978-0-8077-6137-3 (paper)
ISBN 978-0-8077-6169-4 (hardcover)
ISBN 978-0-8077-7775-6 (ebook)

Printed on acid-free paper
Manufactured in the United States of America

Contents

Foreword

Teaching matters. Teachers matter. Preparing teachers with a racial consciousness in mind also matters. Hence, the manner in which teachers are prepared to work, teach, inspire, connect, and lead in today's educational landscape is a vital undertaking. Teaching remains one of the most complex undertakings in the United States and the world. At a time of increasing privatization of public education, the persistence of standardized testing, and greater degrees of accountability, one thing that has remained ever present has been racial and ethnic diversity in schools. This new normal of diversity is embraced by many because it represents a new, more diverse United States, while for others the bustling diversity is symbolic of a change that they would prefer not to see, and long for the day of making "America great again." The tension between what the United States is becoming, and what it once was serves as one of the most important challenges for today's educators and teacher educators.

Some of the most important stakeholders who will serve as arbiters of how the new racial realities will be understood are classroom teachers. Thus, it is vital that racial literacy (Stevenson, 2014) be an essential staple in not only the training of new teachers, but is also incorporated into the framework of teacher learning (e.g., in-service teachers) writ large. Racial illiteracy cannot be allowed to remain as rampant as it is in today's schools and society. In part, racial illiteracy has played a major factor in today's opportunity and outcome gaps that continue to depict students of color as "underachievers." To the contrary, schools have underachieved, and by and large schools of education have underachieved in centering the racial realities in today's schools at the center of their work in preparing future educators. To be clear, incorporating racial realities in teacher education will not be easy, but it is necessary. In this work, Tao Han and Judson Laughter assemble an amazing group of scholars who boldly inform us that race matters in teacher education and how we must respond.

It is important to denote that race is more than just phenotype and physical characteristics. Race delineates power, hegemony, ideology, and a way of seeing the world politically, economically, and socially. The authors in this work interrogate race across space, time, and place, which has important implications for teachers, teacher educators, and teachers in training. No longer can teacher education in the United States rely solely on age-old approaches to teaching and learning. The one-size-fits-all approach must be put to rest. Diversity and differentiation are the order of the day in preparing teachers. It will be imperative to ask new questions, adopt new paradigms, incorporate new theories, and discover innovative pedagogies that inform a reality that many who do this work are grossly unfamiliar.

Teacher education must acknowledge its complicity in some of the very issues that it says it stands against, such as social injustice, anti-Blackness, homophobia, transphobia, hegemony, trauma, power, and control within its own ranks. Far too many teacher candidates of color feel invisible, silenced, violated, and overlooked within their own teacher education programs. Others wonder where are the more critical approaches to teacher education that focus on anti-colonial education, indigenous epistemologies, and education as a praxis of freedom as Paulo Freire teaches us. The works in this book do a compelling job of challenging teacher education as a field, and teacher educators as actors in this field, to do better, teach better, challenge injustice better, and prepare teachers in an authentic way that recognizes racial realities, the persistence of racial injustice, and the demographic realities of our current racial state.

The work of teacher education cannot remain isolated only within its own nation-state context. Ours is a global community, and nations such as the United States have to learn from across its borders to understand how African, Latin, and Australian nations are preparing their teachers within a critical, theoretical, and historical context. We need to interrogate race and racism in education from Asian American and Fijian perspectives. In this work, Andrew Peterson and Rob Hattam ask a poignant question, "Are there common threads across the globe about how we prepare teachers?" One can question if the United States is best prepared to teach teachers in a more racially diverse nation when the very foundation of the country was steeped in what Charles Mills (1997) refers to as a racial contract wherein "white supremacy is the unnamed political system that has made the modern world what it is today" (p. 1). Dismantling White supremacy in teaching and teacher education needs to be a central goal of educators.

Identifying pedagogies, principles, and policies that reclaim the humanity of people of color is essential, and teacher education must be at the forefront of this work. Given the growing diversity in schools with a homogeneous, mostly White teacher and teacher education reality, the challenge can seem daunting, but it is not impossible. Running from race cannot be accepted, avoiding racism needs sharp critique, and any semblance of what Robin DiAngelo (2018) refers to as "white fragility" must be eradicated. Any actions such as fear, guilt, discomfort, or uneasiness around discussing race and racism needs to be viewed as an effort to maintain White supremacy, and all the power dimensions that come along with it. We must do better. Not only are issues of race paramount, but when they intersect with toxic masculinity and patriarchy it has devastating effects for certain populations.

Critical race scholar Kimberlé Crenshaw (2015) reminds us that "the educational, social, and economic factors that funnel Black girls and other girls of color onto pathways to nowhere and render their academic and professional vulnerabilities invisible" (p.15) must be a primary focus of schools.

This work is important because it challenges teacher education to be more racially conscious, not because it is convenient, but because it is the just and right approach to take. The "interest convergence conundrum" must be exposed for what it is, and teacher education must take a stand to show that it sees and understands the melanization of today's global student population or it will cease to exist. *Critical Race Theory in Teacher Education* has put forth a challenge that requires all of our attention. Not only does this work have important implications for teaching and learning in schools, it also provides an epistemological and moral call for us to do justice work with a global framework that captures, reclaims, and restores our humanity.

—Tyrone C. Howard, UCLA

REFERENCES

Crenshaw, K. (2015). *Black girls matter: Pushed out, overpoliced, and under protected*. New York, NY: African American Policy Forum.

DiAngelo, R. (2018). *White fragility. Why it's so hard for white people to talk about racism*. Boston, MA: Beacon Press.

Mills, C. (1997). *The racial contract*. Ithaca, NY: Cornell University Press.

Stevenson, H. (2014). *Promoting racial literacy in schools. Differences that make a difference*. New York, NY: Teachers College Press.

CHAPTER 1

Critical Race Theory in Teacher Education
Coalitions for the Future

Judson Laughter and *Keonghee Tao Han*

This chapter provides a baseline understanding and history of Critical Race Theory (CRT). General tenets of CRT are presented and made available to all succeeding chapters. The authors included in this collection were provided this introduction during the writing of their own chapters and so do not repeat what is included here. We then give an overview of the three sections of this collection, laying out the chapter design in each, and providing a brief abstract of each chapter and how they connect within each section and across the entire book.

INTRODUCTION: CRITICAL RACE THEORY

People have always noticed differences in one another; differing skin tones, facial features, and hair textures appear in the earliest artwork. However, the concept of race is something deeper than phenotype; race represents a product of Enlightenment mythologies:

> The myth of race refers not to the fact that physically distinguishable populations of humans exist, but rather to the belief that races are populations or peoples whose physical differences are innately linked with significant differences in mental capacities, and that these innate hierarchical differences are measurable by the cultural achievements of such populations. (Montagu, 1997, p. 44)

Race delineates a power relationship, not a collection of phenotypic features. During the period of the Enlightenment, promotion of universal human rights created a contradiction between utopian desires and economic realities. The concept of race represents the rationalization, not the transcendence, of that dialectic. Talk of universal human rights could continue because the economic foundations of slave labor (the enslaved persons

1

themselves) were dehumanized, and therefore seen as undeserving of these rights; the naturalization of this distinction followed (Montagu, 1997).

The presence of race in our current society remains the focus of dialectical contradictions from multiple interpretive lenses:

> There is a continuous temptation to think of race as an *essence*, as something fixed, concrete, and objective. And there is also an opposite temptation: to imagine race as a mere *illusion*, a purely ideological construct which some ideal non-racist social order would eliminate. It is necessary to challenge both these positions, to disrupt and reframe the rigid and bipolar manner in which they are posed and debated, and to transcend the presumably irreconcilable relationship between them. (Omi & Winant, 1994, p. 54)

Critical Race Theory descends from several schools of thought attempting to engage this dialectic between essence and illusion, and has given rise to several more specific critical theories both within and beyond the fields of education.

History

Traditional legal discourse viewed the law as a finite set of rules from which judges made decisions (White, 1972). If the law did not directly address or provide precedent for a particular situation, then that situation did not fall under the purview of the law; until laws were passed to address the situation, the court would remain silent. Social forces and historical distance made no difference to the application of the law. In the 1920s and 1930s, realism came to place a strong philosophical influence on the law as its proponents contended that "the application of behavioral sciences and statistical method to legal analysis would lead to better and more creative forms of legal thought and, ultimately, social policy" (Tate, 1997, p. 207).

From this critique, scholars within a movement that came to be known as Critical Legal Studies (CLS) maintained that the ideology inherent in traditional legal discourse only served the hegemony, with a caveat via Gramsci that even the dominated classes offered their support. CLS theorists believed legal doctrine must be situated in its own historical and material moment and gives birth to internal contradictions and external inconsistencies, the transcendence of which drive the development of legal theory (Unger, 1983).

Just as critical theory must always critique itself, the dialectical contradiction harbored within CLS attacked formal structures in the law while avoiding the material lives of the oppressed (Delgado, 1987). A particular critic of CLS brought the presence of race full into the discourse of the law. Derrick Bell took the *Brown v. Board of Education* decision of 1954, the "crown jewel of U.S. Supreme Court jurisprudence" (Delgado & Stefancic, 2001), as the preeminent site of legal critique in America. *Brown* seemed to overturn centuries of racial oppression, but Bell's investigation revealed how the American legal system remained firmly in the hands of the ruling class. A new understanding of the law was necessary before racial oppression would end and Bell's work served as the source of the critical theory now known as Critical Race Theory. CRT was "rooted in the social missions and struggles of the 1960s that sought justice, liberation, and economic empowerment; thus, from its inception, it has had both academic and social activist goals" (Tate, 1997, p. 197).

In successive years, two of Bell's students, Richard Delgado (1987) and Kimberlé Crenshaw (1988), laid out what they felt were the shortcomings of CLS: Race seemed to play at best a supporting role to class in the examination of society. "A movement that has no theory of race and class is apt to seem increasingly irrelevant" (Delgado & Stefancic, 2001, p. 95). Delgado (1987) felt CLS equated racism and classism unfairly, rejected the possibilities of incremental change, and relied on logic and reason too heavily as human directors. Crenshaw (1988) thought that CLS did not analyze society through the reality of those being oppressed, failed to understand the hegemonic power of racism, and minimized the transformative power of an active social theory. The work of Bell and his students addressed inherent contradictions within the law, laying out three primary dialectical contradictions: constitutional contradiction, interest convergence, and threat to social status.

In the U.S. Constitution, the rationalization of race creates a foundational legacy out of the contradiction between human rights and property rights: "When confronted with the decision between White racism and justice, the framers of the Constitution chose racism and the rewards of property" (Tate, 1997, p. 214). The Constitution not only allowed private property, but laid out specific measures to protect it, primarily in granting the franchise only to White landowners.

Interest convergence (Bell, 1980, 2005) represents the contradiction between the interests of humanization and the interests of hegemony. In short, the rights of the racially oppressed will only be supported when they are consistent with the needs of those in power. The contradiction maintains the distinction between the needs of the oppressed and the needs of the oppressor, thereby maintaining the existence of the oppressor and their defining power over the oppressed. In practical terms, the existence in the law of the Fourteenth Amendment or the Civil Rights Act will come to nothing if they diverge from the interests of the oppressor.

A corollary defining the limits of interest convergence is the *threat to social status*, which represents the contradiction between the proclamation of liberation and the rejection of the necessary means. That is, the oppressor will provide immediate retribution should the requests of the oppressed reach too far. The transcendence of any of these contradictions requires a critical theory imbued with the theoretical, active, and reflective critique of race. The transcendence of these contradictions in the United States is the transcendence of race as a dehumanizing category. CRT continues the work of uncovering dialectical contradictions in the United States through the praxis of theory, activity, and reflection focused on race and its social contradiction between essence and illusion.

As a systemic and endemic reality, racism in the United States represents a structure of privilege and oppression correlated to socially created differences that appear normal and natural to many, a universal set of truths to remain unquestioned (Ladson-Billings, 1998; Ladson-Billings & Tate, 1995; Solórzano & Yosso, 2001). This system is reproduced everywhere, but we often fail to see it. It is present in the unspoken benefits offered to people with light skin (McIntosh, 1989). It creates the systems we use to practice science (Scheurich & Young, 1997). It defines us all, even those who fight against it.

The Move to Education

In the years following *Brown* and the dissolution of the *Public School Way Back When* (Ladson-Billings, 1999), teachers and teacher education programs had to face a diversity they were not prepared for and did not accept. The 1960s saw a rash of sociologists and educators defining this new diversity in terms of "culturally deprived" and "culturally disadvantaged": "The school's role was to *compensate* for the children's presumed lack of socialization and cultural resources" (Ladson-Billings, 1999, p. 216, emphasis in original). Schools became sites for continued dehumanization, all under the guise of wanting to benefit those less fortunate. Subtly, the desegregation of the 1950s and 1960s shifted the oppression of the *subaltern* from one of force to one of coercion using the school system as a means of social reproduction. New theories and new applications became necessary to undo this damage, to fight the new forms that racism was taking on.

The work of CRT in the courts caught the attention of theorists who saw connections between the law and education. In 1995, Gloria Ladson-Billings and William Tate proposed the adoption of CRT as an analytical tool for critiquing education theory and notions of multiculturalism. Ladson-Billings and Tate number three primary propositions whose development argues for "a critical race theoretical perspective in education analogous to that of critical race theory in legal scholarship" (p. 47).

Race continues to be a significant factor in determining inequity in the United States. The 2008, 2012, and 2016 presidential contests and recent activism surrounding the policing of Black bodies has brought the issue of race to the forefront of American consciousness like few things have in the past several decades. The presence of race as a significant factor in measuring and understanding inequity is undeniable in the face of condemnatory statistical data concerning "high school dropout rates, suspension rates, and incarceration rates" (Ladson-Billings & Tate, 1995, p. 48). However, the utility of studying and theorizing race has come under question by some postmodern scholars. Ladson-Billings and Tate saw the binary between race as illusion and race as essence as indicative of the questions theorists pose. Primarily, we must address why we continue to use the concept of race if it fails to make sense, if we cannot provide clear definitions of useful and definable distinctions. As compared to class and gender, race remains undertheorized in a society where explanations based on class and gender are insufficient.

U.S. society is based on property rights. On the legal basis of the constitutional contradiction, Ladson-Billings and Tate (1995) stake a claim and also base later work laying out America's confusion between capitalism and democracy. Through concepts like interest convergence, the American hegemony bends even supposed advances in human rights to its own benefit.

The intersection of race and property creates an analytical tool through which we can understand social inequity. If race is still significant for defining inequity in the United States and if we define ourselves through a fundamental confusion of human rights and property rights, then the intersection of these promotes "the construction of Whiteness as the ultimate property" (Ladson-Billings & Tate, 1995, p. 58). Our American mythology of possessing human rights is tied to the possession of property, of which being White is the most important. Even our constitution maintains a difference between *free* and *slave* based on racial characteristics, a precedent followed throughout our judicial and legislative history. The confluence of race and property produces the ultimate objectification, the ultimate dehumanization.

Tenets of Critical Race Theory

As a school of critical thought, CRT represents an evolving collection of ideas useful both as a theoretical framework for designing inquiry and as an analytical framework for working with data. In any application, race remains centered but often intersects and overlaps with other systems of oppression. It is important to remember that CRT is a *theory* and thus does not on its own work to drive method. It is through application of theory to practice that method becomes defined, through work like Critical Race Pedagogy (Lynn, Jennings, & Hughes, 2013) or Critical Race Methodology (Solórzano & Yosso, 2002).

Depending on the specific question or context, a critical race theorist might highlight, uncover, or problematize certain tenets over others. In Table 1.1, we collate several seminal works and align tenets across authors and contexts to establish a collection of tenets commonly appearing in the engagement of CRT. As CRT continues to evolve with the ongoing development of race and racism, we assume these tenets will also respond to these shifts.

OVERVIEW OF THE BOOK

For 30 years, CRT has been a primary driver and advocate for social justice in education. CRT has continued to evolve, ever changing to facilitate the voice of the voiceless. Our focus in this volume is to further infuse CRT in teacher education, as traditional epistemologies that have served and preserved mainstream educational purposes often do not work for diverse populations. This volume examines the history, the present moment, and the future for CRT in teacher education as a tool for social justice. Part I describes the foundations of CRT. Part II examines expansions of CRT into new contexts. Part III looks beyond CRT to other epistemologies often dismissed in White conceptions of teacher preparation. Throughout the chapters within and across this volume, authors collaborate across demographic lines that too often separate us as we work together toward social justice and compassion.

Part I: CRT and Teacher Education

In Part I, we start with the basics, exploring the tradition and longevity of CRT in teacher education. Chapters in this section do not follow a general outline because they are working together to establish a baseline for the rest of the book. DaVonna Graham, Adam Alvarez, Derric Heck, Jawanza Rand, and Rich Milner open this collection by presenting a look at how CRT has been used both as an analytical framework and a tool for improvement in teacher education.

Ashlee Anderson and Brittany Aronson present a chapter paired with that by Cheryl Matias and Jared Aldern to look at two sides of how CRT is useful in driving teacher education, examining teacher diversity and teacher Whiteness. In the last chapter of this section, Gwendolyn Thompson McMillon and Rebecca Rogers present research by two teacher educators (one Black and one White) teaching different sections of the same class.

Part II: Beyond Black and White

In Part II, we present chapters on the second wave of CRT through the presentation of several schools of research that have worked to push CRT beyond a Black/White binary and into the lived experience of multiple intersecting groups. These chapters are not designed to replace CRT but to

Table 1.1. Tenets of Critical Race Theory

General Tenet/ Author	Racism Is Systemic	Rebuke of the System and Neo-liberalism	Activist Theory / Interest Convergence	Use of Voice	Across Disciplines
Milner (2007)	Racism endemic, pervasive, widespread, and ingrained		Interest convergence	Centrality of narrative & counternarratives	
Delgado & Stefancic (2001)	Racism is ordinary, not aberrational	Race and racism are products of social thought; differential racialization; anti-essentialism	Interest Convergence (material determinism) and Colorblind concepts of equality	Unique voice of color	
Solórzano & Yosso (2001)	The centrality and intersectionality of race and racism	The challenge to dominant ideology	The commitment to social justice	The centrality of experiential knowledge	The interdisciplinary perspective
Ladson-Billings (1998)	Racism is normal in American society	Critique of liberalism	Interest convergence	Sometimes employs storytelling to analyze culture	
Tate (1997)	Racism is endemic	Portrays dominant legal claims of neutrality as camouflage	Reinterprets civil rights law in light of its limitations	Insists on a contextual/ historical examination	Racism crosses epistemological boundaries
Ladson-Billings & Tate (1995)	Racism as endemic and deeply ingrained	Challenging claims of neutrality and meritocracy	Reinterpretation of ineffective civil rights law	Naming one's own reality	

build on CRT in ways that acknowledge and benefit more people in more contexts.

Rachel Salas introduces LatCrit and its focus on immigration, linguistic racism, multilingual education, census categories for race and ethnicity, and other issues specific to Latinx contexts. Tao Han discusses AsianCrit and nativist responses to immigration and the myth of a model minority. Angela Jaime and Caskey Russell describes TribalCrit and its use of CRT as a foundation by which to address experiences of tribal people and liminal spaces to which they have been marginalized. Eric Teman introduces QueerCrit in a move beyond race and ethnicity. Finally, Andrew Torres and Lamar Johnson theorize BlackCrit as a response to CRT and how we need specific focus on the marginalization of Black bodies.

Part III: Beyond CRT

In Part I, we lay out the history and theory of CRT and its applications to education and teacher preparation. In Part II, we move beyond a Black/White binary to consider applications of CRT across various groups, contexts, and identities in the United States. Some might consider Parts I and II a complete collection and stop there. However, CRT is a critical theory and must seek tools for its own evolution to continue countering institutionalized, value-laden ideologies like meritocracy, colorblindness, and neoliberalism beyond U.S. contexts.

As Nunn (2000) described, the law (and thus the critique proposed by CRT) is not universal. In fact, Parts I and II are similarly hobbled in that they are relegated to a Euro-American context that might not be the best for moving teacher education forward. If CRT understands social justice as a driving ideal for teacher education, then materialism, competition, individualism, and narcissism are not to be pursued. While CRT fights these tendencies, perhaps looking beyond our Euro-American context will help us imagine new ways of seeing the relationships of our identities and our contexts.

In Part III, we expand CRT with an intention to include indigenous epistemologies from a global context. Both refute a dominant perspective, insisting there ought to be multiple storied truths. While CRT and indigenous epistemologies share commonalities as oppressed thoughts, values, and belief systems, CRT alone cannot suffice for educators and education participants to understand and incorporate indigenous perspectives. To that end, we include the following chapters.

Adeline Borti opens this part with Ghanaian epistemology and examines the effects that colonialism has had on teacher education in Ghana. Then, Cynthia Brock, Ufemia Camaitoga, and Pauline Harris present Fijian research ethics and the concepts of *vanua* and *talanoa*. Lydiah Ngana and John Kambutu continue with Kenyan epistemology. In the last chapter of this section Qi Sun and Reed Scull close by presenting Confucian epis-temologies.

Conclusion

In the closing chapter, Andrew Peterson and Rob Hattam look across the chapters presented and synthesize the lessons to be learned for teacher ed-ucators who want to prepare teachers as agents of social change and com-passion. Are there educational threads common around the world? How do we promote and sustain inter-group dialogue around the preparation of teachers? Let's find out together.

REFERENCES

Bell, D. A. (1980). *Brown v. Board of Education* and the interest-convergence dilemma. *Harvard Law Review, 93*, 518–533.

Bell, D. A. (2005). The unintended lessons in *Brown v. Board of Education. New York Law School Law Review, 49*, 1053–1067.

Crenshaw, K. (1988). Race, reform, retrenchment: Transformation and legitimation in anti-discrimination law. *Harvard Law Review, 101*, 1331–1387.

Delgado, R. (1987). The ethereal scholar: Does critical legal studies have what minorities want? *Harvard Civil Rights–Civil Liberties Law Review, 22*, 301–322.

Delgado, R., & Stefancic, J. (2001). *Critical race theory: An introduction.* New York, NY: New York University Press.

Ladson-Billings, G. (1998). Just what is critical race theory and what's it doing in a "nice" field like education? *International Journal of Qualitative Studies in Education, 11*, 7–24.

Ladson-Billings, G. (1999). Preparing teachers for diverse student populations: A critical race theory perspective. *Review of Research in Education, 24*, 211–247.

Ladson-Billings, G., & Tate, W. F. (1995). Toward a critical race theory of education. *Teachers College Record, 97*(1), 47–68.

Lynn, M., Jennings, M. E., & Hughes, S. (2013). Critical race pedagogy 2.0: Lessons from Derrick Bell. *Race Ethnicity and Education, 16*, 603–628.

McIntosh, P. (1989). White privilege: Unpacking the invisible knapsack. *Peace and Freedom, 49*(4), 10–12.

Milner, H. R. (2007). Race, culture, and researcher positionality: Working through dangers seen, unseen, and unforeseen. *Educational Researcher, 36*, 388–400.

Montagu, A. (1997). *Man's most dangerous myth: The fallacy of race* (6th ed.). Walnut Creek, CA: AltaMira.

Nunn, K. B. (2000). Law as a Eurocentric enterprise. In R. Delgado & J. Stefancic (Eds.), *Critical race theory: The cutting edge* (2nd ed., pp. 429–436). Philadelphia, PA: Temple University Press.

Omi, M., & Winant, H. (1994). *Racial formation in the United States: From the 1960s to the 1990s* (2nd ed.). New York, NY: Routledge.

Scheurich, J. J., & Young, M. D. (1997). Coloring epistemologies: Are our research epistemologies racially biased? *Educational Researcher, 26,* 4–16.

Solórzano, D. G., & Yosso, T. J. (2001). From racial stereotyping and deficit discourse toward a critical race theory in teacher education. *Multicultural Education, 9,* 2–8.

Solórzano, D. G., & Yosso, T. J. (2002). Critical race methodology: Counterstorytelling as an analytical framework for education research. *Qualitative Inquiry, 8,* 23–44.

Tate, W. F. (1997). Critical race theory and education: History, theory, and implications. In M. Apple (Ed.), *Review of research in education* (pp. 195–247). Washington, DC: American Educational Research Association.

Unger, R. M. (1983). The critical legal studies movement. *Harvard Law Review, 96,* 561–675.

White, G. (1972). From sociological jurisprudence to realism: Jurisprudence and social change in early twentieth-century America. *Virginia Law Review, 58,* 999–1028.

Part I

CRT AND TEACHER EDUCATION

CHAPTER 2

Race, Violence, and Teacher Education

An Overview of Critical Race Theory in Teacher Education

DaVonna L. Graham, Adam J. Alvarez, Derric I. Heck,
Jawanza K. Rand, and H. Richard Milner IV

We provide a historical overview of research focused on Critical Race Theory (CRT) and teacher education, outlining three salient themes emerging from the established literature as a call for further study. We hope this chapter challenges researchers to deepen the three themes and to advance what we know about CRT and teacher education. As Solórzano and Yosso (2001) posited, the goal of CRT in teacher education is to establish a "pedagogy, curriculum and research agenda that accounts for the role of race and racism in U.S. education" (p. 3). Moreover, CRT allows teacher educators and teacher education researchers an opportunity to centralize race, racism, and issues of discrimination through analyzing various aspects of the preparation of teachers, including policies and politics of the field (Milner, 2008).

Two guiding questions framed this research: (1) What are pre- and in-service teachers being taught (the curriculum) in teacher education and from a CRT perspective what should they be learning? and (2) What are the racial demographic trends in teacher education and from a CRT perspective what do these demographic trends tell us about the demographic divide between pre-K–12 students and their teachers? Three themes emerged as we systematically reviewed literature on CRT and teacher education: (1) challenging the curriculum, (2) problematizing racial demography, and (3) confronting the overwhelming presence of Whiteness. After discussing the themes, we discuss implications for and theorize about further centering race in teacher education.

REVIEW METHODS

Given this volume's vision, we focus this chapter on a systematic review of refereed journal articles regarding the intersection of CRT and teacher education. We searched for literature between 1995 and 2018 in Academic Search Premier and Educational Research Information Center (ERIC) using key terms "critical race theory and teacher education," "critical race theory and teacher preparation," "critical race theory and teacher training," and "critical race theory and pre-service teachers." We used this timespan because it allowed us to examine articles since Ladson-Billings and Tate (1995) introduced CRT to the field of education.

With our initial criteria, the databases yielded 95 articles, which we narrowed further to 27 by including only publications that directly used CRT as either method or conceptual framework in teacher education contexts. See Figure 2.1 for the distribution of these reviewed articles; specific information about each article can be found in Table 2.1. After sorting our final sample of articles by year, we engaged in a systematic examination of the articles using an inductive theme analysis by summarizing main points from the article, key CRT tenets used, population of focus, and data collection strategies and findings to determine big themes from each article. During the review process, our team developed independent literature syntheses for the purpose of interrater reliability, which we later used to compare and determine emergent themes.

OVERVIEW OF RESEARCH ON CRT AND TEACHER EDUCATION

The majority of literature in this review was published in the past 10 years. In fact, only 6 of the 27 articles on CRT and teacher education that fit our inclusion criteria were published prior to 2008. The growing presence of literature on CRT and teacher education could be related to shifts in more widely held beliefs related to advancing race, equity, and justice. Perhaps the emergence of CRT has provided researchers with tools and strategies to name and critique the institutional systems in which teachers are prepared (Milner & Laughter, 2014). It is also possible that CRT, as a methodological tool, has generated new research design possibilities (Solórzano & Yosso, 2002) for researchers to investigate the voices and experiences of teachers and teacher educators of color (Kohli, 2012).

We organize the remainder of this section by three prominent themes that emerged from our review of literature on CRT and teacher education. Each section defines the theme, provides the number of articles within the theme, and then expounds on subthemes using representative articles.

Challenging the Curriculum of Teacher Education

Thirteen articles in our review critically examined the commitment to social justice and diversity of teacher education programs. These studies tend to draw on CRT's interest convergence (Delgado & Stefancic, 2001) and social justice commitment (Solórzano & Yosso, 2002) to argue for reshaping

Figure 2.1. Distribution of Reviewed Articles

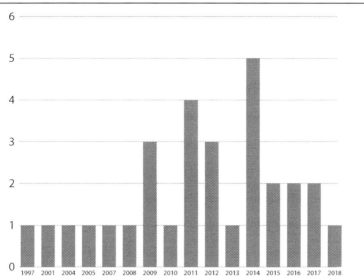

teacher education programs. This research highlighted how CRT has been used to expose contradictions in teacher education programs (Irizarry, 2011; Milner, 2008; Solórzano, 1997; Sleeter, 2017), where teacher education programs purport to be about social justice and diversity while maintaining structural barriers that may exclude future teachers of color from entering the field (Kitchen, Cherubini, Trudeau & Hodson, 2010; Pirbhai-Illich, Austin, Paugh & Farino, 2011; Sleeter, 2017) or insufficiently developing teacher education curricula intended to prepare teachers to be race-conscious (Sleeter, 2017).

To illustrate, Rogers-Ard, Knaus, Epstein, and Mayfield (2012) identified three common barriers preventing teachers of color from entering the teaching force: economic exclusion, standardized testing, and definitions of teacher quality. Many structural barriers were policy-driven. Other researchers noted difficulty among prospective teachers in navigating hostile educational environments; feelings of alienation and silencing were also documented in the literature (Irizzary, 2011). CRT has been useful for challenging systemic barriers to diversifying both teacher education (Sleeter, 2017) and teaching (Irizzary, 2011).

CRT literature has also critiqued teacher education programs for implementing underdeveloped curricula to instill race consciousness and an orientation toward social justice (Milner, 2008). Solórzano (1997) recognized that race, racism, and racial stereotypes, for instance, must be continually discussed in teacher education discourse, particularly in teacher education programs. That is, teacher education programs must design ongoing opportunities for teachers to think and talk about issues related to race and social justice. Studies illustrated how a stronger commitment to social justice in teacher education programs could be addressed through

Table 2.1. Literature Reviewed

Reference	Main Points	CRT Tenets
Bradley, D. (2011). In the space between the rock and the hard place: State teacher certification guidelines and music education for social justice. *Journal of Aesthetic Education, 45*(4), 79–96.	Interrogation of how knowledge is defined and whose knowledge should be prioritized in the teaching of music.	Challenging dominant ideology; counterstorytelling as a method for inclusion; instruction as a tool for social justice
Brown, K. D. (2014). Teaching in color: A critical race theory in education analysis of the literature on preservice teachers of color and teacher education in the US. *Race, Ethnicity And Education, 17*(3), 326–345.	Emphasizes the importance of preparing all teachers as well as recruiting and retaining teachers of color; examines the dominant, pervasive, and normalized culture of Whiteness.	Whiteness as property; endemic nature of racism
Bryant, L. C., Moss, G., & Zijdemans Boudreau, A. S. (2015). Understanding poverty through race dialogues in teacher preparation. *Critical Questions In Education, 6*(1), 1–15.	Authors engage in a dialogical research project within a teacher preparation program to address the dilemma of preparing preservice teachers for educational arenas in which they will interface with students who are socially and economically disadvantaged.	Suggests that the authors pull from all tenets as a lens through which to guide the dialogue
Castagno, A. E. (2012). "They prepared me to be a teacher, but not a culturally responsive Navajo teacher for Navajo kids": A tribal critical race theory analysis of an Indigenous teacher preparation program. *Journal of American Indian Education, 51*(1), 3–26.	Authors discuss a Whiteness, colonialism, and assimilation in White teacher education programs.	Interest convergence

Table 2.1. Literature Reviewed (continued)

Reference	Main Points	CRT Tenets
de los Rios, C., & Souto-Manning, M. (2015). Teacher educators as cultural workers: Problematizing teacher education pedagogies. *Studying Teacher Education, 11*(3), 272–293.	Authors engage in a process of testimonial co-creation to trace Freire's notion of critical pedagogy in their lives as former schoolteachers and current teacher educators.	Collective counterstory
Dixson, A., & Dingus, J. (2007). Tyranny of the majority: Re-enfranchisement of African-American teacher educators teaching for democracy. *International Journal Of Qualitative Studies In Education (QSE), 20*(6), 639–654.	Authors theorize about diversity and the irony in preparing a mostly White teaching force to work with "all" children.	Whiteness as property & counterstory
Hayes, C., Juarez, B., & Escoffrey-Runnels, V. (2014). We were there too: Learning from Black male teachers in Mississippi about successful teaching of Black students. *Democracy & Education, 22*(1).	Authors explore the philosophies of two Black male teachers related to successful teaching of Black children.	Counterstorytelling and challenging dominant ideology
Irizarry, J. (2011). En La Lucha: The struggles and triumphs of Latino/a preservice teachers. *Teachers College Record, 113*(12), 2804–2835.	Analyzes a study that reveals how subordination serves to marginalize students of color by hindering their full, active participation in teacher preparation programs through the silencing of their voices.	Silencing nonmajoritarian voices/narratives; frames discussion around the "central tenets of CRT and LatCrit"
Juarez, B. G., & Hayes, C. (2015). On being named a Black supremacist and a race traitor: The problem of White racial domination and domestic terrorism in US teacher education. *Urban Review, 47*(2), 317–340.	Authors illustrate how Whiteness operates in teacher education.	Draws on all tenets, but focuses mainly on CRT as a method

Table 2.1. Literature Reviewed (continued)

Reference	Main Points	CRT Tenets
Kitchen, J., Cherubini, L., Trudeau, L., & Hodson, J. (2010). Weeding out or developing capacity? Challenges for Aboriginal teacher education. *Alberta Journal of Educational Research*, 56(2), 104–123.	Authors present findings from Aboriginal teacher educators regarding their experiences in programs that aim to prepare teachers for Aboriginal learners.	TribalCrit
Kohli, R. (2009). Critical race reflections: Valuing the experiences of teachers of color in education. *Race, Ethnicity and Education*, 12(2), 235–251.	Teacher education programs can and should draw on the experiential knowledge that TOC bring, particularly around issues of race and racism.	This study uses CRT as a framework for analyzing data
Kohli, R. (2012). Racial pedagogy of the oppressed: Critical interracial dialogue for teachers of color. *Equity & Excellence In Education*, 45(1), 181–196.	Utilizing Freire's conceptual lens and a CRT framework to highlight dialogue about educational experiences of 12 Black, Latina, and Asian American women enrolled in a teacher education program.	Centrality of race and racism; commitment to social justice; valuing experiential knowledge; challenging the dominant narrative; interdisciplinary
Larkin, D. B., Maloney, T., & Perry-Ryder, G. M. (2016). Reasoning about race and pedagogy in two preservice science teachers: A critical race theory analysis. *Cognition And Instruction*, 34(4), 285–322.	Uses critical race theory to examine the manner in which conceptions about race and its pedagogical implications change over time.	
Matias, C. E. (2016). "Why do you make me hate myself?": Re-teaching Whiteness, abuse, and love in urban teacher education. *Teaching Education*, 27(2), 194–211.	Authors use an "emotions-based" approach to understanding Whiteness and discusses the damaging effects of denying race during White childhood via a colorblind ideology.	Centralizes Whiteness a property/priority; critique of liberalism (colorblindness); endemic nature of racism

Table 2.1. Literature Reviewed (continued)

Reference	Main Points	CRT Tenets
Matias, C. E., Viesca, K. M., Garrison-Wade, D. F., Tandon, M., & Galindo, R. (2014). "What is critical Whiteness doing in our nice field like critical race theory?" Applying CRT and CWS to understand the White imaginations of White teacher candidates. *Equity & Excellence In Education, 47*(3), 289–304.	Authors use Critical Whiteness Studies to support CRT to aid in deconstructing the dimensions of White imaginations.	Counterstory
Matias, C. E., & Zembylas, M. (2014). "When saying you care is not really caring": Emotions of disgust, Whiteness ideology, and teacher education. *Critical Studies In Education, 55*(3), 319–337.	Authors interrogate the performative aspect of teacher emotions toward students, particularly the actions of White teachers toward students of color.	Critique of liberalism; endemic nature of racism
Mensah, F. M., & Jackson, I. (2018). Whiteness as property in science teacher education. *Teachers College Record, 120*(1).	Analyzed the experiences of preservice teachers of color enrolled in an elementary science methods course as they gain access to science as White property.	Whiteness as property
Milner, H. R. (2007). Race, culture, and researcher positionality: Working through dangers seen, unseen, and unforeseen. *Educational Researcher, 36*(7), 388–400.	Encourages the researching of self; understanding self in relation to others.	The endemic nature of racism; the importance of the counterstory; converging of interests
Milner, H. I. (2008). Critical race theory and interest convergence as analytic tools in teacher education policies and practices. *Journal of Teacher Education, 59*(4), 332–346.	Author argues that Derrick Bell's (1980) interest convergence can be used as an analytic, explanatory, and conceptual tool in the study and analysis of policies and practices in teacher education.	Interest convergence

Table 2.1. Literature Reviewed (continued)

Reference	Main Points	CRT Tenets
Millner, H. R., & Laughter, J. C. (2014). But good intentions are not enough: Preparing teachers to center race and poverty. *The Urban Review, 47*(2), 341–363.	Authors stress the importance of interrogating race, poverty, and the nexus of the two in their assessment of teacher education programs.	Race as a social construct, interest convergence, colorblindness
Picower, B. (2009). The Unexamined Whiteness of teaching: How White teachers maintain and enact dominant racial ideologies. *Race, Ethnicity, and Education, 12*(2), 197–215.	Investigates how White preservice teachers' life experiences influenced understandings of race and difference.	Racism as an inherent and normalized aspect of American society
Pirbhai-Illich, F., Austin, T., Paugh, P., & Farino, Y. (2011). Responding to "innocent" racism: Educating teachers in politically reflexive and dialogic engagement in local communities. *Journal Of Urban Learning, Teaching, and Research,* 727–740.	Develops a construct of "innocent racism" created by silence or the lack of addressing issues of race within the classroom.	Counterstorytelling; endemic nature of racism; Whiteness as property
Rogers-Ard, R., Knaus, C. B., Epstein, K. K., & Mayfield, K. (2012). Racial diversity sounds nice; Systems transformation? Not so much: Developing urban teachers of color. *Urban Education, 48*(3), 451–479.	Authors highlight a Grow Your Own teacher prep program, "Teach Tomorrow in Oakland (TTO)."	Racism as endemic and standard procedure for schools and society
Sleeter, C. E. (2017). Critical Race Theory and the whiteness of teacher education. *Urban Education, 52*(2), 155–169.	Author examines the overwhelming whiteness that permeates teacher education programs through a critique of the disingenuous claims to diversity, neutrality, and a lack of appreciation for experiential knowledge of TOC	Interest convergence, Whiteness as property, colorblindness

Table 2.1. Literature Reviewed (continued)

Reference	Main Points	CRT Tenets
Solorzano, D. G. (1997). Images and word that wound: Critical Race Theory, racial stereotyping, and teacher education. *Teacher Education Quarterly*, 24(3), 5–19.	Provides specific recommendations, based on Critical Race Theory, to help teacher educators challenge racism and stereotyping in the classroom.	Racial realism, persistence of racism
Solorzano, D. G., & Yosso, T. J. (2001). From racial stereotyping and deficit discourse toward a critical race theory in teacher education. *Multicultural Education*, 9(1), 2–8.	Defines CRT in teacher education as a framework that can be used to theorize the ways and which race and racism impacts structures; seeks to understand how these cultural/social definitions and perspectives influence or justify the treatment of people or color.	Utilizes all five of the tenets of CRT as an analytic tool to "transform the use of racial stereotypes and deficit-based theories in education"
Solórzano, D. G. & Yosso, T. J. (2002). Critical race methodology: Counter-storytelling as an analytical framework for education research. *Qualitative Inquiry*, 8, 23–44.	Authors present an analytical framework for understanding the deficit-based theories used in research with people of color.	Endemic nature of racism, challenging the dominant ideology; commitment to social justice

well-designed curricula that are nuanced and individualized according to teachers' needs (Larkin, Maloney, & Perry-Ryder, 2016; Mensah & Jackson, 2018).

Teachers, mostly White teachers, continue to struggle with incorporating aspects of social justice and race within their work. For example, Milner and Laughter (2014) found that White teachers often do not feel efficacious in their ability to discuss race but rather tend to shift attention to socioeconomic conditions. Further, White teachers often feel uncomfortable reflecting on their own racial identities and those of their Black and Brown students.

By exposing contradictions in many teacher education programs, this literature suggested that teacher education programs and the teaching field are limited by policies that exclude people of color and support ineffective curricula for preparing teachers to be social justice–oriented and race-conscious.

Problematizing the Racial Demography of Teacher Education

Our review yielded 17 articles highlighting the tendency of teacher education programs to undervalue experiential knowledge from preservice teachers of color and teacher educators of color (Hayes, Juarez, & Escoffrey-Runnels, 2014; Kohli, 2009). CRT recognizes experiential knowledge as legitimate and critical to "understanding, analyzing and teaching about racial subordination" (Solórzano & Yosso, 2001, p. 3). Irizarry (2011) advanced that the lived experiences of people of color at Predominantly White Institutions (PWIs) are largely underrecognized and often silenced, particularly regarding issues of racism and discrimination. Refusal to address these issues reifies and legitimates Whiteness within these institutions. Storytelling, narratives, and family histories are useful in drawing on strengths of people of color (Ladson-Billings, 1998; Milner, 2007; Solórzano & Yosso, 2001).

Kohli (2009) shared how 12 preservice teachers of color connected their K–12 school experiences of racism with the experiences of a group of K–12 students of color with whom the preservice teachers worked. While these stories illustrated how experiences with racism can have lasting effects on people of color, more broadly these narratives represent a site of racial knowledge which teacher education programs can tap into to deepen all preservice teachers' understanding of race.

Using a narrative inquiry approach can provide access to racial knowledge and the perspectives of people of color for all teachers and teacher educators to learn from one another and to co-create knowledge (Johnson-Lachuk & Mosley, 2012). Hayes, Juarez, and Escoffrey-Runnels (2014), through exploring two Black male teachers' philosophies and practices, judged that teacher education programs should teach strategies to prepare teachers to engage in transformative pedagogies centering equity, activism, and social literacy.

A CRT framework in teacher education challenges dominant ideologies that perpetuate deficit notions of people of color. Solórzano and Yosso (2001) argued that this framework, which respects individuals' unique lived experiences, also theorizes the intersections between racism and other forms of oppression. Kohli (2012) added that teacher education programs adopting a critical race framework have the opportunity to broaden teachers' multicultural understanding of racial and structural oppression by providing cross-cultural lenses that incorporate experiential knowledge. Moreover, teacher education programs might center racial knowledge to support teachers' navigational awareness of and responsiveness to racial climates and diverse classrooms.

Using the narratives of teacher educators of color can be an insightful CRT approach for challenging a dominant ideology in teacher education (Solórzano & Yosso, 2001). Dixson and Dingus (2007), drawing on their own narratives as teacher educators of color, described how teacher educators of color function primarily as perfunctory symbols of diversity and inclusion. They found that teacher education programs designed for a mostly White teacher force too often rely on the efforts of teacher educators of color to carry the burden of race.

This theme sheds light on the value of experiential racial knowledge for both enhancing teacher education programs and for rejecting practices that perpetuate systemic racism. Decisionmakers in teacher education programs might examine how improving the understanding of prospective teachers and teacher educators of color can increase their presence in predominantly White programs and enhance their experiences within them.

The Overwhelming Presence of Whiteness in Teacher Education

The literature points out the overwhelming presence of Whiteness in teacher education programs. Briefly, Whiteness embodies a complex synergy between racial identity and agency (Jupp, Berry, & Lensmire, 2016), while functioning as a property benefit related to power and privilege.

As in other spaces that privilege White people over people of color (DeCuir & Dixson, 2004; Delgado, 1995; Ladson-Billings, 1998), the functionality of Whiteness works in teacher education to obstruct teacher educators' attempts to center race and disrupt racial injustices. This research establishes that, like other institutions of power and influence, teacher education serves, promotes, and protects White interests, but CRT identifies and rejects such inequitable practices.

For example, Milner (2008) relied on interest convergence to call attention to the manner in which teacher education programs preserve their Whiteness by tolerating the interests of people of color when, and only when, they benefit the interest of White dominance. In other words, institutions intending to sustain their Whiteness are unlikely to make substantive changes to curriculum, policies, courses, or epistemological stances unless these changes benefit or at least do not disturb their own interests (Milner, 2008).

In their study using CRT to analyze Whiteness as property in science teacher education, Mensah and Jackson (2018) argued that preservice teachers are often educated in ways that ignore and sustain systemic inequities. They found institutions tend to adhere to White norms that privilege the voice and perspectives of the majority and neglect the contributions and strengths of people of color. Thus, PWIs develop curricula that assume a White prospective teacher and tend to cater to the interests and emotional sensibilities of a White teaching force (Milner, 2008; Irizarry, 2011; Mensah & Jackson, 2018; Sleeter, 2017). Preservice teachers of color may not be considered in the planning and development of policies, curriculum, and courses, though more recently most programs offer some variation of courses focusing on racial and cultural concerns (Sleeter, 2017).

Juarez and Hayes (2015) used CRT to illuminate how Whiteness refuses to acknowledge racial permanence, cannot coexist with colorblindness, and must accept the myth of meritocracy. Perhaps most significant, the authors showed that White faculty members attempting to advocate for racial justice face consequences for "breaking out of the clan mentality" (p. 336), and that the Whiteness of the institution is ultimately maintained.

Castagno (2012) made a similar assertion, arguing that efforts to adopt a race- and justice-centered approach in teacher education programs can be short-lived, as the influence of colonialism tends to overpower them. Matias, Viesca, Garrison-Wade, Tandon, and Galindo (2014) discovered issues of emotional disinvestment, lack of critical understanding of race, resurgence of White guilt, and recycling of hegemonic Whiteness in White teacher candidates.

This research stresses the significance of CRT in teacher education, particularly for countering the influence of Whiteness in obstructing racial justice. Rogers-Ard and colleagues (2012) considered CRT essential for building a program to advance racial equity in education, and Matias and colleagues (2014) agreed that CRT belongs in teacher education and can be used to help White teachers embrace race and encourage them to work through their emotions of emotional resistance, distress, or deflection toward race.

NEXT STEPS

We have described three salient themes from the literature on CRT and teacher education: challenging the curriculum of teacher education (what gets taught), problematizing the racial demography in teacher education (whose perspectives are silenced), and naming the overwhelming presence of Whiteness of teacher education (who gets to teach). The extant literature addresses these issues, but we need more empirical studies that advance what we know. Thus, we hope teacher education researchers will continue to interrogate, from a CRT perspective, what is taught in teacher education and who is being prepared to teach.

For instance, what role does race play in what is taught in teacher education? Who decides the nature of the curriculum and why? How can teacher education programs couple building content knowledge with racial knowledge in teacher education? Moreover, how can and should teacher education recruit a more racially diverse cadre of teachers? What happens when teachers are mostly White in an increasingly diverse society with students from a variety of diverse spaces?

REFERENCES

Castagno, A. E. (2012). "They prepared me to be a teacher, but not a culturally responsive Navajo teacher for Navajo kids": A tribal critical race theory analysis of an indigenous teacher preparation program. *Journal of American Indian Education, 51*(1), 3–26.

DeCuir, J. T., & Dixson, A. D. (2004). "So when it comes out, they aren't that surprised that it is there": Using critical race theory as a tool of analysis of race and racism in education. *Educational Researcher, 33*(5), 26–31.

Delgado, R., & Stefancic, J. (2001). *Critical race theory: An introduction.* New York, NY: New York University Press.

Jupp, J. C., Berry, T. R., & Lensmire, T. J. (2016). Second-wave white teacher identity studies: A review of white teacher identity literatures from 2004 through 2014. *Review of Educational Research, 86*(4), 1151–1191.

Kitchen, J., Cherubini, L., Trudeau, L., & Hodson, J. (2010). Weeding out or developing capacity? Challenges for Aboriginal teacher education. *Alberta Journal of Educational Research, 56*(2), 104–123.

Kohli, R. (2012). Racial pedagogy of the oppressed: Critical interracial dialogue for teachers of color. *Equity & Excellence in Education, 45*(1), 181–196.

Kohli, R. (2014). Unpacking internalized racism: Teachers of color striving for racially just classrooms. *Race, Ethnicity and Education, 17*(3), 367–387.

Ladson-Billings, G. (1998). Just what is critical race theory and what's it doing in a "nice" field like education? *International Journal of Qualitative Studies in Education, 11*, 7–24.

Ladson-Billings, G., & Tate, W. F. (1995). Toward a critical race theory of education. *Teachers College Record, 97*(1), 47–68.

Milner, H. R., & Laughter, J. C. (2014). But good intentions are not enough: Preparing teachers to center race and poverty. *The Urban Review, 47*(2), 341–363.

Sleeter, C. E. (2017). Critical race theory and the Whiteness of teacher education. *Urban Education, 52*(2), 155–169.

Solórzano, D. G. & Yosso, T. J. (2002). Critical race methodology: Counter-storytelling as an analytical framework for education research. *Qualitative Inquiry, 8*, 23–44.

CHAPTER 3

Teacher Education, Diversity, and the Interest Convergence Conundrum
How the Demographic Divide Shapes Teacher Education

Ashlee Anderson and *Brittany Aronson*

Few educators would argue with the claim that students of color are those most negatively affected by inequalities in the educational system. In terms of race and ethnicity, White and certain groups of Asian American students fare best; in terms of socioeconomics, middle- and upper-class students outperform student populations from other socioeconomic backgrounds on national standardized tests. Ladson-Billings (2006) challenges us to consider how these "achievement gaps" function as symptoms of what she more appropriately termed an *education debt* stemming from historical, economic, sociopolitical, and moral inequities that continue to disproportionately target students of color and students of poverty.

Implicated in this education debt is what educational researchers have labeled the *demographic divide* between diverse student populations and a teaching force that is largely homogeneous (Boser, 2014). The National Center for Education Statistics (NCES) predicts the White student population will continue to decrease, representing only 46% of the public school population by 2024, while Black and Hispanic student populations continue to grow (see Figure 3.1).

In addition to the racial and ethnic diversity that is represented in U.S. classrooms, language and religious diversity is also on the rise. For example, the Democratic Leadership Council estimated that 50 million Americans spoke a language other than English at home, and Eck (2001) called the United States the "most religiously diverse nation on earth" (p. 4). In contrast, the U.S. Department of Education (2016) confirms the racial homogeneity of U.S. teachers, showing that White teachers comprise 82% of the public school teaching force. This homogeneity extends to teacher education as well, though different preparation pathways complicate the picture.

Figure 3.1. Percentage distribution of students enrolled in public elementary and secondary schools by race/ethnicity (Fall 2002, 2012, 2024)

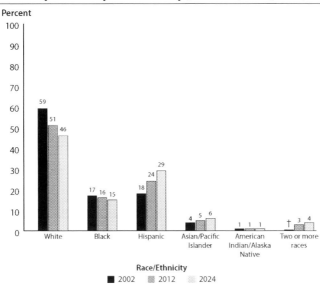

† Not applicable

Note: Prior to 2008, separate data on students of two or more races were not collected. Detail may not sum to totals because of rounding. Data for 2024 are projected.

Sources: U.S. Department of Education, National Center for Education Statistics, Common Core of Data (CCD). "State nonfiscal survey of public elementary and secondary education," 2002–2003 and 2012–2013; and National Elementary and Secondary Enrollment Projection Model, 1972 through 2024. See Digest of Education Statistics 2014, Table 203.50 available at https://nces.ed.gov/programs/raceindicators/indicator_rbb.asp

For example, 75% of students enrolled in traditional teacher preparation programs are White. In contrast, alternative licensure programs tend to enroll a more racially diverse population of preservice teachers (PTs).

Of concern to critical race scholars is how these predominantly White, middle-class, female teachers enter diverse schools with little understanding of the historical, philosophical, sociological, and political foundations that shape them (National Education Association, 2004). This cultural mismatch has focused the attention of education researchers on teachers' (in)ability to effectively teach children who are different from themselves (Howard, 2006; Sleeter, 2001, 2008). Although we certainly agree we must address White teachers' preparation in order to better understand how they might more effectively teach students of color, there is also a need to assess the recruitment, preparation, and retention of teachers of color within this largely homogeneous teaching force. This area of scholarship has not been well developed.

A majority of the literature related to "teacher diversity" addresses this demographic divide in the context of the cultural mismatch between a predominantly White teaching force and a diversifying student population; there is significantly less literature discussing experiences of teachers of color in teacher education and in classrooms (Kohli, 2014; Lee, 2013). Few studies have critically analyzed specific features of teacher education, and even fewer have employed Critical Race Theory as the primary lens of analysis (Brown, 2014; Jackson, 2015).

For example, much of the research surrounding teachers of color within teacher education has focused on teacher distributions or the (in)ability of specific licensure pathways to recruit and retain a more diverse teaching force (Cochran-Smith, Cannady, McEachern, Mitchell, Piazza, Power, & Ryan, 2012). Receiving far less attention in the academic literature are the experiences of PTs of color in teacher preparation.

Brown (2014) represents one of the largest reviews of literature (more than 80 articles through 2012) on the experiences of PTs of color in U.S. teacher education. Brown used CRT to organize the primary themes that were identified: (1) *recruitment and retention*, (2) *perspectives and voices*, and (3) *experiences in teacher preparation*. While the first theme addressed the need for students of color to interact with teachers who share similar backgrounds, the second theme described the general optimism that PTs of color felt about the teaching field as a whole, which included the finding that African American teachers exhibited higher rates of optimism than Asian American/Pacific Islander PTs.

Finally, the third theme discussed teacher preparation programs whose objectives might be inconsistent with the needs of PTs of color (i.e., coursework designed for White students), and so leave them feeling invisible. Brown's (2014) analysis represents a wide array of studies and illustrates the challenges that PTs of color face when navigating teacher education programs serving mostly White students and staffed with predominantly White teacher educators (Milner & Self, 2014; Picower & Kohli, 2017).

AUTHOR POSITIONALITY

Our own positionalities have significantly informed the arguments that we include herein. We are two racially White women who are former public school teachers, one prepared via an alternative licensure program and the other trained in a traditional teacher education program. These experiences have informed our interest in teacher preparation, as well as our joint commitment to racial justice, as the result of which we work to center the voices and experiences of people of color.

Having been an under-prepared White teacher in a racially integrated and predominantly low-income school, Anderson (Author 1) is interested in the (in)equity effects of education, especially the ways in which schools, teachers, and teacher education have the potential to be both transformative and/or oppressive. She is classed with moderate material wealth and education (notwithstanding an impoverished upbringing), gendered cis-hetero and female, able-bodied, and committed to progressive politics.

Aronson (Author 2) is interested in how to prepare a predominantly White teaching force to embody anti-oppressive teaching practices in schools. As a racially White, middle-class, Christian, able-bodied, cis-hetero female, she shares many qualities with the current teaching force and has experienced many of the same "epiphanies" as the predominantly White students whom she teaches. She is also ethnically Latina (Colombian) and, through her own re-education, has grappled with her internalized Whiteness and the ways that she erased her Latina identity for much of her life.

Returning to Ladson-Billings's (2006) call to action via the education debt, then, we believe it is our moral obligation as privileged White women to work to make schools more equitable for students of color. Acknowledging that many educational inequalities are the consequences of larger societal realities (Anyon, 2014; Kozol, 2006), we do not subscribe to the belief that (White) teachers alone contribute to student achievement disparities. We do, however, believe that teachers have a great deal of potential to positively affect their students (or not). Our work with CRT has been the natural outgrowth of our moral commitment to racial justice.

TEACHER EDUCATION, DIVERSITY, AND THE INTEREST CONVERGENCE CONUNDRUM

To frame this project, we discuss the historical context in which the demographic divide exists, paying particular attention to the experiences of Black teachers as one example of how various inequities have played out. Next, we describe the ways in which the coded language of diversity has been implicated in the demographic divide, after which we outline the concept of interest convergence and how it informs the marginalization of teachers of color in both teacher education and in classrooms. We offer several examples of interest convergence with respect to the experiences of teacher educators of color, after which we conclude by discussing the implications of this research and providing specific recommendations for teacher education and K–12 schools.

Historical Context

The demographic divide was created by various historical realities that fundamentally directed the trajectory of teaching and teacher education. Beginning in the 1850s, formal teacher education developed as a space exclusively for White women, as they were the primary image of "teacher" (Hill-Jackson, 2017). At the end of the Civil War, a dual system of schooling was created with separate schools for White and Black children and teachers (Anderson, 1988; Fultz, 1995). Despite a 90% illiteracy rate among formerly enslaved Black populations, which itself was the result of their being denied basic literacy skills, a powerful movement to self-educate was catalyzed by Black leaders, particularly Black women (Hill-Jackson, 2017).

By the turn of the 20th century, there were nearly 60,000 Black teachers, again mostly women (Foster, 1997), which expanded to nearly 90,000 prior to the 1954 *Brown* decision. However, as Hill-Jackson (2017) points out, the post-*Brown* period of school desegregation was marked by significant damage to the Black community, including the reassignment of Black teachers to integrated schools, if not their outright dismissal. As an additional harm, during this period Black children were forcibly bussed to integrated schools where they were met with hostility and taught by White teachers who were either unprepared or unwilling to develop relationships and to teach in culturally relevant ways.

Since the 1970s, the U.S. has witnessed the mass departure of Black teachers from teacher education. The publication of *A Nation at Risk* in 1983 ushered in a new set of priorities that were accompanied by a noticeable decline in the numbers of Black women teachers despite attempts to address dwindling numbers of "minority teachers." Displacement, or the "systemic and involuntary aspect of teachers' departures from urban schools due to federal, state, and district school reforms" (White, 2016, p. 3), has been the intentional concomitant of what Hill-Jackson (2017) identifies as largely hidden culprits in the mass exodus of Black teachers, including requirements for certification, state licensing tests, teaching reforms and accountability, as well as overall career opportunities within the teaching profession. Though some reforms perceivably *advanced* racial justice, the effects negatively affected Black teachers and communities.

The Coded Language of Diversity

Contemporary research surrounding the demographic divide is saturated with watered-down understandings of diversity that do little to critically engage demographic trends, particularly as they pertain to teachers of color. Arce-Trigatti and Anderson (2018) recently identified two primary features animating public discourses surrounding diversity in education:

1. *Diversity as an economic input*, wherein the overall goal of diversity becomes conflated with various economic realities and incentives
2. *Diversity as a democratic input*, which positions diversity as a potential means by which to facilitate intercultural dialogue and collaboration as well as to further the cause of social justice (p. 2, italics in original)

Thus, diversity is held to provide specific economic advantages, like the benefit of a multicultural workforce at a time when global markets are becoming increasingly diverse.

Diversity also "holds the capacity not only to facilitate intercultural dialogue and collaboration, but also to further the cause of social justice by providing all students, not just a select, privileged few, access to equal educational opportunities and outcomes" (Arce-Trigatti & Anderson, 2018, pp. 10–11). However, Arce-Trigatti and Anderson go on to assert that the oversimplification of an exceedingly complex term leads to confusion and a lack of meaningful, effective policies.

We contend that this overall lack of definitional clarity and narrowed understanding of a complex feature such as diversity engenders the use of what ultimately amounts to coded language that inequitably targets people of color. Diversity becomes something to be capitalized upon, both economically and democratically, but its existence at the margins of policy discourses does little to create more equitable educational environments for students and teachers of color.

The Interest Convergence Conundrum

We focus on one of CRT's tenets, interest convergence, to guide our analysis. Originally theorized by Derrick Bell (1980) in his powerful critique of the *Brown* decision, the concept of interest convergence is animated by two primary ideas: "the interest of blacks in achieving racial equality will be accommodated only when it converges with the interests of whites"; and even with convergence, a remedy will be nullified whenever it "threatens the superior societal status of middle and upper class whites" (p. 523). In terms of education, then, any policy or practice that perceivably advances racial justice must also serve the interests of Whites. In terms of teacher education, we see an overall lack of effort in the recruitment of a more diverse teaching force and in the support of teachers of color, who often become the means by which training programs are able to claim an interest in diversity.

The current debate over the relative merits and challenges of alternative versus traditional teacher education provides a helpful example of the intricacies of this process. Some advocates call for more alternative pathways, which typically embrace the perceived advantages of on-the-job training over traditional, university-based certification programs requiring extensive preservice preparation. Supporters of alternative programs cite these programs' ability to attract a more diverse teaching force, while advocates of extensive preservice training express concerns that our most underserved students (i.e., those in "hard-to-staff" schools) are exposed to the least prepared and experienced teachers.

We contend that neither of these arguments suggests real reforms to teacher education that would benefit teachers of color. Although we applaud alternative programs' ability to recruit more teachers of color, our concern lies primarily with the reality that those teachers face once they enter their respective programs (Lapayese, Aldana, & Lara, 2014), as well as the potentially negative outcomes for existing teachers of color (White, 2016). Similarly, when supporters of traditional teacher education programs vilify alternative licensure programs, whose inclusion of teachers of color characteristically outpaces their own, teachers of color become targeted.

Retention has become a lightning rod for critiques of teacher education. Supporters of traditional teacher training programs often target alternative licensure options for their high rates of attrition. However, retention data typically reflects the career trajectories of White teachers, not teachers of color who often exhibit higher rates of retention within the schools they serve (Irizarry & Donaldson, 2012), which are disproportionately hard-to-staff schools (Ingersoll & May, 2011).

This debate represents just one of the ways in which interest convergence operates in teacher education. Certainly, the recruitment of more teachers of color should be part of the conversation, but that inclusion should not exploit the labor of teachers of color in an effort to diversify. Similarly, programs must provide meaningful and nonexploitative interventions serving the unique interests of teachers of color.

Many existing teacher education programs primarily target the needs of White teacher candidates. At the same time that training programs lessen requirements for courses in social foundations, multicultural education, or social justice (Aronson & Anderson, 2013), when these courses are offered, they often cater to the "development, conceptual, pedagogical, philosophical, and curricular needs of White students" (Milner & Self, 2014, p. 13). The ultimate outcome of this process is the recentering of White teachers at the expense of teachers of color, who are excluded from the curriculum, reflecting and perpetuating the system of White supremacy (Picower & Kohli, 2017).

There is also a need to increase the numbers of teacher educators of color as a potential means by which to attract more teachers of color into teacher education. However, just as the cycle is created to maintain Whiteness in teacher education, there are similar cycles for teacher educators of color who inevitably will work at Predominantly White Institutions (PWIs) with predominantly White female preservice teachers. Matias (2016) explained how the pain of Whiteness is exacerbated when her White teacher candidates profess a readiness to teach urban students of color while simultaneously confirming harmful color-evasive ideologies.

Similarly, Johnson and Bryan (2017) illuminated how Black males working at PWIs are "metaphorically murdered in the academy" (p. 3). This happens when faculty of color are silenced or outright disrespected in their teaching (when hired to do racial justice work) from unsupportive White faculty or resistant students. We contend that recruitment constitutes but one part of the realities that teacher educators of color experience. Where those realities involve the exploitation of their labor, or their exclusion from a curriculum that is largely geared toward White teachers, we contend that interest convergence is at play.

NEXT STEPS: THE MORAL OBLIGATION FOR TEACHER EDUCATION

We have addressed the demographic divide as it pertains to teacher education using CRT, specifically the tenet of interest convergence, to highlight inequities that persist in schools, not only for students of color but also for preservice and practicing teachers of color. In our descriptions of both the historical and contemporary contexts in which these inequities exist, we have shown the ways in which Black teachers, as one example, were pushed out of schools in favor of Whitestream ways of teaching and learning.

Similarly, we have traced several examples within teacher education that maintain an inequitable status quo, despite seeming advances in racial justice via the diversification of teacher education. These realities lead us to the conclusion that the demographic divide is less the result of circumstantial phenomena than an intentional act executed by actors who overtly and covertly perpetuate White supremacy. Ultimately, this has serious implications for teacher education and for researchers and policymakers whose work affects preservice and practicing teachers of color.

Given the complexity of the historical and contemporary contexts of teacher education, we extend critique to the sorts of falsely erected binaries that maintain what Milner (2008) called a *false racial innocence* in which "change is often *purposefully* and *skillfully* slow" (p. 334). Milner (2008) pointed to the activation of this false racial innocence when decisions are made within teacher education policy that disregard the ways in which race shapes and privileges certain perspectives (allowing, for example, White teacher educators to choose not to examine their own racialized privileges). What makes this innocence false is the ability of White teacher educators to claim ignorance while simultaneously making decisions that negatively affect people of color. Examining both the historical and contemporary contexts of teacher education deeply challenges this sort of willful ignorance.

Given the moral obligation of educators to address issues of race and racism (Ladson-Billings, 2006), we too have an obligation to address these issues within teacher education. As long as a demographic divide persists, we must continually reexamine the intentional origins of the divide in order to shed light on how interest convergence has played a role in both its conception and its maintenance. We must also continue to ask questions we may not readily have answers to: What happens when we bring faculty of color to teacher education at PWIs? How is this different from recruiting teachers or color to urban schools serving Black and Brown children (which we know is beneficial) versus bringing teacher educators of color to PWIs (which we know *abuses* them)? Is it possible to balance this need to diversify with the consequences of such abuse?

REFERENCES

Anderson, J. D. (1988). *The education of Blacks in the South, 1860–1935*. Durham, NC: University of North Carolina Press.

Anyon, J. (2014). *Radical possibilities: Public policy, urban education, and a new social movement* (2nd ed.). New York, NY: Routledge.

Arce-Trigatti, A., & Anderson, A. (2018). Defining diversity: A critical discourse analysis of public educational texts. *Discourse: Studies in the Cultural Politics of Education*. DOI: 10.1080/01596306.2018.1462575

Aronson, B., & Anderson, A. (2013). Critical teacher education and the politics of teacher accreditation: Are we practicing what we preach? *Journal for Critical Education Policy Studies*, *11*(3), 244–262.

Bell, D. A. (1980). *Brown v. Board of Education* and the interest-convergence dilemma. *Harvard Law Review*, *93*, 518–533.

Boser, U. (2014). Teacher diversity revisited: A new state-by-state analysis. *Center for American Progress*. Retrieved from https://eric.ed.gov/?id=ED564608

Brown, K. (2014). Teaching in color: A critical race theory in education analysis of the literature on preservice teachers of color and teacher education in the U.S. *Race Ethnicity and Education*, *17*(3), 326–345.

Cochran-Smith, M., Cannady, M., McEachern, K., Mitchell, K., Piazza, P., Power, C., & Ryan, A. (2012). Teachers' education and outcomes: Mapping the research terrain. *Teachers College Record*, *114*(10), 1–49.

Eck, D. L. (2001). *A new religious America: How a "Christian" country has become the world's most religiously diverse nation*. New York, NY: Harper.

Foster, M. (1997). *Black teachers on teaching*. New York, NY: The New Press.

Fultz, M. (1995). African American teachers in the South, 1890–1940: Powerlessness and the ironies of expectations and protest. *History of Education Quarterly*, *35*(4), 401–22.

Hill-Jackson, V. (2017). . . . And then there were none: Reversing the exodus of Black women from the teaching profession. In A. Farinde-Wu, A. Allen-Hardy, & C. W. Lewis (Eds.), *Black Female Teachers: Diversifying the United States' Teacher Workforce* (pp. 9–48). Bingley, UK: Emerald Publishing Limited.

Howard, G. H. (2006). *We can't teach what we don't know: White teacher, multiracial schools* (2nd ed.). New York, NY: Teachers College Press.

Ingersoll, R. M., & May, H. (2011). The minority teacher shortage: Fact or fable? *Phi Delta Kappan*, *93*(1), 62–65.

Irizarry, J. & Donaldson, M. L. (2012). Teach for America: The Latinization of U.S. schools and the critical shortage of Latina/o teachers. *American Educational Research Journal*, *49*(1), 155–194.

Jackson, T. O. (2015). Perspectives and insights from preservice teachers of color on developing culturally responsive pedagogy at predominantly White institutions. *Action in Teacher Education*, *37*(3), 223–237.

Johnson, L., & Bryan, N. (2017). Using our voices, losing our bodies: Michael

Brown, Trayvon Martin, and the spirit murders of Black male professors in the academy. *Race Ethnicity and Education*, 20(2), 163–177.

Kohli, R. (2014). Unpacking internalized racism: Teachers of color striving for racially just classrooms. *Race Ethnicity and Education*, 17(3), 367–387.

Kozol, J. (2006). *Shame of the nation.* New York, NY: HarperCollins.

Ladson-Billings, G. (2006). From the achievement gap to the education debt: Understanding achievement in U.S. schools. *Educational Researcher*, 35(7), 3–12

Lapayese, Y. V., Aldana, U. S., & Lara, E. (2014). A racio-economic analysis of Teach for America: Counterstories of TFA teachers of color. *Perspectives on Urban Education*, 11(1), 11-25.

Lee, V. (2013). Teachers of color creating and recreating identities in suburban schools. *The Qualitative Report*, 18(16), 1–16. Retrieved from www.nova.edu/ssss/QR/QR18/lee16.pdf

Matias, C. E. (2016). "Why do you make me hate myself?" Re-teaching Whiteness, abuse, and love in urban teacher education. *Teaching Education*, 27(2), 194–211.

Milner, H. R. (2008). Critical race theory and interest convergence as analytic tools in teacher education policies and practices. *Journal of Teacher Education*, 59(4), 332–346.

Milner, H. R., & Self, E. A. (2014). Studying race in teacher education: Implications from ethnographic perspectives. In A. D. Dixson (Ed.), *Researching race in education: Policy, practice, and qualitative research* (3–29). Charlotte, NC: Information Age Publishing.

National Education Association. (2004). Assessment of diversity in America's teaching force: A call to action. Retrieved from www.nea.org/assets/docs/HE/diversityreport.pdf

Picower, B., & Kohli, R. (Eds.). (2017). *Confronting racism in teacher education: Counternarratives of critical practice.* New York, NY: Taylor & Francis.

Sleeter, C. E. (2001). Preparing teachers for culturally diverse schools: Research and the overwhelming presence of Whiteness. *Journal of Teacher Education, 52,* 94–106.

Sleeter, C. E. (2008). Preparing White teachers for diverse students. In M. Cochran-Smith, S. Feiman-Nemser, & D. J. McIntyre (Eds.), *Handbook of research on teacher education: Enduring questions in changing contexts* (pp. 559–582). New York, NY: Routledge.

U.S. Department of Education, Office of Planning, Evaluation and Policy Development, Policy and Program Studies Service. (2016). *The state of racial diversity in the educator workforce.* Retrieved from www2.ed.gov/rschstat/eval/highered/racial-diversity/state-racial-diversity-workforce.pdf

White, T. C. (2016). Teach for America's paradoxical diversity initiative: Race, policy, and Black teacher displacement in urban schools. *Education Policy Analysis Archives*, 24(16), 1–42.

CHAPTER 4

"I See Whiteness"
The Sixth Sense of Teacher Education

Cheryl E. Matias and *Jared J. Aldern*

In the popular film *The Sixth Sense*, Malcolm (played by Bruce Willis) is a renowned child psychologist who, after deflecting and projecting onto Cole (played by Haley Joel Osment), a boy who claims to see dead people, comes to realize that he is the one who is dead. Throughout the movie, Malcolm counsels Cole as if Cole were mistaken, never entertaining the possibility that the mistake is within Malcolm himself.

In this way, the movie is about Malcolm projecting from a belief that Cole was not reasoned in his reality of seeing dead people. Malcolm gaslights the young boy into thinking that what he sees is not true when it *is* true. Why does Malcolm refuse to see the truth? Because Malcolm is an award-winning child psychologist with all his stature, accolades, and accomplishments, his mindset is ontologically predetermined to undermine a child; a child's true reality could not (moreover, has no right to) hold a candle to Malcolm's false reality.

It is important to note how power is exercised here because we find it operates similarly in teacher education. When Malcolm holds his reality above Cole's, even if the upheld reality is patently false, it becomes narcissistic because he does so with an air of arrogant entitlement. Yet the movie plays on our own arrogance, entitlement, and narcissism too. In the end, movie watchers reflect on all the scenes so much so that they question their own overlooking of the truth. Perhaps the audience has its own sense of narcissism, or worse yet an obedience to the performativity of narcissism such that they too refuse to see the truth. Therein lies the problem. To what extent will society kowtow to narcissists and how does narcissism like that in this film also play out with regard to Whiteness in teacher education?

We begin this chapter with *The Sixth Sense* because we find its prophetic moral sadly applicable to the state of teacher education. Although Sleeter (2001) pointed out the overwhelming presence of Whiteness 17 years ago, teacher education narcissistically acts as if that reality is not true by refusing to teach about Whiteness, acknowledge that Whiteness is operating, or be active in dismantling White supremacist practices. And, in refusing this obvious truth, it continues business as usual. It is as if teacher education gaslights teachers to believe that while we acknowledge Whiteness is a reality, we refuse to see it, respond to it, or call it by its name.

In this refusal, teacher education inadvertently recycles that which it proclaims to abhor: social injustice, educational inequity, and racially biased teaching. Therefore, in respecting our sixth sense of education, we focus on *seeing* Whiteness in teacher education as a way to combat the tendency to overlook its demoralizing and pervasive presence in teacher education.

"I SEE [WHITE] PEOPLE":
WHITENESS, EMOTIONALITY, AND TEACHER EDUCATION

An oft-invoked trope of preservice teachers is their desire to "help" or "give back" to urban schools, communities of color, or students of color. While this socially acceptable rhetoric is commonly viewed as altruism, empathy, or genuine care from teachers (who are predominantly White) toward their soon-to-be K–12 students of color, CRT and critical Whiteness studies urge us to be skeptical of such readily accepted pageantries. What if, in fact, such routinely performed rhetoric is nothing but a mask covering deeper, less glamorous issues? Should teacher educators blindly accept assertions of "I love kids" as an important litmus test of aptitude for teaching? If so we, the authors, respond with, "But so do pedophiles."

Despite its crassness, such a rebuttal nonetheless gets to the point of our argument here: There must be a deeper and more comprehensive understanding of a teacher's stated intentions and their actual effect because embedded in such pageant-like answers is a complex web of emotions that are, as Matias and Zembylas (2014) suggested, mere *sentimentalizations*. That is, they are surface displays of ego-construction that function to mask underlying and hidden emotions not deemed socially acceptable. Or, as Matias (2016a) proffered, these White emotions are just surface emotions that stem from "White emotionalities" that are deeper racialized emotions socially construed with respect to the hegemony of Whiteness and one's submission to and complicity with White supremacy.

To this end, Critical Whiteness Studies (CWS) is an interdisciplinary approach to race that offers a specific set of tools for unmasking and unmaking Whiteness in teacher education that CRT does not. While CRT focuses on the effects of racism on people of color, CWS focuses on how Whiteness is exerted in ways that are racially microaggressive to people of color. When using both CRT and CWS in concert, we can unveil Whiteness *and* its effect on people of color.

Take, for example, the common presumption in teacher education of aptitude and readiness. It is narcissistic for preservice teachers to presume they are helping without embodying the proper credentials, experiences, and knowledge sets of the very communities or people they believe they are helping. Bonilla-Silva's (2006) empirical study suggested that Whites lay claim to having a Black best friend when in actuality they do not. White respondents made such claims, then, when asked to list five of their best friends, none of those five was Black. Respondents could not even recall the name of their Black "bestie." This suggests that Whites created fictitious friendship with Blacks (Matias, 2016b), folks of color, and anyone deemed "Other" to ostensibly disassociate themselves from being racist.

Applied to teacher education, the presumed aptitude for being ready to "help" students of color, when actual relationships with people of color have not been experienced, is a narcissistic unexamined privilege. To be a qualified candidate for teaching in diverse urban U.S. schools with students of color, one must have experienced connection with people outside the insular bubble of Whiteness and be cognizant of their position in the racial hierarchy. Or, as Mills (1997) argued, they must be keenly aware of the racial contract that ensures their elevated status within the existing racial hierarchy.

To better illustrate this point, we draw from a recent interaction between one of the authors (a female of color) to a White male audience member during a panel presentation at the 2018 American Educational Research Association (AERA) conference in New York City. Along with many other audience members, the man appeared concerned over the lack of diversity in teaching. Eager to demonstrate his commitment, he described his role as a diversity specialist at his institution, and asked the panelists, "What can I do?" His terminologies were correct. His intention to diversify was also on point. However, his ontological understanding of what constitutes diversity and why we are in need of it was not.

Yancy (2018) described how, if racial justice–minded folks were not in tune with their orientations to Whiteness, such a demand on folks of color served as yet another convenient way to maintain privilege by passing over one's burden of White responsibility. By avoiding and thus not having to feel the weight of the racial pain and fatigue people of color experience, and by expecting to be served up ready-made solutions by people of color, Whites circumvent the only process that will ultimately ensure their sustained commitment to a just society, what Yancy (2018) called tarrying with the discomfort.

In fact, this man at AERA narcissistically refused to acknowledge Whiteness, let alone his own complicity in it. Never in his discourse did he mention his White identity, Whiteness, or larger structural issues of White supremacy. He simply needed a checklist. One panelist (a White female doing work on critical Whiteness in education) got flustered with this line of questioning, commenting that these questions are often posed to her by the very chief diversity officers, diversity specialists, and other positions in that capacity (many of whom were White themselves) who professed to be experts in diversity. So the panelist asked, "Aren't you the diversity expert?" The man became emotionally unfettered, outwardly displaying his White fragility, and reverted to making racially biased claims and engaging in normalized discourses of Whiteness. At first, he refused to respond to the panelist's question, as if it were too unintelligible for him to comprehend. In doing so, he maintained the racial contract whereby he is never made to feel as if he is the object of study, for he assumes his subjectivity (Mills, 1997).

In his rhetoric, he was able to see the racial Other by pointing out racial achievement gaps and lack of teacher diversity but at the same time was blinded by his own Whiteness. He refused to see his own entitled White identity politics whose position as "specialist" meant nothing if he were not aware of his power and privilege. This is especially striking when considering he had just listened to a 1.5-hour-long panel on the White hegemonic alliance in education. He altogether refused to address Whiteness or even acknowledge his role in repositioning people of color as the objects of study, thereby attempting to deflect any direct gaze on Whites. Furthermore, he reverted to assuming teachers of color may not be qualified. Lastly, he maintained an assumption that White teachers are qualified by finding it shocking for someone to offer a contrary notion.

The point here is not that diversity specialists should ignore the needs of teachers, faculty, and/or students of color. Absolutely not. To the contrary, what must be considered is one's ontological understanding of what constitutes diversity with respect to one's own identity within White supremacy. To find it too obtuse to entertain Whiteness when we know it is a real issue is narcissistic. And narcissism colludes with false realities, just as teacher education romanticizes teachers' roles as missionaries or saviors for urban communities sans recognition of how suburbia was established through denial and restriction of resources and freedoms of peoples of color in preference of Whites (Massey & Denton, 1993; Oliver & Shapiro, 2006).

Another example is the rhetoric of "giving back" in teacher education. This popular parlance is often invoked to explain why teachers, many of whom are White and not from the communities they seek to teach, choose to teach in diverse urban schools. Upon its utterance, the White-approved discourse is readily accepted as normal. In fact, the normalization is such that the remark does not typically cause another person to pause and ask, "What have you taken that you feel the need to give back?" Emotionally speaking, feeling compelled in this way connotes the idea that one has taken something and thus feels the need to return it to its rightful owner.

Yet, when asked about what it is they need to give back, teachers often reveal they are aware that they grew up in "nice" communities with "good" schools unlike some of the schools they seek to teach in. Pushing deeper, why does coming from these nice communities and good schools make one feel guilty enough to want to return the niceties and goodness? Or perhaps more astutely, how were these privileges realized at the expense of "others"?

What was taken from other communities and schools in order to have middle- and upper-class White communities filled with good schools and ample economic opportunities?

As suggested above, White wealth was accumulated at the expense of Black wealth (Oliver & Shapiro, 2006) through FHA-insured home loans for Whites only, legal redlining of communities of color, racially restrictive covenants, and police-endorsed terrorism when Blacks and people of color sought to move into White neighborhoods (Rothstein, 2017). Yet in today's discourse many Whites invoke the popularized cultural rhetoric that birds flock together as a way to justify why White communities are mainly White (Bonilla-Silva, 2006).

This same ahistorical, amnesiac, or distorted historical understanding is seen in teacher education. In efforts to diversify, teacher education blindly refuses to acknowledge its racist past and present. Namely, discussions or questions within teacher education include the following: *Why don't teachers of color want to be teachers? Why aren't there enough teachers of color? Why is teacher education replete with White teachers?*

Irvine and Irvine (1983) offered some vision of unintended consequences of school desegregation: decreased diversity and increased educational White Eurocentricity. Years later, Tillman (2004) argued that the effect of *Brown v. Board of Education* was the firing, delegitimizing, and subjection to racially discriminatory hiring practices of Black teachers and administrators, and also claimed these (un)intended consequences ultimately produced a "'manufactured crisis' in the education of African American children" (p. 301)—a chain of crises manifesting in racial achievement gaps, racial disproportionality in special and gifted and talented education, and punitive disciplinary actions.

One should not have an ahistorical approach to why diversity lacks in areas, fields, and industries that are predominantly White today. Simply, it was made to be that way. Denying this historical reality is in and of itself a blatant exertion of White racial privilege, power, narcissism, and arrogance—an act of racism. That is, to deny and willfully turn a blind eye to the reality of White supremacy in teacher education is a slap in the face to teachers of color, people of color, and communities of color. Yet teacher education does often turn that blind eye.

Henceforth, the ability to see White people, let alone Whiteness in general, in teacher education becomes vital to ensure a more racially just educational system. For if one lacks the ovaries to bear witness to the depravities caused by White supremacy, they will remain living a surreal existence in a false reality forever engaging, enacting, and hoping for practices, remedies, or policies lacking real weight in the real world. Essentially, they willfully remain a marked perpetrator knowing full well they will never be labeled as such because a White supremacist educational system refuses to see the historical realities and be held responsible for them.

"I'M READY TO TELL YOU MY SECRET NOW": THE DIRTY SECRET OF WHITENESS

In the commitment to see teacher education engage in racially just practices, we, the authors, talk matter-of-factly about the dirty secrets of Whiteness. However, it should be clearly noted that doing so is not for pleasure. In doing the work of understanding how the overwhelming presence of Whiteness operates in teacher education, per Sleeter (2001), we, the authors, have been targeted by hate groups; ostracized from our programs and departments; and subjected to bullying, harassment, and unjust treatment from folks who believe they are engaging in socially just practices in education. The hope behind such bullying practices is for critical scholars of race to simply shut up about race and Whiteness.

We say this to highlight the genuinely risky nature of speaking aloud this dirty little secret, the elephant in the living room, or the "Lord Voldemort" of education: That which cannot be spoken aloud only gains power in silence. For example, revealed in private communications with philosopher George Yancy, political science professor George Lipsitz, CRT attorney Kimberlé Crenshaw, and English professor Lee Bebout, all of whose work focuses on Whiteness in critical ways, is the fact that they too are targeted for merely engaging in this work. In fact, before one of the authors went up for tenure she was warned by a senior White male professor that she would not earn tenure if she kept "making up" words like *Whiteness*. Not only was this an indirect threat to her job security, it was a blatant dismissal of the field of Whiteness and race studies, as if Whiteness is just make-believe, a unicorn.

This is of grave importance because it should be forever recognized that dismantling White supremacy in an institution built by it is dangerous, isolating, and abusive. In doing racially just work to call out White supremacy, anti-Blackness, and the destructive nuances of everyday Whiteness, institutions like teacher education may engage in abusive practices, attempting to gaslight you in ways that inappropriately characterize the "whistleblower" as the "bad guy" for simply bringing up the racialized lives of White people.

At the 2018 Critical Race Studies in Education Association Conference in New Mexico, the moderator presented a panel with commonly asked questions for scholars doing research in Whiteness and White supremacy specific to education. Interspersed throughout the commentaries of the panelists, audience member after audience member nodded heads, snapped their fingers (as a way to indicate an acknowledgment of hidden truth), and felt compelled to share their stories in dealing with White emotionality.

One Latina junior professor relayed a story about how she sat on a master's thesis committee for a student and when she disagreed with the White female thesis chair about the inclusion of race and White supremacy in the student's thesis, the chair started crying during the defense. Later, the Latina professor got an email from the dean of the school claiming that he needed to meet with her because of her lack of civility; "civility" here used as a way to police the Latina professor. Not much unlike the Panopticon (Foucault, 1977), Whiteness surveils in ways that enforces the racial contract. If one were to step out of line of the contract, as the Latina professor did, there are punitive measures that Whites, like this dean, can take in attempting to reinforce the racial contract.

In this case, the White tears of this White thesis chair were strategically used as a semantic maneuver (Bonilla-Silva, 2006) to control the discourse of race without ever uttering the word race. And, as the dean placated the emotionalities of the White female thesis chair by engaging in punitive measures and quickly assuming the Latina professor was uncivil, he was complicit in maintaining the racial contract as well. Cheryl offered this rebuttal: Instead of readily assuming that the professor of color who brings up race is the problem, why not consider that the person with the real problem is the White female professor who cries at the mere mention of race?

Using CRT's intersectional approach on race *and* gender provides a more complex understanding of the dynamics that happen after the dirty secret of Whiteness is exposed. In this situation, because the Latina professor was quickly assumed to be "the problem," we clearly see how race is operating. Racial stereotypes of angry Brown women and the assumed innocence of Whiteness are invoked.

Alongside race, gender is also presenting itself. The dynamics here are between the two women (one of color and one who is not of color) as race is upheld by the White male dean rescuing the crying White lady. To better understand, we draw from feminist theories. Hooks (1994) describes how during the feminist movement White feminists treated Black feminists as servants to the cause, thus reinforcing the old servant–served paradigm. This idea is again manifested in academia when Gutiérrez y Muh, Flores Nieman, González, and Harris (2012) dedicated an entire anthology to how female faculty of color are presumed incompetent. Berry and Mizelle (2006) discussed the ways in which female faculty of color were treated poorly by White counterparts and particular "skinfolk" who ascribe to Whiteness ideology, albeit through a different operating mechanism as field whip in the neoplantation politics of the academy.

Yet, the dynamics between two women of different races is also about how each *raced* gender is upheld. White women, as Godfrey (2010) articulated, have erroneously been given the racial and gendered characterization of innocence such that when there are White female tears, they are in need of protecting. Inscribed on the White woman's body is the stereotype of virgin-like purity, high morality, and innocence, whereby White men have historically produced laws (e.g., antimiscegenation laws) and engaged in terroristic policing tactics (e.g., Emmett Till) to protect it.

In fact, the field of teaching itself, though originally occupied by men, was later considered a feminine field due to White women's assumed moral status (Kliebard, 1995; Spring, 2016). Along with this insight is Baldwin's (1963) assertion that a White sense of morality cannot be understood without the context of framing Blackness as immoral. That is, just as a valley cannot be conceptualized without the context of its surrounding mountains, Whiteness has erroneously defined itself as moral only in juxtaposition with something perceived to be immoral. That is why Baldwin, in his 1963 talk to teachers, states the Negro does not need the White man as much as the White man needs the racially biased stereotypes of the Negro in order to justify his own existence.

Circling back to race and gender, then, when a White woman is given an ontological definition of purity, innocence, and morality, she will need an archnemesis to embody her antithesis: the woman of color. Therefore, anything that a woman of color does that upsets, unsettles, or discomforts White women is seen as attacking the morality of humanity itself. And in this sad struggle between White goodness and Black/Other badness, women of color are often readily assumed to be the problem even if they are professionally revealing the dirty secret of race.

DE PROFUNDIS CLAMO AD TE, DOMINE: RECONCILIATION OF TRUTHS IN NEXT STEPS

The Sixth Sense ends with a sense of completeness and peace even though Malcolm comprehends his own death. The peace stems from him finally seeing the gruesome reality of his own death despite difficulties in doing so. Essentially, or psychoanalytically, he had two deaths: physical and metaphysical. On the one hand, he realizes he is physically dead, which in and of itself is hard to swallow. On the other hand, he also realizes his metaphysical death. Suffice it to say that this metaphysical death is simply realizing he can no longer interact in a reality of which he once thought he was a part *and* from which he built his identity. In fact, his death at the hands of Vincent (a former patient who ended up killing Malcolm in the beginning of the film due to Malcolm's failure to properly counsel him) is a prophetic lesson to Malcolm to not be too narcissistic in his assumption that he is saving, helping, and/or giving back to his patients in savior-like grandeur, a lesson from which teacher education can learn.

Applied to teacher education, Whiteness, with all its gruesomeness, narcissism, and emotionalities, needs to take a hard stare in the mirror. It needs to see a metaphysical death whereby it realizes its wrongful interpellation to a false reality, a reality from which White teachers then build their White racial identities. More precisely for teacher education, the Whiteness in teacher education needs to realize its wrongful overlooking, dismissing, and/or refusing to see a raced reality leading to the manufacturing of White curriculum, White normative pedagogies, intervention practices, preservice teacher selection protocols, and White privileging found in standardized exams and educational policies. It must see its narcissistic and emotionally manipulative tendencies that continue to deny its own reflection as some perverse way of justifying its unearned elevated position.

Finally, it needs to bear witness to a more humane reality wrought with historical atrocities, slavery, discrimination, and White racial affirmative actions. Only when this happens can teacher education reconcile its sixth sense of Whiteness.

SPECIAL NOTE

To those who bear witness and refuse to look away for the sake of a more humane educational system. Also, to my La Doña and twinnies for nurturing my heart as I continue to endure the burden of bearing witness. Finally, for my baby boy, you know I see you.

REFERENCES

Baldwin, J. (1963, December 21). "A talk to teachers." *Saturday Review.* Retrieved from www.zinnedproject.org/materials/baldwin-talk-to-teachers

Berry, T. R., & Mizelle, N. D. (2006). *From oppression to grace: Women of color and their dilemmas in the academy.* Sterling, VA: Stylus Publishers.

Bonilla-Silva, E. (2006). *Racism without racists: Color-blind racism and the persistence of racial inequality in the United States.* Lanham, MD: Rowman & Littlefield Publishers.

Foucault, M. (1977). *Discipline and punish* (Trans. A. Sheridan). New York, NY: Pantheon.

Godfrey, P. (2010). "Sweet little (White) girls"? Sex and fantasy across the color line and the contestation of patriarchal White supremacy. *Equity & Excellence in Education, 37*(3), 204–218.

Gutiérrez y Muhs, G., Flores Niemann, Y., González, C.G., & Harris, A.P. (2012). *Presumed incompetent: The intersections of race and class for women in academia.* Louisville, CO: University Press of Colorado.

hooks, b. (1994). *Teaching to transgress: Education as the practice of freedom.* New York, NY: Routledge.

Irvine, R., & Irvine, J. (1983). The impact of the desegregation process on the education of Black students: Key variables. *The Journal of Negro Education, 52*(4), 410–422.

Kliebard, H. M. (1995). *The struggle for the American curriculum: 1893–1958* (2nd ed.). New York, NY: Routledge.

Massey, D. S., & Denton, N. A. (1993). *Segregation and the making of the underclass.* Cambridge, MA: Harvard University Press.

Matias, C. E., & Zembylas, M. (2014). "When saying you care is not really caring": emotions of disgust, whiteness ideology, and teacher education. *Critical Studies in Education, 55*(3), 319–337. DOI: 10.1080/17508487.2014.922489

Matias, C. E. (2016a). *Feeling White: Whiteness, emotionality, and education.* Rotterdam, Netherlands: Sense Publishers.

Matias, C. E. (2016b). White skin, Black friend: A Fanonian application to theorize racial fetish in teacher education. *Educational Philosophy and Theory, 48*(3), 221–236.

Mills, C. (1997). *The racial contract.* Ithaca, NY: Cornell University Press.

Oliver, M. & Shapiro, T. (2006). *Black wealth/ White wealth: A new perspective on racial inequality.* New York, NY: Routledge.

Rothstein, R. (2017). *The color of law: A forgotten history of how our government segregated America.* New York, NY: Liveright Publishing Corporation.

Sleeter, C. (2001). Preparing teachers for culturally diverse schools: Research and the overwhelming presence of Whiteness. *Journal of Teacher Education, 52*(2), 94–106. DOI: 10.1177/0022487101052002002

Spring, J. (2016). *Deculturalization and the struggle for equality: A brief history of the education of dominated cultures in the United States* (8th ed.). New York, NY: Routledge.

Tillman, L. C. (2004). (Un)Intended consequences?: The impact of the *Brown v. Board of Education* decision on the employment status of Black educators. *Education and Urban Society, 36*(3), 280–303.

Yancy, G. (2018). *Backlash: What happens when we talk honestly about racism in America.* Lanham, MD: Rowman & Littlefield.

CHAPTER 5

Racial Literacy
Ebony and Ivory Perspectives of Race in Two Graduate Courses

Gwendolyn Thompson McMillon and *Rebecca Rogers*

In our work as teacher educators, specifically charged with the preparation of literacy teachers, we intentionally incorporate issues of racism, racial violence, and anti-racism in our course curricula. Because of the complexities of this pursuit, we have had many discussions over the years concerning victories and challenges in our courses, as well as progress and obstacles in our research and community engagement activities. This chapter tells the story of a research study with a naturalistic design that crossed geographic, racial, and university boundaries. We asked our students to read Edwards, Thompson McMillon, and Turner's (2010) *Change Is Gonna Come* and the National Council of Teachers of English (NCTE) statement affirming #BlackLivesMatter (2015) and to respond in writing to a prompt we called "Black Literate Lives Matter: Taking Pedagogical Action."

As an interracial research team, we analyzed artifacts of students' learning to address the following research questions: What variation in racialized understandings exist in written responses generated by literacy education graduate students across racialized lines? How do we, as White (Rebecca) and Black (Gwendolyn) professors, read and interpret the themes and discourse patterns in students' essays? Foreshadowing our findings, we also asked: How does our cross-racial analysis contribute to the expansion of our own racial literacy?

Our scholarship is grounded in Critical Race Theory (CRT) and the pedagogical application of racial literacy. CRT scholars understand that racism is an enduring facet of American life and is perpetuated in policies, texts, and interactions. Racism and capitalism intersect to create the conditions for the continued violation of Black and Brown bodies. Racial literacy is an interactive process that reads racism and anti-racism in all their (global) psychological, interpersonal, and structural dimensions. We believe that if racism is perpetuated through policies and micro-practices, so, too, is racial equity work (Lazar, Edwards, & Thompson McMillon, 2012).

46

OUR HERSTORY

We were introduced to one another by a mutual friend at the Literacy Research Association (LRA) annual conference in San Antonio. We discussed our family literacy and parent engagement–focused research as well as our teaching. While conversing, we became aware of commonalities among our work within the organization and in our home communities. Since our initial meeting, we have proudly affirmed and celebrated special moments in each other's life, such as professional awards and our children's accomplishments.

We worked together on LRA's Executive Board at a time when the organization was focused on racial equity issues. We collaborated on writing a section of the strategic plan focused on diversity, equity, and inclusion. Rebecca cherishes Gwendolyn's insight, wisdom, humor, spirituality, and willingness to work across racial divides. At times, Rebecca feels that Gwendolyn is more forgiving of White people's ignorance and privilege than she should be. Gwendolyn acknowledges that she is able to get to this position because of her spirituality. Gwendolyn appreciates the passion with which Rebecca has thought about issues of racism, White privilege, and equity. They have confided in each other about personal and professional concerns, and have proven to be trustworthy friends to each other. Gwendolyn often says that Rebecca has a good heart, wants to move things forward quickly, and has little patience for anyone who gets in the way. But she reminds Rebecca that sustained change is more likely when progress occurs at a gradual, continuous pace that allows people's transformed hearts and minds to be manifested by actions.

In almost every conversation we have, we talk about the effect of racism on our lives, and the lives of the people we work with and care about. We share our own pain, struggles, and hopes. This, in turn, adds to the lenses we are able to bring to our own teaching and our lives in a society permanently scarred with structural racism. It was these insights we sought to raise to the surface in our analysis.

Our teaching and research was a form of critically conscious scholarship that crossed geographic and institutional boundaries (Willis, Montavon, Hall, Hunter, Burke, & Herrera, 2008). We committed to creating conditions where our students can contribute to racial justice through literacy practices. To do this, we centered issues of racism, racial violence, power, and equity in our literacy education graduate courses. In 2016, we decided we would both give the same assignment (called "Taking Pedagogical Action: Black Literate Lives Matter") to our classes. In designing the pedagogical intervention, we wanted to examine more closely our students' responses to become better able to support their racial literacy practices. We invited the members of our classes to contribute artifacts of their written work for this study after the class had ended. We also examined our own racialized discourses and what this means for the design of critically conscious sites of teaching and research.

Gwendolyn's course was a doctoral class entitled "Examining Culture, Race, Equity, and Power in Education." Core readings and assignments focused on topic-related theories: sociocultural theory, critical theory, Critical Race Theory, critical pedagogy, culturally relevant pedagogy and culturally sustaining pedagogy. The university is a public university located in a suburban area, with a student population that is 76% White, 8.8% African American, 6.3% Asian, 3.3% Hispanic, 1% Native American, and 4.3% Other.

Rebecca's class was a required master's-level class called "Literacy Acquisition for Diverse Students." The course was online and divided into eight modules that covered topics such as multiliteracies, second language acquisition, racial literacy, and critical literacy. Rebecca's university is a land grant university with students coming from the following racial/ethnic groups: 68% White, 19% African American, 7% not specified/other, 4% Latino, and 3% Asian. Across both classes, a total of 11 participants were included in the study.

Our data set included 11 essays that were written in response to an assignment we called "Taking Pedagogical Action: Black Literate Lives Matter." The assignment asked students to engage with Chapter 5 in Edwards, Thompson McMillon, and Turner's (2010) book and NCTE's statement affirming #BlackLivesMatter. Chapter 5 is called "The Road to Redemption: Moving from Victims to Victors" and focuses on different steps that educators can take to "maintain a healthy village" (p. 136).

The assignment description and guidelines that we both gave to our students stated:

> In Chapter 5, the authors present solutions relevant to a number of stakeholders (e.g., policymakers, teachers, teacher educators, community members). After reading their proposed solutions, reflect on which resonate the most with you and why. Next, read NCTE's statement affirming #BlackLivesMatter and create a 250-word synthesis/reflection that draws together the authors' proposed solutions and the NCTE statement. Your synthesis should include your own ideas for pedagogical action.

We recognize the genre we requested was a hybrid one. It was an academic essay and it openly invited students to take "pedagogical action" and opened a space to engage with racial equity and justice.

RACIAL AWARENESS AND COMMITMENT ACROSS RACIAL LINES

Racial literacy is a complex, interactive process that develops across time, people, and contexts (Mosley & Rogers, 2011; Sealey-Ruiz, 2011). We found evidence of varying levels of racial literacy distributed across our students. We also observed a great deal of complexity and contradictions in racial literacy practices *within* individuals. For example, a teacher may use racial terms and concepts but not identify themselves as working toward racial equity. Conversely, a teacher may identify as an anti-racist educator but not take responsibility for their actions.

Our analysis included the emergent categories of racial awareness, pedagogical change, social change, and individual responsibility. The first category, racial awareness, is divided into two parts. General racial awareness is shown when students discuss racism on a general level in society, such as institutional racism in education. Individual racial awareness requires students to identify themselves in their writing.

The second category emphasizes pedagogical change. Students may discuss specific practices that are or will be utilized to fight racism. The next category considers a macro perspective of change that involves institutional or societal impact. Finally, the last category assesses whether the student takes ownership in the action(s) discussed.

Overall, both classes' responses included a moderate commitment to racial literacy. Regardless of whether they were writing to an African American or White professor, most of the students' essays demonstrated examples of racial awareness and a commitment to taking action to promote racial equity in their classrooms and schools. Each of our groups also included students who expressed high and low commitment to racial literacy. To give more detailed examples of the variation in written responses, we have chosen three essays that correspond with a gradient of commitment to racial literacy.

Low Commitment to Racial Literacy

Joanne was a White teacher with 11 years of classroom experience. She worked as an instructional coach in a middle school that serves mainly African American children. Joanne's essay included distancing language with solutions embedded in preservice teacher education, something outside her locus of control. Her essay was written in a very objective and matter-of-fact way, without appraisal or ownership.

Throughout the essay, Joanne used unmarked racial terms and coded racialized talk, distancing her from taking responsibility. Integration in her essay did not center marginalized voices but simply brought them into a lesson plan. Furthermore, Whiteness was never identified as a racial identity or construct and, therefore, was beyond the purview of the curriculum. Her writing did not include the vocabulary of racial equity efforts. Also, Joanne assumed that teachers will automatically embrace the idea of "learning about others," when in fact teachers often prefer not to discuss or learn how to properly address problems of racism, racial violence, and White privilege.

Moderate Commitment to Racial Literacy

Amy was a White teacher working as a literacy specialist in an elementary school that mainly serves Black students. She had 10 years of teaching experience, including 4 years as an instructional coach. In her essay, she identified her students as African Americans, but she left her own racial identity unmarked. She acknowledged that she has received almost no professional development focused on making instruction culturally relevant to students' lives.

Amy's essay included evidence of racial awareness and a commitment to action. However, she also failed to identify herself racially and presented dichotomous thinking. For example, she noted wanting to change her literacy instruction, to focus less on technical support and to "begin to take on conversations of race, identity." It appeared she did not yet see the possibility of integrating an emphasis on racial equity within accelerative literacy sessions. She relied heavily on a past success story without acknowledging Black students who perhaps were not engaged in a so-called culture of resilient reading. A great amount of emphasis was placed on schoolwide libraries for the culture of resilient reading.

High Commitment to Racial Literacy

Tamara was a Black educator with 2 years of teaching experience in a middle school serving mainly Black students. She integrated ideas about racial equity across her ideas and proposed pedagogic actions. She named herself and her students as part of Black culture. She said it was her "responsibility" to teach African American history. She even acknowledged her own growth and learning.

She positioned herself in alliance with the ideas of #BlackLivesMatter. Her actions were curriculum based and built on what she was already doing. Indeed, she used many personal pronouns to position herself in the essay as an insider. Her actions were focused on sharing her passion to motivate students to take action in their community. We noted that Tamara's essay was an example of "social equity teaching in action" (Lazar, Edwards, & Thompson McMillon, 2012). She used her classroom as a space and place to help students develop skills and strategies needed to improve their lives and their communities.

RACIALIZED INTERPRETATIONS

Our interracial research alliance assisted us to create a more complex reading of our students' essays. What follows are three examples of how our initial interpretations were deepened because of the intersections of our racialized epistemologies.

Bedtime Reading as Racialized Practice

Amy was a White graduate student and practicing teacher of 10 years. In her essay, she commented on books she was reading that would help her dismantle systems of power and oppression in her own classroom. In particular, she noted her bedtime reading of Coates's (2015) book *Between the World and Me*. Gwendolyn picked up on the phrase "bedtime reading" and commented that it was interesting that she reads Coates's book as "leisure reading."

To Gwendolyn, reading before bed was dismissive or not a serious engagement with material that dealt with racial injustice. She visualized someone reading a book like *Between the World and Me* in a more serious manner, not as bedtime reading. Rebecca, contrastingly, had interpreted this part of Amy's writing to mean that racial justice issues are so much a part of her that she wants to engage with these issues even in her quietest time, before she goes to bed. Many White people, Rebecca thought, might not choose either to read the book or to continue their thinking about racism into their bedroom. Gwendolyn made the point that if she read the book before bed, as a Black woman—especially a mother of Black sons—she would not be able to sleep. The experiences are too real and immediate for her. Rebecca had not considered that "bedtime reading" means something different for those who are living daily with racial privilege and for those who experience racial oppression.

We lingered in this space of multiple interpretations and seemed to both rest with the idea that this image of "bedtime reading" could and would mean different things to both of us based on our lived experiences. We also discussed the kinds of racial vocabulary that people use to signal their racial identities. It seemed to Rebecca that Amy infused her language with markers to signal that she is not the kind of White person who rests on the invisible culture of Whiteness but tries actively to disrupt it. Gwendolyn noted that Amy's use of the phrase "de-education of African American youth" echoed Woodson's concept of the "mis-education of the Negro" and wondered if Amy had read this important historical text.

Performative Silences and Directness of Discourse

The culture and ideology of Whiteness has a stranglehold on teacher education that often results in people of color being silenced (Delpit, 2006; Haddix, 2012). In reflecting on this assignment, we were both aware of ideas our Black students, in particular, did not articulate. While this assignment was explicit in requesting students to engage with racism and equity and develop "pedagogical actions," students may have struggled with finding their voice in this genre, particularly as they were writing for a grade and for professors who crossed racial lines. Two essays demonstrate how we pushed each other to think again about the complexity of racial literacy, particularly interpretations that cut across racial lines.

Delores was a Black administrator. She had taught for 14 years, including being an administrator for 8 years. She currently worked in the district office as an instructional facilitator. Her essay identified professional development and teacher education as her pedagogical solution. When Rebecca read the essay, she was surprised by the self-monitoring and silencing that she thought she read. The sentence "not only African American students but *all students*" particularly caught her attention. In this statement, Rebecca heard echoes of arguments used against the #BlackLivesMatter movement. Rebecca struggled with this because it felt to her as though Delores, a Black woman, might be adding a qualifying phrase that she thought a White professor would want to hear. She did not step into the essay and claim a stance toward racial equity.

Gwendolyn helped Rebecca see that clearly Delores thought that Black lives matter. She expressed this in concluding her essay arguing for the use of the narrative voices of Black women in books used in her teaching/pedagogic action. This prompted a discussion between Rebecca and Gwendolyn about the kinds of racialized risk involved for teachers of color in predominantly White settings of teacher education. As an experienced administrator, Delores had undoubtedly been challenged to share racial ideologies in socially palatable ways that would not offend her colleagues, but instead motivate them toward progress. In her professional environment, performative silence may have served her well, but her indirectness raised a red flag in the class of a White professor who wanted her to genuinely share her authentic self.

Sydney was a doctoral student with a unique set of experiences. She had been in the criminal justice field for over 20 years. Gwendolyn was highly critical of Sydney's essay because she focused on the election of Donald Trump, the political environment, and a negative outlook for Blacks and all students in general. She did not take the immediate pedagogical stance that Gwendolyn wanted to see. For Rebecca, the directness of Sydney's writing contrasted with Delores's indirectness of discourse.

In the first line of her essay, Sydney called out literacy researchers for perpetuating deficiencies of Black children. She saw racism in this country as thinly veiled during the Obama administration; racist actions were emphasized by the words and actions of Donald Trump. She called Trump's words and actions "ignorant." She directly named the United States as having "racist ways," embodying White culture and dominance. Gwendolyn pointed out the strength of the phrase "country's history of apartheid." We both acknowledged that the statement Sydney picked up on from NCTE was not one that we specifically remembered ourselves. Sydney was writing an essay that she knew would be read by a Black professor.

Rebecca helped Gwendolyn to think again about Sydney's essay by asking, "Why are you so irritated? What's really bugging you?" Gwendolyn responded that she had very high expectations, especially for Black students, because she knew that they would be held to a higher standard. She did not want to be harsh, but at the same time, she felt compelled to push them harder. She internally cheered for them to cross every *t* and dot every *i*, and when they did not quite meet that standard, she was disappointed.

Finally, Rebecca asked Gwendolyn if she thought her response was a by-product of internalized oppression (Pérez, Johnson, & Kohli, 2006). Gwendolyn's first response was to tell Rebecca: "Now, you know I'm very pro-Black!" Rebecca's suggestion triggered major cognitive dissonance for Gwendolyn. She told Rebecca that she needed some time to think about it. They scheduled another analysis session and went their separate ways. Gwendolyn shared her thinking with her husband and sons, and came to the conclusion that perhaps she was indeed experiencing internalized oppression. When we met for the follow-up session, Gwendolyn expressed anger with herself for allowing her racist education to affect her mentality to the point that she may be too hard on some of her Black students, but at the same time she feels she must prepare them for success within the culture of power (Delpit, 2006).

NEXT STEPS

With the confluence of the #BlackLivesMatter movement in St. Louis and the 2016 presidential election, the timing of the assignment affected most students' responses and may have influenced our analyses as well. Certainly, the intersections of our identities helped us to see more fully the ways in which racism is structurally encoded and interactionally enacted. We have foregrounded a version of intersectionality that focuses on the new knowledge that is created when people from diverse backgrounds intersect to make meaning in educational contexts. We need to recognize that assigning levels to students' racial literacy awareness is certainly an imperfect measure. Yet it helped us make sense of the complexity of meanings and provided a basis from which we could discuss the essays and imagine pedagogical recommendations.

When we began this project, we thought perhaps there would be obvious differences in how students encoded racial meanings in their essays based on whether they were writing for an African American or White professor. What we came to understand is that we both provided space to learn about race, language, literacy, and power in meaningful ways in our courses. This laid the groundwork for students to trust they could write honestly about issues of racism and racial justice. We acknowledged that it was easier for us as instructors to step into the perspective of those students whose racial consciousness seemed to align most readily with our own. This was both an affordance and constraint in our reflections. We learned that our supposed understanding could, in fact, hold hidden racial biases and blinders. It was here that our cross-racial dialogues helped expand our possible responses to our students.

For years, we have shared the difficulties of incorporating race, racism, and racial violence in our teacher education courses. When we launched this study, we were eager to better understand how racialized meanings were encoded in our preparation of literacy teachers. As we started data analysis, we realized that we would need many sessions because the essays were laden with intersectionality, symbolism, and multiple layers of identity. We were reminded that centering race, racism, and racial violence in our literacy education courses is not only about the topic, readings, and our students' stances. It also involves the racialized work we engage in our interpretations of students' work. Entering into a research collaboration that invited us to dialogue about our racialized interpretations expanded the range of reading paths available to us. This, in turn, heightened our awareness of the various ways we might respond to our students' essays to support and encourage continued growth and contributions to racial equity.

It is vital at this juncture to warn all cross-racial teams that the most important component of a cross-racial team is trust. This cannot be over-emphasized. We took the time to develop a relationship that was built on longstanding admiration and trust. Data analysis sessions were long, challenging, and at times very uncomfortable; however, because of our relationship, we were able to stop abruptly, reschedule, return to the conversation, challenge, prod, irritate, recommend, and confess. For example, when Rebecca asked Gwendolyn if she thought she might be exhibiting internalized oppression, she took a major risk. Gwendolyn could have cut her off immediately, become silent or superficial. Instead, Gwendolyn was comfortable ending the session without being concerned about hurting Rebecca's feelings. Rebecca immediately responded with assurance that they could reschedule whenever Gwendolyn was ready. After several days we met for another data analysis session. Rebecca simply listened while Gwendolyn shared a deep self-analysis. We talked about internalized oppression and what it meant in the context of the research.

As we move toward the goal of a racially literate society, we support the Call to Action written by Edwards, Thompson McMillon, and Turner (2010) and NCTE's statement affirming #BlackLivesMatter (2015). We recognize that a "parallel revolution" is necessary at all levels. We also know that the parallel revolution must begin within ourselves. According to Jennings and Lynn (2005), self-reflection is an important component of critical race pedagogy. Everyone has a story, and one's own narrative is birthed out of their experiences. Each narrative is written between the lines of spoken and written words. It is imperative for each person to identify their own narrative and understand how it affects their mindset, actions, and even refusals to act.

In conclusion, we believe that our parallel revolution requires us to form cross-racial alliances. We reflect that whenever there has been a major social improvement, it has always required cross-racial alliances. As we move toward racial literacy in our society, like our foremothers and forefathers who fought for their own rights and the rights of others, we must lock arms together to fight racism at every level and exemplify the spirit of the song "Ebony and Ivory" by Paul and Stevie that urges us to live together in harmony.

REFERENCES

Coates, T. (2015). *Between the world and me.* New York, NY: Spiegel & Grau.

Delpit, L. (2006). *Other people's children: Cultural conflict in the classroom.* New York, NY: The New Press.

Edwards, P., Thompson McMillon, G., & Turner, J. (2010). *Change is gonna come: Transforming literacy education for African American students.* New York, NY: Teachers College Press.

Haddix, M. (2012). Talkin' in the company of my sistas: The counterlanguages and deliberate silences of Black female students in teacher education. *Linguistics & Education, 23*, 169–181.

Jennings, M. E., & Lynn, M. (2005). The house that race built: Critical pedagogy, African-American education, and the re-conceptualization of a Critical Race Pedagogy. *Educational Foundations, 19*(3–4), 15–32.

Lazar, A., Edwards, P., & Thompson McMillon, G. (2012). *Bridging literacy and equity: The essential guide to social equity teaching.* New York, NY: Teachers College Press.

Mosley, M., & Rogers, R. (2011). Inhabiting the tragic gap: Pre-service teachers practicing racial literacy. *Teaching Education, 22*(3), 303–324.

National Council of Teachers of English. (2015). Statement affirming #BlackLivesMatter. Retrieved from www.ncte.org/governance/pres-team_9-8-15

Pérez, L., Johnson, R., & Kohli, R. (2006). Naming racism: A conceptual look at internalized racism in U.S. schools. *Chicano-Latino Law Review, 26*, 183–206.

Sealey-Ruiz, Y. (2011). Learning to talk and write about race: Developing racial literacy in a college English classroom. *English Quarterly: Journal of the Canadian Council of Teachers of English Language Arts, 42*(1), 24-42.

Willis, A., Montavon, M., Hall, H., Hunter, C., Burke, L., & Herrera, A. (2008). *On critically conscious research: Approaches to language and literacy research.* New York, NY: Teachers College Press and National Conference on Research in Language and Literacy.

Part II

BEYOND BLACK AND WHITE

CHAPTER 6

Latino Critical Race Theory (LatCrit)

A Historical and Compatible Journey from Legal Scholarship to Teacher Education

Rachel Salas

Latino Critical Theory (LatCrit) is a theoretical perspective illuminating the complexity of Latinx[1] (DeGuzman, 2017) and other subordinated groups' identities and speaks to racism, sexism, classism, and other forms of oppression (Delgado Bernal, 2002; Solórzano & Delgado Bernal, 2001; Valdes, 1998; Villenas, Deyhle & Parker, 1999). LatCrit challenges paradigms that situate the Latinx community and other outgroups within a deficit view based on race, language, immigration status, and economic situation.

While LatCrit shares many tenets with Critical Race Theory (CRT), a LatCrit lens is "concerned with a progressive sense of coalitional Latina/ Latino pan-ethnicity and addresses issues often ignored by critical race theorists such as language, immigration, ethnicity, culture, identity, phenotype, and sexuality" (Solórzano & Delgado Bernal, 2001, p. 311). LatCrit focuses on domestic and global issues that center the Latinx community through a multidimensional and inclusive perspective (Arriola, 1998; Delgado Bernal, 2002).

A LatCrit perspective provides analytical lenses to identify and target racialized structures contributing to legal, social, and educational subordination and oppression of ethnic, linguistic, and other diverse groups. A LatCrit perspective critiques the majoritarian narrative through "stories, parables, chronicles, narratives and counterstories" (Delgado, 1988, p. 2413). Borrowing the storytelling genre from CRT, LatCrit scholars use fictional and nonfictional narratives to critique majoritarian structures, and offer tales that counter the dominant viewpoint that historically marginalized and subordinated the Latinx community and other oppressed groups (Delgado, 1988; Valdes, 1998). Storytelling is an integral part of CRT and LatCrit and is used both in legal scholarship (Delgado, 1988, 1997) and in educational research (Solórzano & Delgado Bernal, 2001; Solórzano & Yosso, 2001).

LatCrit's roots are historically tied to CRT. Many of the legal minds who emerged as LatCrit scholars began theorizing for a more inclusive method to find voice for the Latinx community's and other outgroups' central concerns, such as issues of language, class, economics and immigration status, that were integral to their survival and existence.

HISTORY

Valdes (1998) argued, "LatCrit theory is first and foremost an intellectual and discursive movement striving to create a culture of understanding about Latinas/o and the law" (p. 7). Latino Critical Race Theory emerged and benefitted from the legal thought and work of CRT and Critical Feminism (Hernandez-Truyol, Harris, & Valdes, 2006; Valdes, 1998). A group of legal scholars theorized how best to serve local and global communities beyond the Black/White binary of CRT (Espinoza & Harris, 1997; Trucios-Haynes, 2001; Valdes, 1998) and to "test alternative approaches to the design of academic venues for outsider scholarship" (Hernandez-Truyol, Harris, & Valdes, 2006, p. 183).

At the 1995 Hispanic National Bar Association annual meeting in San Juan, Puerto Rico, a group of legal scholars from the Latino Law Professor section met to discuss how best to proceed with organizing a more inclusive agenda to meet the needs of Latino communities and perspectives (Arriola, 1998). The term *LatCrit,* or *Latino Critical Theory,* was coined at this gathering and the first LatCrit conference was conceived and held in La Jolla, California, in 1996 (Hernandez-Truyol, Harris, & Valdes, 2006).

Prior to convening this first meeting, stakeholders met multiple times to formulate a set of salient functions and guideposts as a guiding structure for the group's work and future scholarship. These functions and guideposts were formulated based on the social and legal needs of Latinos and other diverse communities at the time with the understanding that they were dynamic and would evolve as the legal and social needs of the diverse communities grew (Hernandez-Truyol, Harris, & Valdes, 2006).

The four functions formulated were as follows:

- *The production of knowledge*: the formulation and generation of ideas and knowledge that focus a lens on issues that pertain to Latinos and the law. This knowledge base expands understanding of Latino communities, society, and the global community. The production of knowledge is a catalyst that moves the theory forward for the betterment of society and the law;
- *The advancement of social transformation*: the practicability of ideas and knowledge that set forth a path of improvement and transformation for Latinos, other marginalized groups, and society

as a whole. Praxis, acting and reflecting on the world in order to change it (Stovall, Lynn, Danley, & Martin, 2009), is an integral component to LatCrit;

- *The expansion and connection of antisubordination struggles*: the Latinx community is diverse, both domestically and globally, and interconnected to other subordinated groups in the fight for justice; and
- *The cultivation of community and coalition*: LatCrit comprises a collective of scholars, activists, educators, and others who have joined together as a community to improve the social and legal environment for Latinos and others. (Hernandez-Truyol, Harris, & Valdes, 2006; Valdes, 1998)

These functions, while described individually, work together, are interrelated, and are not intended to be stand-alone functions.

Along with these functions, seven guideposts were designed to focus theorizing forward toward praxis for the LatCrit community and other subordinate groups:

- Recognize and accept the inevitable and political nature specific to legal scholarship in the U.S.: This guidepost promotes a realistic understanding of the need to navigate politics and jurisprudence in the U.S. in order to promote social justice.
- Recognize that critical outsider scholars must become academic activists both within and beyond our institutions, professions, or local situations: This guidepost is the call to engage actively in antisubordination theorizing and praxis for the benefit of the Latinx and marginalized communities.
- Commit to building intra-Latina/o communities and intergroup coalitions: This guidepost focuses a collaborative lens on praxis and the multidimensionality, diversity, and interrelatedness of the LatCrit community at large.
- Find commonalities while respecting differences: In order to respect knowledge building of the community, an understanding of common themes, needs, and foci, as well as individual and group differences, is needed.
- Appreciate, incorporate, and apply the jurisprudential past: This guidepost recognizes the advancements and achievements of the past work that informs current and future work.
- Commit to a continual engagement in self-critique (individually and collectively): This guidepost recognizes the need to engage in ethical theorizing and praxis within individual and collective work products with a focus on promoting antisubordination academic activism.

- Recognize both specificity and diversity in the construction of LatCrit theory, praxis, and community: This guidepost is a call to continued authentic work product and collaboration that moves the democratic process forward. (Bender & Valdes, 2011)

The guideposts steer the LatCrit movement in a unified and progressive manner. Although the functions and guideposts were crafted by legal Lat-Crit scholars, they have application to the educational community as well.

FROM CRT TO LATCRIT IN EDUCATION

LatCrit, like CRT, emerged from and is grounded in legal thought and scholarship (Valdes, 1998). With the introduction of CRT in education by Gloria Ladson-Billings and William Tate (1995), educational researchers such as Solórzano (1997, 1998), Solórzano and Villalpando (1998), and Villenas, Deyhle, and Parker (1999) began to explore the use of CRT as a lens to examine the social inequalities and lived experiences of Latinos in education broadly. Much of this research focused on elementary, secondary (K–12), and higher education.

Solórzano (1997), Solórzano and Yosso (2001), and Smith-Maddox and Solórzano (2002) were the first to use a CRT analytical lens to look at teacher education specifically. Soon these same researchers, followed by others, began to lay the groundwork for using both CRT and LatCrit as analytical lenses to critique the social and educational lives and environment of the Latinx community (Delgado Bernal, 2002; Fernández, 2002; Solórzano & Delgado Bernal, 2001; Solórzano & Yosso, 2002; Villalpando, 2003, 2004; Yosso, 2005, 2006). While many researchers continued to combine the use of CRT and LatCrit, LatCrit began to emerge as a legitimate analytical tool increasingly used by more educational researchers in the field.

Figure 6.1 shows the development of LatCrit from its inception as a part of the LatCrit legal scholarship to its use in education and teacher education. Moving from a CRT lens to include a LatCrit perspective, Solórzano and Yosso (2001) posited that "A LatCrit theory in education is a framework that can be used to theorize and examine the ways in which race and racism explicitly and implicitly impact on the educational structures, processes, and discourses that affect People of Color generally and Latinas/os specifically" (p. 479). Furthermore, they argue, "LatCrit theory in education is conceived as a social justice project that attempts to link theory with practice, scholarship with teaching, and the academy with the community. LatCrit theory in education is transdisciplinary and draws on many other schools of progressive scholarship" (p. 479).

Just as legal scholars used narratives (Delgado, 1988, Valdes, 1998), Latinx researchers also studied their community by telling stories and

Figure 6.1: Historical Diagram of LatCrit in Teacher Education

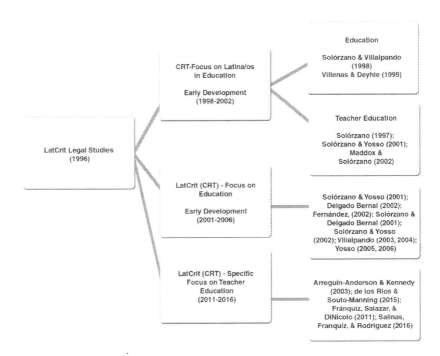

producing counterstories that were empowering and emancipatory, combating stereotypical and dehumanizing majoritarian narratives. These stories or counterstories are used both to counter the dominant narrative and as a method of analysis in research.

According to Yosso (2006), majoritarian storytelling "is a method of recounting the experiences and perspectives of those with racial and social privilege" (p. 9). This form of majoritarian narrative often perpetuates myths and situates people of color in economically and socially deprived contexts. Majoritarian narratives can contain overt and covert deficit and delimiting descriptive language of people of color that are written and often accepted as "truths."

Solórzano and Yosso (2002) outlined five ways counterstorytelling can be used within a pedagogical context:

- to create a common community within nondominant groups;
- to question dominant thought and perspective (especially about how nondominant groups are perceived);
- to bring clarity and new perspectives to nondominant groups, show them there is solidarity in their struggle and provide a lens to new and potential possibilities;

- to show members of nondominant groups how they can co-construct a better life by weaving elements of counterstories and their daily reality; and
- to provide a discourse of possibility to counter dominant belief systems. (p. 156)

Counterstories can be developed as autobiographical, biographical, and composite (Yosso, 2006).

Counterstorytelling has been used as a method of developing voice and power in racially and socially marginalized people. These stories provide a legitimate and valued vehicle for marginalized groups to voice their lived experience and perspectives. They can shine light on experiences and issues of social and racial injustice. Ultimately, counterstorytelling in education is used to confront majoritarian tales that provide a singular lens and distorted representation of the Latinx community and other nondominant groups (Yosso, 2006).

RESEARCH SYNTHESIS: LATCRIT IN TEACHER EDUCATION

The majority of the research in education using LatCrit as a theoretical tool has focused on K–12, undergraduate, and graduate students (Revilla, 2001; Gonzalez & Portillos, 2007; Pérez Huber, 2010; Rodriguez, Amador & Tarango, 2016; Freire, Valdez & Delavan, 2016; Stein, Wright, Gil, Miness, & Ginanto, 2017). There are a few studies focusing an analytical lens on LatCrit and teacher education specifically, which are described here. The first three studies focus specifically on LatCrit and bilingual preservice teachers.

Fránquiz, Salazar, and DiNicolo (2011) looked at the preparation of bilingual teachers. The researchers challenged the assumption that teachers of color know everything about diversity and do not need additional support in teaching culturally and linguistically diverse (CLD) students. They felt it was important for all teacher candidates to experience a program that assisted in deconstructing views and myths about CLD student populations. In addition, LatCrit should be used to challenge the deficit views educators may have about bilingual learners and to support collaboration and coalition between teachers and students. The bilingual preservice teachers learned to used counterstories to challenge assumptions and deficit views about the language.

Arrequín-Anderson and Kennedy (2013) used a specific language planning experience for their preservice bilingual teachers involved in an environmental science workshop. Using the Project Wild curriculum sponsored by the Council for Environmental Education and usually administered in English, they created a Spanish language agenda and program for all participants. The 6-hour workshop was held entirely in Spanish to challenge the omission of Spanish-speaking students' home language in the environmental science curriculum. The preservice teachers were involved in the use of Lat-Crit to challenge majoritarian language policies and center the students' language as a source of strength.

Salinas, Fránquiz, and Rodriguez (2016) looked at bilingual preservice teachers as well. The researchers worked with preservice teachers in a social studies methods course to deconstruct historical inaccuracies and to support the construction of counterstories and narratives addressing those inaccuracies. The preservice teachers, using primary sources and historical data, also created narratives for instrumental people of color who played a significant role but were ignored and left out of the social studies curriculum. Using a LatCrit lens, these bilingual preservice teachers learned to challenge and question dominant ideologies.

De los Rios and Souto-Manning (2014) focused on their own lived experiences as former teachers and current teacher educators. They utilized a LatCrit perspective and *testimonio* to detail their thoughts on how teacher preparation needs to change to better prepare teachers to work with all students. They used Pérez Huber's (2009) description of *testimonio* as "a verbal journey of a witness who speaks to reveal the racial, classed, gendered, and nativist injustices they have suffered as a means of healing, empowerment, and advocacy for a more humane present and future" (p. 644) to tell their stories. Through their counterstory, de los Rios and Souto-Manning called for a critical pedagogy of teacher education so teachers are prepared for a diverse society and learn to "approach issues of inequity in real and authentic ways" (p. 287).

Each of these studies integrated one or all of the four functions of LatCrit by (1) advancing the needs of the Latinx community through the creation of knowledge, (2) encouraging social transformations that involve praxis, (3) focusing on antisubordination struggles, and (4) bringing scholars together to improve the educational environment for the Latinx population.

NEXT STEPS

A growing body of literature focuses on LatCrit as an analytical lens and framework to analyze K–12 and higher education, but little research is specific to teacher education. There are several immediate reasons to increase LatCrit teacher education research.

First, the Latinx community in the United States continues to grow rapidly (Bauman, 2017), while less than 20% of the teacher workforce identify as people of color (Brown & Ulrich, 2017). This continued cultural and linguistic mismatch between teachers and students may not bode well for the academic success of the CLD student population in the United States. (Egalite & Kisida, 2017). Teacher preparation programs should make every effort to provide teacher candidates with culturally relevant pedagogy (de los Rios & Souto-Manning, 2015) and a deep understanding of how to successfully educate an increasingly culturally and linguistically diverse student population.

Second, we continue to live in a racist society. The Latinx community, as well as other racial minority groups, is under constant siege by the current White House administration. The Latinx population has been referred to by dehumanizing terms: *criminals*, *drug dealers*, *rapists*, *murderers* (Simon, 2018) and *animals* (Davis, 2018). This oppressive and subordinating language affects the Latinx population directly and also barrages prospective teachers, teacher educators, and dominant-population students who are regularly exposed to it from the media. Teacher preparation programs should provide teacher candidates with authentic and supportive field experiences with opportunities to work with CLD students, families, and communities so that they can learn firsthand of the funds of knowledge (Gonzalez, Moll, & Amanti, 2005), strengths, and support systems these students possess.

Finally, the Latinx student population continues to be overrepresented in special education referrals, identification, and placement (Moreno & Segura-Herrera, 2014) and underrepresented in gifted-and-talented classrooms or programs (Harris, Plucker, Rapp, & Martinez, 2009; Del Siegel et al., 2016). Teacher education must prepare teachers to be able to identify giftedness in Latinx and CLD student populations and understand the differences between a language difference and a disability. In 2011 the National Association for Gifted Children (NAGC) released a position statement that is a clear call for educators to do more to increase the identification of CLD students for gifted programs.

A sense of urgency should be felt by all teacher education researchers to use a LatCrit analytical lens and framework in all the areas mentioned above to learn how best to prepare teachers who can provide high-quality and equitable educational experiences for Latinx students and all CLD students. In addition, the four functions laid out by the LatCrit legal scholars should be adapted and used for a LatCrit theoretical lens on teacher education:

- Production of knowledge with a focus on teacher education;
- Advancement of social transformation as praxis in teacher education;
- Expansion and connection of antisubordination struggles through teacher education global awareness; and
- The cultivation of community and coalition beyond the classroom.

The goal of LatCrit research in teacher education should be to generate ideas and knowledge on how best to serve the Latinx community and other outgroups through transformative educational practice, and to foster connections and relationships within and beyond the Latinx community for a truly educated populace and a just society.

NOTE

1. The term *Latinx* is used to describe the Latina/o community in my writing and to be gender inclusive. When writing from the LatCrit legal and educational studies, I use the term used by the author(s).

REFERENCES

Arreguín-Anderson, M. G., & Kennedy, K. D. (2013). Deliberate language planning in environmental education: A CRT/LatCrit perspective. *Journal of Environmental Education, 44*(1), 1–15. DOI: 10.1080/00958964.2012.665098

Arriola, E. R. (1998). Difference, solidarity and law: Building Latina/o communities through LatCrit theory: Foreword. *Chicano-Latino Law Review, 19*(1), 1–67.

Bauman, K. (2017, August 28). School enrollment of the Hispanic population: Two decades of growth. [Blog post]. Retrieved from www.census.gov/newsroom/blogs/random-samplings/2017/08/school_enrollmentof.html

Bender, S., & Valdes, F. (2011). LatCrit XV symposium afterword—at and beyond fifteen: Mapping LatCrit theory, community, and praxis. *Harvard Latino Law Review, 14*, 397–445.

Brown, C., & Ulrich, B. (2017, September 17). Revisiting the persistent teacher diversity problem. Retrieved from www.americanprogress.org/issues/education-K–12/news/2017/09/28/415203/revisiting-persistent-teacher-diversity-problem/Center for American Progress

Davis, J. H. (2018, May 16). Trump calls some unauthorized immigrants "animals" in rant. *New York Times*. Retrieved from www.nytimes.com/2018/05/16/us/politics/trump-undocumented-immigrants-animals.html

De los Rios, C., & Souto-Manning, M. (2015). Teacher educators as cultural workers: Problematizing teacher education pedagogies. *Studying Teacher Education, 11*(3), 272–293.

DeGuzmán, M. (2017). Latinx: ¡Estamos aquí!, or being "Latinx" at UNC-Chapel Hill. *Cultural Dynamics, 29*(3), 214–230.

Delgado Bernal, D. (2002). Critical Race Theory, Latino critical theory and critical race-gendered epistemologies: Recognizing students of color as holders and creators of knowledge. *Qualitative Inquiry, 8*(1), 105–126.

Delgado, R. (1988). Storytelling for oppositionists and others: A plea for narrative. *Michigan Law Review, 87*, 2411–2441.

Delgado, R. (1997). Rodrigo's fifteenth chronicle: Racial mixture, Latino-critical scholarship, and the Black-White binary. *Texas Law Review, 75*, 1181–1201.

Del Siegel, Gubbins, O'Rourke, Langley, Mun, Luria, Little, McCoach, Knupp, Callahan, & Plucker, (2016). Barriers to underserved students' participation in gifted programs and possible solutions. *Journal for the Education of the Gifted, 39*(2), 103–131.

Egalite, A. J., & Kisida, B. (2017). The effects of teacher match on students' academic perceptions and attitudes. *Educational Evaluation and Policy Analysis*, 40(1), 59–81.

Espinoza, L., & Harris, A. P. (1997). Afterword: Embracing the tar baby: LatCrit theory and the stick mess of race. *California Law Review*, 85, 1585–1645.

Fernández, L. (2002). Telling stories about school: Using Critical Race and Latino Critical theories to document Latina/Latino education and resistance. *Qualitative Inquiry*, 8(1), 45–65.

Freire, J. A., Valdez, V. E., & Delavan, M. G. (2016). The (dis)inclusion of Latina/o interests from Utah's dual language education boom. *Journal of Latinos and Education*, 16(4), 276–289. DOI: 10.1080/15348431.2016.1229617

Fránquiz, M. G., Salazar, M. d. C., & DeNicolo, C. P. (2011). Challenging majoritarian tales: Portraits of bilingual teachers deconstructing deficit views of bilingual learners. *Bilingual Research Journal*, 34(3), 279–300.

González, J. C., & Portillos, E. L. (2007) The undereducation and overcriminalization of U.S. Latinas/os: A post–Los Angeles riots LatCrit analysis. *Educational Studies*, 42(3), 247–266. DOI: 10.1080/00131940701634643

Gonzalez, N., Moll, L. C., & Amanti, C. (Eds.). (2005). *Funds of knowledge: theorizing practices in households, communities, and classrooms*. Mahwah, NJ: Lawrence Erlbaum.

Harris, B., Plucker, J. A., Rapp, K. E., & Martínez, R. S. (2009, Spring). Identifying gifted and talented English language learners: A case study. *Journal for the Education of the Gifted*, 32, 368–393, 442. Retrieved from unr.idm.oclc.org/login?url=https://search-proquest-com.unr.idm.oclc.org/docview/222340733?accountid=452

Hernandez-Truyol, B., Harris, A., & Valdes, F. (2006). Beyond the first decade: A forward-looking history of LatCrit theory, community and praxis. *Berkeley La Raza Law Journal*, 17, 169–216.

Ladson-Billings, G., & Tate, W. F. (1995). Toward a critical race theory of education. *Teachers College Record*, 97(1), 47–68.

Moreno, G., & Segura-Herrera, T. (2014). Special education referrals and disciplinary actions for Latino students in the United States. *Multicultural Learning and Teaching*, 9(1), 33–51. DOI: http://dx.doi.org.unr.idm.oclc.org/10.1515/mlt-2013-0022

National Association for Gifted Children. (2011). *Position statement: Identifying and serving culturally and linguistically diverse gifted students*. Washington, DC: NAGC. Retrieved from www.nagc.org/sites/default/files/Position%20Statement/Identifying%20and%20Serving%20Culturally%20and%20Linguistically.pdf

Pérez Huber, L. (2009). Disrupting apartheid of knowledge: Testimonio as methodology in Latina/o critical race research in education. *International Journal of Qualitative Studies in Education*, 22 (6), 639–654.

Pérez Huber, L. (2010). Using Latina/o critical race theory (LatCrit) and racist nativism to explore intersectionality in the educational experiences of undocumented Chicana college students. *The Journal of Educational Foundations*, 24(1), 77–

96. Retrieved from unr.idm.oclc.org/login?url=https://search-proquest-com.unr.idm.oclc.org/docview/205234632?accountid=452

Rodríguez, C., Amador, A., & Tarango, B. A. (2016). Mapping educational equity and reform policy in the borderlands: LatCrit spatial analysis of grade retention. *Equity & Excellence in Education*, 49(2), 228–240. DOI: 10.1080/10665684.2016.1144834

Revilla, A. T. (2001). LatCrit and CRT in the field of education: A theoretical dialogue between two colleagues. *Denver University Law Review*, 78 (4), 623–632.

Salinas, C. S., Fránquiz, M. E., & Rodriguez, N. N. (2016). Writing Latina/o historical narratives: Narratives at the intersection of critical historical inquiry and LatCrit. *Urban Review*, 48, 264–284.

Simon, D. (2018). Trump's other insensitive comments on race and ethnicity. *CNN Politics*. Retrieved from www.cnn.com/2018/01/11/politics/president-trump-racial-comments-tweets/index.html

Smith-Maddox, R., & Solórzano, D. G. (2002). Using critical race theory, Paulo Freire's problem-posing method, and case study research to confront race and racism in education. *Qualitative Inquiry*, 8(1), 66–84.

Solórzano, D. (1997). Images and words that wound: Critical Race Theory, racial stereotyping, and teacher education. *Teacher Education Quarterly*, 24, 5–19.

Solórzano, D. (1998). Critical Race Theory, racial and gender microaggression, and the experiences of Chicana and Chicano scholars. *International Journal of Qualitative Studies in Education*, 11, 121–136.

Solórzano, D., & Delgado Bernal, B. (2001). Examining transformational resistance through a critical race and LatCrit theory framework: Chicana and Chicano students in an urban context. *Urban Education*, 36(3), 308–342.

Solórzano, D., & Villalpando, O. (1998). Critical Race Theory: Marginality and the experiences of students of color in higher education. In C. Torres & T. Mitchell (Eds.), *Sociology of education: Emerging perspectives* (pp. 211–224). Albany, NY: State University of New York Press.

Solórzano, D. G., & Yosso, T. J. (2001). From racial stereotyping and deficit discourse toward a critical race theory in teacher education. *Multicultural Education*, 9, 2–8.

Solórzano, D. G., & Yosso, T. J. (2002). Critical race methodology: Counter-storytelling as an analytical framework for educational research. *Qualitative Inquiry*, 8(1), 23–44.

Stein, K. C., Wright, J., Gil, E., Miness, A., & Ginanto, D. (2017). Examining Latina/o students' experiences of injustice: LatCrit insights from a Texas high school. *Journal of Latinos and Education*, 17(2), 103–120. DOI: 10.1080/15348431.2017.1282367

Stovall, D., Lynn, M., Danley, L., & Martin, D. (2009). Critical race praxis in education. *Race Ethnicity and Education*, 12(2), 131–132.

Trucios-Haynes, E. (2001). Why "race matters:" LatCrit theory and Latina/o racial identity. *La Raza Law Journal*, 12, 1–42.

Valdes, F. (1998). Under construction: LatCrit consciousness, community, and theory. *La Raza Law Journal, 10,* 1–55.

Villalpando, O. (2003). Self-segregation or self-preservation? A Critical Race Theory and Latina/o critical theory analysis of a study of Chicana/o college students, *International Journal of Qualitative Studies in Education, 16*(5), 619–646, DOI: 10.1080/0951839032000142922

Villalpando, O. (2004). Practical considerations of critical race theory and Latino critical theory for Latino college students. *New Directions for Student Services, 105,* 41–50. DOI: 10.1177/002248710730841

Villenas, S. Deyhle, D., & Parker, L. (1999). Critical Race Theory and praxis: Chicano(a)/Latino(a) and Navajo struggles for dignity, educational equity, and social justice. In D. Deyhle, L. Parker, & S. Villenas (Eds.*), Race is—race isn't: Critical Race Theory and qualitative studies in education* (pp. 31–51). Boulder, CO: Westview Press.

Yosso, T. (2005). Whose culture has capital? A Critical Race Theory discussion of community cultural wealth. *Race Ethnicity and Education 8*(1), 69–91.

Yosso, T. (2006). *Critical race counterstories along the Chicana/Chicano educational pipeline.* New York, NY: Routledge.

CHAPTER 7

Exploring Asian American Invisibility in Teacher Education
The AsianCrit Account

Keonghee Tao Han

At the inception of Critical Race Theory (CRT), Robert Chang (1993) initiated AsianCrit by denouncing ahistoricism, color-blindness, White meritocracy, and the Black–White binary to chronicle Asians' lived experiences in the U.S. context. Subsequently, Asian scholars have defined legal, educational, and political realities specific to Asian Americans (Ancheta, 2006; Lee, 2001; Museus, 2014). In this chapter, I first present AsianCrit as a framework to recount the history of Asian racial reality; then I examine how this historical contextualization helps us understand how an invisible Asian presence exists in American education and teacher education. I conclude the chapter with a look at next steps for AsianCrit pertinent to teacher education.

TENETS OF ASIANCRIT:
A HISTORICAL-CONTEMPORARY FRAMEWORK

In building on CRT, AsianCrit focuses on issues unique to Asian Americans. AsianCrit tenets include Asianization, transnational context, intersectionality, storytelling as legitimate knowledge, and social justice activism.

Asianization

Historically as well as today, Asian Americans suffer a nativist racism associated with xenophobia (Chang, 1993; Gee, 1999). Asians' perpetual foreigner images are fashioned to subordinate us as forever foreigners who cannot assimilate to American life (Suzuki, 2002). Beginning in the 1800s, Asian Americans were depicted as an invading "yellow peril" who undermined American cultural life. As Gold Rush railroad workers and coal miners, Chinese immigrants were represented as coolies and slaves and suffered economic and racial harassment (Lowe, 1996).

The epithet "yellow peril" named a fear that included economic and military invasion, competition for work, and interracial marriage (Ancheta, 2006; Museus, 2014). In response to this fear, the Chinese Exclusion Act of 1882 banned Chinese immigrant laborers, and it was not until the McCarran-Walter Act of 1952 revised the 1924 Immigration Act that this near-total ban was lifted (though Asian immigration remained tightly limited). During the Second World War, Japanese American citizens were forcibly sent to internment camps (Chang, 1993; Suzuki, 2002).

The 1965 Immigration Act brought better-educated Asian immigrants to the U.S. (Lowe, 1996). Thereafter, the image of Asians changed from yellow peril to hardworking and successful "model minority" (Suzuki, 2002). *Model minority* sounds like a compliment, depicting Asian Americans as successfully assimilated to American culture. But despite this new image among mainstream scholars, media, and society, Asian Americans have not fully achieved economic and sociopolitical benefits or status (Lowe, 1996).

For example, East Asian Americans show excellent high school and college graduation rates (Yu, 2006). However, several problems are hidden in the model minority idea. First, there are multiple Asian nationalities and identities who struggle in school (e.g., Pacific Islanders; Southeast Asians from Vietnam, Cambodia, Laos, and Hmong), but, due to model minority assumptions, many do not receive needed academic and economic aids (Lee, 2001; Lei, 2006; Pang, Han, & Pang, 2011; Yu, 2006).

Second, despite high achievements and credentials, there exists a glass ceiling characterized by visibly fewer leadership positions occupied by Asians in the academic and sociopolitical arenas (Kiang, 2004; Nielson & Kiang, 2013). Moreover, the glass ceiling includes lower earnings and tenure, promotion, and reappointment rates for Asian faculty when compared to White faculty (Yan & Museus, 2013).

Third, by selectively portraying one minority group as a model, the mainstream society has concocted a meritocracy argument for Asians against other minoritized groups that covers up structural inequality and ideological hegemony to reinforce the racial hierarchy—White-top, Asian-middle, and Black-bottom (Chang, 1993; Pang, Han, & Pang, 2011; Yu, 2006). As such, in a divide-and-conquer manner, interethnic conflict has been forged and White supremacy is further maintained (Lei, 2006; Min, 2004; Suzuki, 2002; Yu, 2006).

Transnational Contexts

Though the model minority may be a myth, overall Asian American educational and economic successes continue to rise (Yu, 2006). The Pacific Rim nations' economic growth has made them a collective world superpower over the past several decades. This change creates different (inter)national geopolitical dynamics and influences the lives of Asian Americans—the

United States, now has to accept alternative reactions from other superpowers like Brazil, Russia, India, and China (Kupchan, 2012).

Intersectionality

Asian women experience layered racism and sexism just as many other ethnic or racial minority women do (hooks, 2015). They face a combination of oppressions that remain largely undocumented and unrecognized (Han, 2014, 2018). To reconstruct bigotry and racism, intersectionality of racism, gender, class, sexual orientation, and national origin for both men and women of Asian descent, new analyses and interpretations are possible that can contribute to the existing literature in the K–12 and higher education contexts.

To date, women of color and Asian women have been silenced and marginalized in most professional arenas, including teacher education and academia (Han, 2014, 2018; Li & Beckett, 2006). Asian women's situated narratives documenting both struggles and successes still need to be researched and recognized as a foundation for activism and the further development of Asian American women's contributions to the academy (Han, 2014, 2018; Hune, 1997, 2006; Matsuda, 1997).

Storytelling as Legitimate Knowledge

Asian voices are particularly situated to document histories of immigration (e.g., Chinese Exclusion Act of 1882), economics (e.g., exploitation and massacre of Chinese workers, 1885), education (e.g., shifting affirmative action policies and practices; see Tekagi, 1992), and administrative or military action (e.g., Japanese internment camps). Too often, the Asian American intellectual canon, experiential knowledge, and voices are unheard in education (An, 2016; Kiang, 2004; Museus, Maramba, & Teranish, 2013). These silenced voices and epistemologies ought to be infused as a guide to future teacher education.

Social Justice Activism

Historical construction of Asian American identity as immigrants, foreigners, or model minorities was interposed within the Black/White binary, reflecting political construction of stereotypical Asian American identity. As we are placed critically in the middle in the White-top-and-Black-bottom racial hierarchy, we must create a constructive narrative that includes the voices and contributions of Asian Americans in order to achieve equality and social justice (Chang, 1993). Just as Bell (1992) declared, we ought to combat and struggle for human dignity and liberation for Asians (ourselves) and all Others in a colonized American life.

TEACHER EDUCATION: WHY ARE ASIAN AMERICANS INVISIBLE?

Teachers of color have not kept up in education (Haddix, 2015). Asian Americans in particular are significantly underrepresented in the teaching profession (Rong & Preissle, 2014). Asian American teachers historically and currently have been a small percentage of the teaching force and an even smaller fraction in teacher education, making up about 1–2% of all U.S. K–12 teachers (Ng, Lee, & Pak, 2007). Gordon's (2000, 2005) research interviewing Asian student teachers revealed possible explanations for the shortage of Asian American teachers. First, Asian parents stress high status, respect, and income for their children and because teaching in the U.S. is not highly acknowledged, parents pressure their children to enter other merit-based fields (e.g., engineering, medicine, or computer science).

Also, Asian Americans feel individual inadequacy gaining access to the dominant American pedagogy, which balances social interactions and interpersonal relations differently from Asian traditions. In Confucian-heritage cultures, teachers are considered masters, and teacher-centered, top-down instructional approaches are practiced (Alon & McIntyre, 2005). Asian American educators therefore approach teaching differently compared to mainstream classroom practices: Asian-descent educators see their role as moral agents and expect to encounter their own culturally ingrained reverence for education (Han & Scull, 2012; Nguyen, 2008). Moreover, Asian American teachers are concerned about White racism stemming from cultural and linguistic discrimination, especially if they have an accent and related English proficiency problems. In sum, existing research explains that Asians' cultural expectations of saving-face and fears of White racism affect Asians' career choices and lead them to avoid entering the teaching profession in the U.S. (Gordon, 2000, 2005; Rong & Preissle, 2014; Tang, 2002).

In higher education settings, Asians are just as invisible, as they are Othered by mainstream policy and practices (Han & Leonard, 2017). Numerically, they are a minority: In fall 2015, of all full-time faculty at degree-granting postsecondary institutions, Asian/Pacific Islander males composed 6%, females 4%, of all faculty members (National Center for Education Statistics, 2015). The glass ceiling effects manifest in income disparity (Lee, 2002), skewed power relations between Whites and Others (Han, Scull, Nganga, & Kambutu, 2018), invisibility in high-ranking positions (Kiang, 2004; Nielson & Kiang, 2013), and multilayered racialized and gendered discrimination among women faculty (Han, 2014, 2018; Hune, 2006; Li & Beckett, 2006).

Absence of Asian American Content in Curriculum

All racialized groups' histories, heritage, and cultures are distorted and misrepresented in curriculum and textbooks. Asian perspectives and history are misrepresented in school curriculum (An, 2016; Sheets & Chew, 2002). Textbooks and curricular materials have documented Whites' perspectives that present individuals as bad guys instead of critically considering the roots of those portrayals in structural and cultural White supremacy (Brown & Brown, 2010).

Asians' histories continue to be absent from K–12 curricula (An, 2016; Suh, An, & Forest, 2015) and teacher education programs (Kiang, 2004; Ng et al., 2007; Nguyen, 2008; Sheets & Chew, 2002). If Asian history and contributions are included, they are limited to a few representations, such as Chinese immigration in relation to transnational railroad construction and Japanese internment camps, eliding other Asian groups' history and contributions as invisible and distorted (An, 2016).

Similarly, teacher education remains White in epistemological content and practices (Han, 2018; Han et al., 2018). Statewide curriculum content, frameworks, and teacher competency assessments exclude Asian and Other epistemological and cultural content and pedagogy (Han, 2018; Kiang, 2004). The consequence of teacher education primarily inculcating Whiteness in content, personnel, competency tests, classroom practices (Jupp, Berry, & Lensmire, 2016), and governance/administration (Han & Leonard, 2017; Kiang, 2004; Yan & Museus, 2013) is that teacher education has not kept up with globalized times. The one-Whiteness-size-fits-all system has propelled achievement and wealth gaps in all education levels, especially for the growing number of Asian and Other ethnic descent students in K–12 schools (Apple, 2004).

Power Positioning and Racial Relations in Teacher Education

Han, Scull, Nganga, and Kambutu (2018) described disparate power dynamics among White governance and racial positioning of faculty of color (FOC) in a rural teacher education context. Counternarratives of FOC in this study problematized three major issues: (1) In the White-top-heavy academy, Whites occupy and maintain most decisionmaking positions; (2) FOC are often not included as leaders and excluded from decision making processes; and (3) ethnic, race-based research is undervalued. This study thus cautions race scholars to interrogate White supremacy: When dominant groups exclude Others from policy and decisionmaking processes, epistemological White supremacy is sustained.

NEXT STEPS: DEVELOPING ASIANCRIT IN TEACHER EDUCATION

An overwhelmingly White teaching faculty and teacher education force have fostered an educational dilemma surrounding achievement and wealth gaps between White students and students of color, as well as the Othering of FOC. Not only does this cultural and racial mismatch constitute the educational dilemma, but it also generates misunderstanding of and discrimination against diverse students by monocultural, monolingual White teachers (Lea, 2009). Similarly, White cultural norms alienate and marginalize FOC while leaving both White and diverse teachers unprepared.

The Need for Teacher/Faculty Diversity

From critical research, we know the following: (1) Teacher–student race matching—when students are matched with same-race teachers—can result in positive student achievements (Cherng & Halpin, 2016; Egalite, Kisida, & Winters, 2015) and lower rates of absence and suspensions (Holt & Gershenson, 2015); and (2) critical and culturally relevant pedagogues have enhanced student academic performance (Ladson-Billings, 2009). Because critical pedagogues respect diverse students' cultural identities and can emulate cultural practices of home cultures, they shift students from school failure toward excellence.

Yet teacher education remains White (Han et al., 2018; Ladson-Billings, 1995) and current classroom practices continue to reify mainstream biases (Hill-Jackson, 2007; Jupp, Berry, & Lensmire, 2016; Seattlage, 2011). Education urgently needs to diversify teaching faculty at the K–12 levels (Boser, 2014; Haddix, 2015) and the academy (Han et al., 2018). To address personnel diversification, it is crucial that people of color be represented at all levels of education, as well as in administrative governance and policy decisionmaking positions (Kiang, 2004; Nakanishi, 1996; Turner, Gonzalez, & Wood, 2008).

Diversify Teacher Education Curriculum and Pedagogy

Current curricular and pedagogical practices both widen achievement and wealth gaps and lead to further excluding Others. Without broadening the curriculum and embracing Other epistemologies in teacher education, the education system enables already antagonistic interethnic conflicts and hostile racial relations. Teacher education must expand its curriculum and pedagogy to include critical, multicultural, global content and more inclusive institutional and classroom practices. Other ways of knowing and doing ethnic, race-based research should be respected (Han et al., 2018; Turner et al., 2008).

The inclusion of Asian history and its indigenous intellectual canon is vital if teacher education is to develop along with the 21st-century global world (Kincheloe, 2017). Critical scholars cannot emphasize enough the need for transformative, global education so that teacher education provides space for pedagogy to develop a critical consciousness for educational and social equality in our teachers (Chapman, 2013; Kincheloe, 2017; Lei, 2006).

Reconstruct Asian Identity and Positioning in Teacher Education

Before the emergence of CRT and AsianCrit, Asian educators did not have a racial paradigm and vocabulary to ascertain the manifestations of historical and contemporary race relations in American life and education. With AsianCrit, we can create progressive racial relations and assert Asian American identity and positions in teacher education. AsianCrit ought to continue to recognize tensions and alienation among Asian Americans and interethnic racial relations as manipulated by dominant groups.

Today, Asians and Others face an ominous racial hegemony generated by the result of the 2016 election and the current administration. As the U.S. confronts tremendous challenges (inter)nationally in reestablishing democratic and diplomatic cultural, religious, and racial relations, Asian Americans should be watchful of the current political climate. AsianCrit scholars must speak up to counter Whiteness and its dominance. By raising our voices and reconstructing Asian American history and current narratives across education, we march toward vigorous, forceful activism for educational equity in teacher education.

Raise Consciousness to Form Coalitions

Today more serious and blatant backlash is on the rise in academia and in all American life. People of color are Othered on campus: Asian and diverse students and faculty have been subjected to hate speech, racial slurs and stereotypes, and injuries on campus (Han, 2018; Yan & Museus, 2013). Racial victims in academia often leave the profession or conform to its demands. To remedy hate speech, racism, and White backlash on university campuses, AsianCrit scholars advocate consciousness raising and speaking up, establishing and opening up safe spaces to learn to talk nonconfrontationally about race, gender, class, sexuality, and other -isms (Han, 2018; Matsuda, 1997). Interventions like sustained multicultural workshops for administrators, faculty, and students ought to be required (Chapman, 2013; Han & Leonard, 2017; Sleeter & Milner, 2013).

As positioned in the middle of the racial hierarchy, our racial consciousness is critical (Matsuda, 1997). Asian Americans must not be the coopted model minority, behaving as honorary Whites, but ought to exterminate White oppression by rejecting White supremacy (Matsuda, 1997). We should not sell our spirits just to obtain *"enhanced-super standing status"* inside the White colonizers' system (Bell, 1992, p. 115). We should not criticize fellow minoritized brothers and sisters just for individual gains. Buying and being sold into the fashionable power game will not get us saved; if we succumb to a neo-plantation attitude to please our White masters, we are only allowing White supremacy to replicate our own colonization.

Through media and under the current administration, we are taught racial hatred and we are short of compassion toward human dignity. What we need is compassion and coalition among all of us, Others and Whites, if we are to achieve institutional and structural changes (Delgado, 1989; Frankenberg, 1993). Critical race scholars have advocated alliance and coalition-forming but have not fully described how we can build trust to take the first step toward that coalition. Teacher education might initiate this project by embracing Others and Other epistemologies. Teacher educators ought to pioneer coalition-building, justice-seeking, and global-mindedness, fostering education so that future teachers can cultivate pliable young minds early on to develop their critical consciousness and understanding of Others.

REFERENCES

Alon, I., & McIntyre, J. R. (2005). *Business and management education in China: Transition, pedagogy, and training*. Hackensack, NJ: World Scientific Publishing.

An, S. (2016). Asian Americans in American history: An AsianCrit perspective on Asian American inclusion in state U.S. history curriculum standards. *Theory & Research in Social Education, 44*(2), 244–276.

Ancheta, A. N. (2006). *Race, rights, and the Asian American experience*. New Brunswick, NJ: Rutgers University Press.

Apple, M. W. (2004). *Ideology and curriculum*. New York, NY: Routledge Falmer.

Bell, D. (1992). *Faces at the bottom of the well: The permanence of racism*. New York, NY: Basic Books.

Boser, U. (2014). A new state-by-state analysis. Retrieved from www.scribd.com/doc/221645148/Teacher-Diversity-Revisited-A-New-State-by-State-Analysis

Brown, K. D., & Brown, A. L. (2010). Silenced memories: An examination of the sociocultural knowledge on race and racial violence in official school curriculum. *Equity & Excellence in Education, 43*, 139–154. DOI: 10.1080/l0665681003719590

Chang, M. J. (1993). Toward an Asian American legal scholarship: Critical race theory, poststructuralism, and narrative space. *California Law Review, 81*, 1241–1323.

Chapman, T. K. (2013). A Critical Race Theory analysis of past and present institutional processes and policies in teacher education. In A. F. Ball & C. A. Tyson (Eds.), *Studying diversity in teacher education* (pp. 237–256). New York, NY: Rowman & Littlefield.

Cherng, H. S., & Halpin, P. F. (2016). The importance of minority teachers: Student perceptions of minority versus white teachers. *Educational Researcher, 20*, 1–14.

Delgado, R. (1989). Storytelling for oppositionists and others: A plea for narrative. *Michigan Law Review, 81*, 2411–2441.

Egalite, A. J., Kisida, B., & Winters, M. A. (2015). Representation in the classroom: The effect of own-race teachers on student achievement. *Economics of Education Review, 45,* 44–52.

Frankenberg, R. (1993). *White women, race matters: The social construction of whiteness.* Minneapolis, MN: University of Minnesota Press.

Gee, H. (1999). Beyond black and white: Selected writings by Asian Americans within the critical race theory movement. *St. Mary's Law Review, 30,* 759–800.

Gordon, J. A. (2000). Asian American resistance to selecting teaching as a career: The power of community and tradition. *Teachers College Record, 102*(1), 173–196.

Gordon, J. A. (2005). In search of educators of color. *Leadership, 35*(2), 30–35.

Haddix, M. M. (2015). *Cultivating racial and linguistic diversity in literacy teacher education: Teachers like me.* New York, NY: Routledge.

Han, K. T. (2014). Moving racial discussion forward: A counterstory of racialized dynamics between an Asian-woman faculty of color and White preservice teachers in traditional rural America. *The Journal of Diversity in Higher Education, 7*(2), 126–146. DOI: 10.1037/a0036055

Han, K. T. (2018). A demographic and epistemological divide: Problematizing diversity and equity education in traditional rural teacher education. *International Journal of Qualitative Studies in Education.* DOI: 10.1080/09518398.2018.1455997

Han, K. T., & Leonard, J. (2017). Why diversity matters in rural America: Women faculty of color challenging Whiteness. *The Urban Review, 49*(1), 112–139. DOI: 10.1007/s11256-016-0384-7

Han, K. T., & Scull, W. R. (2012). Listening to Hyun-woo: What can we learn from a Korean American English learner? *The Clearing House, 85,* 23–32. DOI: 10.1080/00098655.2011.606244

Han, K. T., Scull, W. R., Nganga, L., & Kambutu, J. (2018). Voices from the red states: Challenging racial positioning in some of the most conservative communities in America. *Race, Ethnicity, and Education.* DOI: 10.1080/13613324.2018.1468751

Hill-Jackson, V. (2007). Wrestling whiteness: Three stages of shifting multicultural perspectives among White preservice teachers. *Multiple Perspectives, 9*(2), 29–35.

Holt, S. B., & Gershenson, S. (2015). *The impact of teacher demographic representation on student attendance and suspensions.* IZA Discussion Paper no. 9554. Retrieved from papers.ssrn.com/sol3/papers.cfm?abstract_id=2708367

hooks, b. (2015). *Ain't I a woman: Black women and feminism.* New York, NY: Routledge.

Hune, S. (1997). Higher education as gendered space: Asian American women and everyday inequities. In C. R. Ronai, B. A. Zsembik, & J. Feagin (Eds.), *Everyday sexism in the third millennium* (pp. 191–196). New York, NY: Routledge.

Hune, S. (2006). Asian Pacific American women and men in higher education. In G. Li & G. H. Beckett (Eds.), *"Strangers" of the academy: Asian women scholars in higher education* (pp. 15–36). Sterling, VA: Stylus Publishing.

Jupp, C. J., Berry, T. R., & Lensmire, T. J. (2016). Second-wave White teacher identity studies: A review of White teacher identity literature from 2004 through 2014. *Review of Educational Research, 86*(4), 1151–1191.

Kiang, P. N. (2004). Checking Southeast Asian American realities in Pan-Asian American agendas. *AAPU Nexus: Policy, Practice & Community, 2*(1), 48–76.

Kincheloe, J. L. (2017). The knowledges of teacher education: Developing a critical complex epistemology. In A. Darder, R. D. Torres, & P. Baltodano (Eds.), *The critical pedagogy reader* (3rd ed., pp. 503–517). New York, NY: Routledge.

Kupchan, C. A. (2012). *No one's world: The West, the rising rest, and the coming global turn.* New York, NY: Oxford University Press.

Ladson-Billings, G. (1995). Toward a theory of culturally relevant pedagogy. *American Educational Research Journal, 32*(3), 465–491.

Ladson-Billings, G. (2009). *The dream keepers: Successful teachers of African American children.* San Francisco, CA: Jossey-Bass.

Lea, V. (2009). Unmasking Whiteness in the teacher education college classroom: Critical and creative multicultural practice. In S. R. Steinberg (Ed.), *Diversity and multiculturalism: A reader* (pp. 57–76). New York, NY: Peter Lang.

Lee, S. J. (2001). More than "model minorities" or "delinquents": A look at Hmong American high school students. *Harvard Educational Review, 71*(3), 505–529.

Lee, S. M. (2002). Do Asian American faculty face a glass ceiling in higher education? *American Educational Research Journal, 39,* 695–724. DOI: 10.3102/00028312039003695

Lei, J. (2006). Teaching and learning with Asian American and Pacific Islander students. *Race, Ethnicity, and Education, 9*(1), 85–101.

Li, G., & Beckett, G. (Eds.). (2006). *"Strangers" of the academy: Asian women scholars in higher education.* Sterling, VA: Stylus.

Lowe, L. (1996). *Immigrant acts: On Asian American cultural politics.* Durham, NC: Duke University Press.

Matsuda, M. J. (1997). *Where is your body?: And other essays on race, gender and the law.* Boston, MA: Beacon Press.

Museus, S. D. (2014). *Asian American students in higher education.* New York, NY: Routledge.

Museus, S. D., Maramba, D. C., & Teranishi, R. T. (2013). *The misrepresented minority.* Sterling, VA: Stylus Publishing.

Nakanishi, D. T. (1996). Asian American in higher education: Faculty and administrative representation and tenure. In C. S. V. Turner, M. Garcia, A. Nora, & L. I. Rendon (Eds.), *Racial and ethnic diversity in higher education.* ASHE reader series (pp. 361–375). Boston, MA: Pearson Custom Publishing.

National Center for Education Statistics. (2015). Fast facts: Race/ethnicity of college faculty. Retrieved from nces.ed.gov/fastfacts/display.asp?id=61

Nielson, P. A., & Kiang, P. N. (2013). Introduction: Asian American and Pacific Island leaders in higher education. In S. D. Museus, D. C. Maramba, & R. T. Teranishi (Eds.), *The misrepresented minority* (pp. 245–248). Sterling, VA: Stylus Publishing.

Nguyen, H. T. (2008). Conceptions of teaching by five Vietnamese American preservice teachers. *Journal of Language, Identity, and Education, 7*, 113–136.

Rong, X. L., & Preissle, J. (2014). *Educating immigrant students in the 21st century: What educators need to know.* Thousand Oaks, CA: Corwin Press.

Seattlage, J. (2011). Counterstories from White mainstream preservice teachers: Resisting the master narrative of deficit by default. *Cultural Studies of Science Education, 6*, 803–836.

Sheets, R. H., & Chew, L. (2002). Absent from the research, present in our classrooms: Preparing culturally responsive Chinese American teachers. *Journal of Teacher Education, 53*(2), 127–141.

Sleeter, C. E., & Milner, H. R. (2013). Researching successful efforts in teacher education to diversify teachers. In A. F. Ball & C. A. Tyson (Eds.), *Studying diversity in teacher education* (pp. 81–104). New York, NY: Rowman & Littlefield.

Suh, Y., An, S., & Forest, D. (2015). Immigration, imagined communities, and collective memories of Asian American experiences: A content analysis of Asian American experiences in Virginia U.S. history textbooks. *Journal of Social Studies Research, 39*(1), 39–51.

Suzuki, B. H. (2002). Revisiting the model minority stereotype: Implications for student affairs practice and higher education. *New Directions for Student Services. 97*, 21–32.

Tang, M. (2002). A comparison of Asian American, Caucasian American, and Chinese college students: An initial report. *Journal of Multicultural Counseling and Development, 30*(2), 124–134.

Tekagi, D. (1992). *The retreat from race: Asian American admissions and racial politics.* New Brunswick, NJ: Rutgers University Press.

Turner, C. S. V., Gonzalez, J. C., & Wood, J. L. (2008). Faculty of color in academe: What 20 years of literature tells us. *Journal of Diversity in Higher Education, 1*, 139–168.

Yan, W., & Museus, S. D. (2013). Asian American and Pacific Islander faculty and the glass ceiling in the academy. In S. D. Museus, D. C. Maramba, & R. T. Teranishi (Eds.), *The misrepresented minority: New insights on Asian American and Pacific Islanders, and the implications for higher education* (pp. 249–265). Sterling, VA: Stylus Publishing.

Yu, T. (2006). Challenging the politics of the "model minority" stereotype: A case for educational equity. *Equity & Excellence in Education, 39*(4), 325–333.

CHAPTER 8

Tribal Critical Race Theory

Angela M. Jaime and *Caskey Russell*

This chapter covers the basic tenets of Tribal Critical Race Theory (Tribal-Crit or TCRT). There is a vital need for theoretical frameworks directly tied to Native and Indigenous people[1] in the discourse of race, colonization, decolonization, White supremacy, and settler colonialism. This chapter seeks to explain how TribalCrit might help analyze and explicate the unique and complex nature of Native and Indigenous peoples' lived experiences in regard to race, ethnicity, and nationality, both historically and presently. As we are Native people, TribalCrit has played a major role in our research. The ability both to use a theory in research and to see ourselves through its theoretical lens has had major effects on our own writing, on how we read and evaluate the writings of Native authors, and on our teaching.

Of course, the tenets of TribalCrit do not cover all of our lived experience; for instance, TribalCrit fails to address the issues and concerns of gender nonconforming people, though it may be possible to make TribalCrit more receptive to examining and analyzing intersectional issues of gender and "two-spiritedness." That being said, it is important that there is a theory like TribalCrit for Native/Indigenous people to help us theorize and tell our stories and experiences in our own voices. TribalCrit provides a framework for us to define ourselves rather than being defined by non-Native notions of who we should be.

INTRODUCTION OF TRIBAL CRITICAL RACE THEORY

In 2005, Bryan McKinley Jones Brayboy wrote the seminal article on Tribal-Crit, "Toward a Tribal Critical Race Theory of Education." Brayboy recognized a need to distinguish the distinctive differences and cultural experiences of Indigenous people from those of other groups commonly examined by Critical Race Theory:

> TribalCrit emerges from Critical Race Theory (CRT) and is rooted in the multiple, nuanced, and historically- and geographically-located epistemologies and ontologies found in Indigenous communities. Though they differ depending on

time, space, place, tribal nation, and individual, there appear to be commonalities in those ontologies and epistemologies. TribalCrit is rooted in these commonalities while simultaneously recognizing the range and variation that exists
within and between communities and individuals. (Brayboy, 2005, p. 427)

Of course, there are both many similarities and many differences among the
Indigenous peoples of the world, which makes any generalizing in comparative Indigenous studies difficult.

One of the major commonalities Indigenous people share is the experience of colonization. Brayboy (2005) stated that CRT and other CRT spin-
off theories maintain the "basic premise of CRT that racism is endemic in
society. In contrast, the basic tenet of TribalCrit emphasizes that colonization is endemic to society" (p. 429). Colonization, both historical and
ongoing, is an ever-present reality for Indigenous people across the world. It
permeates all aspects of life: social, political, sexual, and judicial—especially the manner in which laws and policies regarding Indigenous people are
designed and implemented.

Though TribalCrit does not dismiss racism as a key element in oppression, racism against Native people is intertwined with colonization. Brayboy
(2005) went on to explain this in deeper context: "This process of colonization and its debilitating influences are at the heart of TribalCrit; all other
ideas are offshoots of this vital concept" (p. 429). According to Brayboy, the
nine key tenets of TribalCrit are as follows:

1. Colonization is endemic to society;
2. U.S. policies toward Indigenous peoples are rooted in imperialism,
    White supremacy, and a desire for material gain;
3. Indigenous peoples occupy a liminal space that accounts for both the
    political and racialized natures of our identities;
4. Indigenous peoples have a desire to obtain and forge tribal sovereignty,
    tribal autonomy, self-determination, and self-identification;
5. The concepts of culture, knowledge, and power take on new meaning
    when examined through an Indigenous lens;
6. Governmental policies and educational policies toward Indigenous
    peoples are intimately linked around the problematic goal of
    assimilation;
7. Tribal philosophies, beliefs, customs, traditions, and visions for the
    future are central to understanding the lived realities of Indigenous
    peoples, but they also illustrate the differences and adaptability
    among individuals and groups;
8. Stories are not separate from theory; they make up theory and are,
    therefore, real and legitimate sources of data and ways of being; and
9. Theory and practice are connected in deep and explicit ways such
    that scholars must work toward social change.

In the following sections of this chapter, these tenets and their relation to teacher education will inform our discussion.

TRIBALCRIT ON IMPROVING TEACHER EDUCATION

Each TribalCrit tenet touches on various aspects of education, yet none directly speaks to how to improve teacher education. In this chapter, we are interested in thinking about praxis, especially as outlined in tenet 9 above: We want to explore ways in which TribalCrit can be implemented within the classroom. In order to get at that praxis, it is essential that we discuss briefly the history of federally mandated education for Native students to better understand why TribalCrit should be included in teacher education.

The forcing of Western education on Indigenous peoples is a painful subject. For the Indigenous peoples of the United States, federal policies were implemented and enforced requiring Indigenous tribes to send their children to boarding schools that were usually far away from those Native communities. The schools stripped the children of their languages, cultures, and identities—often using corporal punishment—and tried to assimilate the children into White American ideals.

The brutality of these boarding schools created intergenerational cycles of mistrust toward education systems, cycles that still affect the performance of today's Native students (Butterfield & Pepper, 1991). As we wrote in 2010:

> What is now recognized as the boarding school era began in 1879 with the opening of U.S. Training and Industrial School at Carlisle, in Carlisle, Pennsylvania. The mission of the boarding schools was to eradicate all facets of Indian culture (language, religion, dress, history, etc.) and to assimilate Indians into mainstream white America. (Jaime & Russell, 2010, p. 148)

Boarding schools instructed Native children in standard curriculum—reading and writing English, basic arithmetic—but the primary focus was vocational and military training (Jaime & Russell, 2010). "Except for a limited number of students, the promise of the boarding school was a lie: the damage done to the identities and self-images of many students outweighed the benefits of the boarding schools. Moreover, boarding schools were training Indian students to supposedly succeed in a country that was both racist and averse to accepting Indians as equals" (p. 148).

Within a decade of the founding of Carlisle, there were 26 off-reservation U.S. government boarding schools (as well as many more on-reservation government-run boarding schools), and by 1893 Congress authorized the commissioner of Indian Affairs to enforce attendance of all American Indian children of appropriate age—even by withholding food rations and annuity payments from the children's families, if necessary (Calloway, 2004; Jaime & Russell, 2010).

The boarding school policy began to decline in the 1930s, due to the closure of many schools for financial reasons, and following governmental reports and legislation, such as the Merriam Report (1928) and the Indian Reorganization Act (1934), aimed at mitigating the deficiencies found in those schools. However, the boarding school era did not really end until the 1960s, with the growing Red Power and Self-Determination movements (Calloway, 2004; Jaime & Russell, 2010). In 1969, Senate subcommittee reports delineated the appalling state of contemporary Indian education. The subcommittee called their findings "shocking," and their report signaled the end of the kill-the-Indian-save-the-man boarding school policies (Josephy, Nagel, & Johnson, 1999; U.S. Senate Special Subcommittee, 1969).

With this history of federally enforced boarding school education in the United States as context, we can begin to discuss the need for TribalCrit in teacher education. As delineated by Brayboy, TribalCrit tenets 1, 2, and 6 focus on the U.S. government's policies of colonization and imperialism and how they affect all major institutions within the U.S., including the educational system.

Tenet 1 states that colonization is endemic to society, which includes the educational system (the boarding school era speaks directly to that fact). Curricula have been created within the contexts of colonization to promote and justify the ultimate aim of colonization, which is to fully control the mental and physical universes of the colonized. The curricula have been written and approved by those who occupy the administrative and legislative levels of education and the textbook companies that often have little to no knowledge or understanding of Indigenous histories and cultures. These groups have traditionally approved curricula that celebrated the accomplishments and conflicts of settler/European Americans and situated people of color as sidebar information, which reinforced their marginalization. When we recognize that colonization is endemic in our education system, we can then theorize how colonization has affected the classroom and curriculum and take the necessary steps to decolonize both.

Tenet 6 states, "Governmental policies and educational policies toward Indigenous peoples are intimately linked around the problematic goal of assimilation" (Brayboy, 2005, p. 429). To start the process of decolonizing classrooms and curriculum, we must be able to identify and call attention to the problematic goal of assimilation historically and in the present day in classrooms and curricula across the country. We must be able to articulate why assimilationist educational policies are destructive and how those policies seek to abolish the rights and identities of Indigenous peoples. TribalCrit provides a theoretical grounding for that articulation.

Tenet 3 recognizes the unique identity of Native people in the U.S. as both politicized and racialized beings. Too often in the classroom Native students are seen as only a racialized minority group; teachers do not know that Native students are citizens of Native nations. Moreover, curricula and textbooks relegate Natives to the past—rarely are they allowed into the 20th century—which makes it easy for teachers to not know or respect the political identities of Native students in their classrooms. Brayboy noted how the "liminal" space that Native people occupy accounts for both political and racial identities. TribalCrit is unique in providing a theoretical framework for understanding that liminal space. If TribalCrit were part of teacher education in the U.S., it would help teachers understand the nature of Native dual identity and perhaps even aid in strategizing ways to revamp curricula to respect this dual identity and begin to address Native liminality.

Tenet 4 relates directly to tenet 3: Bringing TribalCrit into the classroom has the potential to affect both Native and non-Native students through the acknowledgment, acceptance, and inclusion of issues such as tribal sovereignty, tribal autonomy, self-determination, and self-identification within the classroom. Within the TribalCrit framework, teachers and students are asked to consider the broad implications of tribal sovereignty and self-determination. More than 300 treaties were signed between Indigenous nations and the U.S. government, with subsequent legislation affirming the rights of Native nations to seek self-determination.

TribalCrit asks teachers to go beyond simple racial formulations of Native identity into these larger political considerations. "Currently, the different circulating discourses around what it means to be Indian as well as what constitutes American Indian education establish a context in which American Indians must struggle for the right to be defined as both a legal/ political and a racial group" (Brayboy, 2005, p. 433). Affirming Native students in the classroom by way of acknowledgment and inclusion of their tribal rights instills pride and self-determination in our present and future generations, and also teaches non-Native students the importance of Natives as political actors within the United States.

Tenets 5, 7, and 8 provide concrete examples of how Indigenous people can aid teachers in understanding the value of Indigenous traditions, cultural knowledge, beliefs, and stories; moreover, these tenets validate rather than disparage Indigenous identities and communities. The belief that "American" values (i.e., White Euroamerican values) are the norm, as well as the most academically valid, marginalizes and silences those outside the dominant group. "The ability to determine a place in the world (power) is enabled by knowledge American Indian communities have that is rooted in both Indigenous and European sources of knowing" (Brayboy, 2005, p. 436).

Finally, as mentioned earlier, the last tenet demands praxis: There must be a component of action or activism in any theoretical framework—the other eight tenets are only words until put into practice, especially in the classroom. Teacher education should train future teachers to become the best possible teacher for each and every student, and not just the best teachers for wealthy or middle-class White children. We demand excellence from our educators and should expect them to be inclusive and open-minded to the diverse student population of the United States. "TribalCrit research and practice—or better still, praxis—moves us away from colonization and assimilation and towards a more real self-determination and tribal sovereignty" (Brayboy, 2005, p. 440).

TRIBALCRIT AND THE RESEARCH

Teacher education specifically focuses on preparing people to be teachers, using theory, practice, and curriculum to prepare them for a career in classrooms across the U.S. This very specific training in education lacks infused or intense instruction and immersion in multicultural education, social justice, and critical education. Some institutions value these areas of emphasis more than others, but most teacher education programs have only one or two classes focused on a survey of marginalized groups.

Some of these classes cover disability studies, ESL, ethnic diversity, globalization, gender and women's education, as well as all peripherally oppressed groups. This approach often oversimplifies marginalized groups and seeks to see them as generally the same. These oversimplifications and generalizations about a shared minority experience create stereotypes for students that are not easily unlearned, due to the lack of in-depth knowledge about any one particular group and the differences among minority groups.

This limited attention to issues of diversity in teacher education can also be due to *interest convergence* (Delgado & Stefancic, 2001) in colleges and schools of education: Those in power and in charge of curriculum only grudgingly include diversity when they feel that *not* to do so would threaten their control. Tokenism—and the notion of a shared minority experience— is often the outcome.

After a careful search for published works that used TribalCrit in teacher education, searching in the areas of Native American education, Indigenous education, and First Nations education, we were dismayed to find very few such works. Outside the article by Bryan Brayboy defining TribalCrit, there were only a small number of papers employing TribalCrit in discussing teacher education. This finding is alarming given that TribalCrit is a useful framework for analyzing and understanding colonization, narratives of Indigenous experiences, culture and knowledge, tribal sovereignty, tribal autonomy, self-determination, and self-identification, all of which should be of concern when working with Indigenous youth. The few articles that were uncovered used TribalCrit in parts, but never holistically.

For example, Castagno (2012) stated that her university "prepared me to be a teacher, but not a culturally responsive Navajo teacher for Navajo kids" (p. 4). Castagno argued that "federally-funded Indigenous teacher preparation programs housed at mainstream, predominantly White universities can be colonial and thus require significant focused work in order to ensure that they are not" (p. 4). Castagno utilized only five of the nine tenets of TribalCrit, all of which focused on colonization, U.S. government influence or involvement with Indigenous communities, issues of sovereignty, and social change. The intent of her article was to share her story of an Indigenous teacher preparation program that attempted to prepare culturally responsive Navajo teachers for Navajo schools (Castagno, 2012). Of the articles we reviewed, this one was most clearly related to improving teacher education programs using TribalCrit.

Haynes Writer (2008) employed Critical Race Theory and TribalCrit together as a theoretical framework to interrogate teacher education, curriculum, and pedagogy. While utilizing both CRT and TribalCrit seems redundant, it becomes clear that Haynes Writer is calling for teacher education programs to incorporate the two theories into their programs to better educate future teachers and begin to decolonize the system. She stated, "Belief becomes practice. Reading through a CRT and TribalCrit lens, I add to Mankiller's statement and say that public perceptions also fuel public practice" (p. 8). If teachers are not educating students with accurate information about Indigenous people, then those students grow up continuing the cycle of colonization.

Haynes Writer (2008) further explained the need for both theories in teacher education:

> Thus CRT and TribalCrit are useful tools in telling the stories of historical and contemporary issues affecting Indigenous Peoples among those complex intersections. This facilitates the examination of whiteness as property, which interrogates white privilege and dislocates the normativity of whiteness. Colonization is disrupted, allowing for the reclaiming and re-centering of Indigenous knowledges, experiences, and perspectives. (pp. 9–10)

Although there is a gaping hole in the direct use of TribalCrit in teacher education, several articles reflect the use of TribalCrit in the areas of higher education and education peripherally.

Castagno and Lee (2013) used TribalCrit and the notion of interest convergence to highlight the use of Native mascots and institutional policies affecting Native students in a specific university. They expanded this to include what they call *ethnic fraud* in higher education. The authors focused on three of the nine tenets centered around colonization and government relations with Indigenous peoples. The authors utilized TribalCrit as a theoretical lens to view interest convergence as the focal point of the ethnic fraud.

Quijada Cerecer (2013) wrote to "examine hostile school policies and leadership practices and student responses in a public high school with a majority population of American Indian students who reside on a reservation"

(p. 591). While the central focus of this article was not about improving teacher education programs, it does indirectly reflect on teacher preparation by shedding light on the school in the article, which neglected students' educational needs and views and marginalized Native students through specific policies.

The final article we retrieved claiming to use TribalCrit (Mendez & Mendez, 2013) stated the authors' intention to use TribalCrit as a theoretical framework in their analysis, but did not specify which tenets applied to their study. This article focused on Native students and financial aid in higher education.

Overall, the lack of research in teacher preparation utilizing TribalCrit is disappointing and alarming. We feel that the potential of TribalCrit has not been realized within teacher education and, consequently, within K–12 classrooms. We see Brayboy's seminal article in 2005 as a call for scholars and educators to take up the theoretical framework of TribalCrit and use it to fight for curricular and classroom decolonization. Unfortunately, this call was ignored or forgotten. We'd like to revive that call.

NEXT STEPS: WHERE DOES TRIBALCRIT GO NOW?

In our 21 years in education across several universities, we have rarely found TribalCrit used in teacher education curricula. With so little use of TribalCrit in teacher education, and in light of its importance to the field of Indigenous and Critical Studies, the theory should be better implemented in the literature and research across teacher education programs. In Native American and Indigenous education, TribalCrit lends itself to creating space for dialogue around ways in which educators can address the unique needs of Indigenous students in education.

Educators serving any Native student should have a basic understanding of history as told from the Native perspective and of current research and discourse in Indigenous education; TribalCrit should be embedded in the curriculum:

> Today, TribalCrit would argue, education for American Indians is not always rooted in the goal of assimilation, although some assimilation seems to be an inevitable outcome of education that occurs through the formal structures of western schooling. Education, according to TribalCrit, might also teach American Indian students how to combine Indigenous notions of culture, knowledge, and power with western/European conceptions in order to actively engage in survivance, self-determination, and tribal autonomy. (Brayboy, 2005, p. 437)

Even teachers who do not teach Native or Indigenous students might benefit from some knowledge of TribalCrit so that they might more effectively critique the curricula present in their classrooms.

Two state governments in the Rocky Mountain region have passed legislation to ensure that teacher education programs include Indigenous history and education in their curriculum. Montana and Wyoming have both passed Indian Education for All Acts (Wyoming in 2018 and Montana in 1999) to require teacher preparation for teachers in the areas of history, curriculum, and pedagogy to better meet the needs of Native students in their states. This legislation holds teacher education programs accountable to teach their preservice teachers in elementary social studies and secondary social studies/history the histories and culture of the Indigenous people from within and outside their own states.

We are not advocating mere 1-day "TribalCrit Sensitivity Training" models, but rather the use of Critical Race Theory in the creation of curriculum as a means to address diverse student populations in all teacher education training programs. Further, if teachers are interested in working with Indigenous populations or know they will be working within these populations, they should be required to complete coursework specific to working with Indigenous students, much like in Montana and Wyoming. These programs should be based on a TribalCrit framework, infusing the nine tenets to better serve the Indigenous students.

In the interest of this book's concern with methods to improve teacher education, we provide a short list of suggested readings to further understanding of the history of Indigenous peoples from their perspective. It is our intention to influence others to learn the historical reality of the United States (Dunbar-Ortiz, 2014) rather than the myths we are currently taught in school.

In conclusion, TribalCrit works to dismantle the historical trauma and present-day oppression imposed on Indigenous people in an effort to heal and move forward into a decolonized future of education and generational health.

NOTE

1. The terms *Native* or *Indigenous People* are used interchangeably throughout the chapter. For us, it is more inclusive and indicative of our community than using a general term. When appropriate, we will use the tribal name when referring to a specific group.

SUGGESTED READINGS

Dunbar-Ortiz, R. (2014). *An Indigenous peoples' history of the United States*. Boston, MA: Beacon Press.

Fletcher, M. L. M. (2008). *American Indian education*. New York, NY: Routledge.

Klug, B. J., & Whitfield, P. T. (2003). *Widening the circle: Culturally relevant pedagogy for American Indian Children*. New York, NY: Routledge Falmer.

Reyhner, J., & Eder, J. (2004). *American Indian education.* Norman, OK: University of Oklahoma.

Stannard, D. E. (1992). *American holocaust: The conquest of the new world.* New York, NY: Oxford University Press.

Wilkinson, C. (2005). *Blood struggle: The rise of modern Indian nations.* New York, NY: W.W. Norton & Company.

REFERENCES

Brayboy, B. M. J. (2005, December). Toward a tribal critical race theory in education. *The Urban Review,* 37(5), 425–446.

Butterfield, R. & Pepper, F. (1991). Improving parental participation in elementary and secondary education for American Indian and Alaska Native students. *Indian nations at risk task force commissioned papers.* (ERIC Documents Reproduction Services ED 343763)

Calloway, C. (2004). *First Peoples: A documentary survey of American Indian history.* Boston, MA: Bedford/St. Martin's Press.

Castagno, A. E., & Lee, S. L. (2013). Native mascots and ethnic fraud in higher education: Using Tribal Critical Race Theory and the interest convergence principle as an analytical tool. In A. D. Dixson, D. Gillborn, G. Ladson-Billings, L. Parker, N. Rollock, & P. Warmington (Eds.), *Critical Race Theory in education,* (Vol. 3, pp. 329–347). New York, NY: Routledge.

Delgado, R., & Stefancic, J. (2001). *Critical Race Theory: An introduction.* New York, NY: New York University Press.

Dunbar-Ortiz, R. (2014). *An Indigenous peoples' history of the United States.* Boston, MA: Beacon Press.

Haynes Writer, J. (2008). Unmasking, exposing, and confronting: Critical Race Theory, Tribal Critical Race Theory and multicultural education. *International Journal of Multicultural Education,* 10(2), 1–15.

Jaime, A. M., & Russell, C. C. (2010). Reaching Native American families to increase school involvement. In Miller Marsh, M., & Turner-Vorbeck, T. *(Mis) understanding families: Learning from real families in our schools* (pp. 145–161). New York, NY: Teachers College Press.

Josephy, A., Nagel, J., & Johnson, T. (1999). *Red power: The American Indians' fight for freedom* (2nd ed.). Lincoln, NE: University of Nebraska Press.

Mendez, J. P., & Mendez, J. (2013). Students' perceptions of American Indian financial aid. *Journal of American Indian Education,* 52(1), 45–64.

Quijada Cerecer, P. D. (2013). The policing of native bodies and minds: Perspectives on schooling from American Indian youth. *American Journal of Education,* 119, 591–616.

U.S. Senate Special Subcommittee on Indian Education. (1969). *Indian education: A national tragedy—A national challenge.* Senate Report No. 91–501. Washington, DC: Author.

CHAPTER 9

Queer Theory: QueerCrit

Eric D. Teman

Queer theory is relatively new among critical social science theories, having emerged in the early 1990s (Sedgwick, 1990). With roots in women's studies, queer theory challenges sexual identities as part and parcel of one's essential self (Marinucci, 2016). This mirrors feminism's challenge of sex as essential. Queer theory also extends the field of queer studies, which traditionally focused on homosexual behaviors, to include all sexual identities (Ingraham, 1996). Queer theorists argue against stable genders, sexes, and sexualities (McIntosh, 1996; Weeks, 1996), which are considered unstable and multiple (Chauncey, 1994; McNair, 2017; Pfeffer, 2012; Shahani, 2008).

DISRUPTING, DECENTERING, AND SUBVERTING

Via queer theory, we can disrupt, decenter, and subvert dominant beliefs to wrest queer narrative from the hands of "positivistic, pathologizing researchers with the focus of fixing 'the broken'" (Teman & Lahman, 2012, p. 344). Queer theory sheds light on the privilege of heterosexuality (particularly male), institutional normalization practices, and discriminatory societal powers used to oppress those outside said systems of power (Bower-Phipps, 2017; Goldberg & Allen, 2018; Hermann-Wilmarth & Bills, 2010; McCormack, Anderson, & Adams, 2014; Wilkinson & Pearson, 2009).

As a critical lens, queer theory permits examination of social processes by destabilizing presumed categorization of identity into heteronormative boxes (Barber & Clark, 2002; Hartman, 2017; Williams, 2016). Queer theory is a primary tool through which we can problematize binaries in gender, sex, sexuality, and desire—this affords us the ability to complicate what has been (and what is) considered the "norm" or "normal" (Ozturk, 2014; Rumens, 2012). Queer theory seeks to halt the perpetuation of ill-conceived simple classifications of individuals into boxes that do not fit one's true identity—all queer identities are allowed to manifest, exist, and flourish (Callis, 2009).

A WAY OF LIVING

More broadly, queer theory is a way of living, a way of being, and a way of knowing (Marinucci, 2016). Identifying as a queer theorist transcends the pursuit of scholarly, academic research. That is, we queer theorists see the world through a filter, we view events in certain ways, and we always question society's role in othering us (Chauncey, 1994; Sedgwick, 1990; Shahani, 2008).

Queer theory is inexorably intertwined with feminism; in fact, queer theory in the historical context in which it arose cannot exist separately from feminism (Marinucci, 2016). The queer, like women, are similarly oppressed by the dominant, paternalistic, hegemonic, White male. Queers do not view themselves as perpetual victims, as they are strong, relentless, and most persistent survivors in their activism and fight for equality (Sedgwick, 1990).

THE EPISTEMOLOGICAL CLOSET

Being queer is an immutable characteristic (Green, 2017; Mucciaroni & Killian, 2008). For so many years, the debate over nature versus nurture was center stage, with many arguing that no one is born other than heterosexual: Gays and lesbians were socially nurtured in some, probably unintentional, way, and hence are not entitled to equal protection under the law, and discrimination against queer individuals should proceed with full force (Yoshino, 2002). This contention has led to the queer having to hide their true identities in order to fit in and be granted a false acceptance in society (Yoshino, 2002).

The gay-bashing era (not implying it is over) produced the creatively crafted "homosexual panic" defense, used successfully to stop convictions or lessen the sentences of those who claimed a right to physically assault and batter gay men. The argument was one of diminished capacity: The accused would assert "a pathological psychological condition, perhaps brought on by an unwanted sexual advance from the man whom he then attacked" (Sedgwick, 1990, p. 19). This trivializes the queer plight and demoralizes the individual suffering the heinous beating.

Queer individuals have experienced having their rights toyed with; one minute they have rights, the next minute those same rights are stripped away. Queer individuals live their lives on the ballot (Schieble, 2012). Queer lives are political. No matter how much "progress" we make toward equality, history will forever be indelibly stained with the blood of those who were not White, heterosexual males (Teman, 2016).

Eve Sedgwick (1990) framed the sexual orientation issue quite aptly when she proposed that "many of the major nodes of thought and knowledge in twentieth-century Western culture as a whole are structured—indeed, fractured—by a chronic, now endemic crisis of homo/heterosexual definition, indicatively male" (p. 1). In other words, probably nothing of modern culture can be understood without first being processed through a binary lens of homo/hetero understanding. This is a damaged lens we look through, one with a history of terming those seen as sexually deviant as homosexual, thereby terming the normal as heterosexual (Sedgwick, 1990).

RESEARCH ON QUEER TEACHERS: WHAT DO WE KNOW ABOUT THE QUEER TEACHING FORCE AND IMPROVING TEACHER EDUCATION?

There is some research on queer classroom teachers, queer approaches to teaching, and queer school culture. Queer theory is the framework within which many of these studies are built. In the literature, the difficulty and political upheaval is apparent when teachers are open about gender or sexual identities that deviate from the bifurcated, heterosexual male–female relationship model. This leads to stifling open dialogue about sexuality and gender issues in the classroom.

Invisible Queer Teachers

Despite progress toward equal rights for lesbian, gay, bisexual, transgender, queer, questioning, ally (LGBTQQA+) individuals, schools remain problem institutions in which diverse sexualities or genders continue to be marginalized and silenced (Bower-Phipps, 2017; Ferfolja & Hopkins, 2013). If teachers fear being open about their gender or sexuality, we cannot progress adequately as a society—the marginalized will continue to be silenced (Teman, 2018; Teman & Lahman, 2012). Schools need to introduce appropriate and accurate explanations of what sexuality and gender are (Connell & Elliott, 2009). If teachers cannot be open, students' sexual and gender expressions will remain stifled (Teman, 2018).

Bower-Phipps (2017) discussed issues surrounding LGBTQQA+ teachers' decisions to disclose their own sexuality and/or gender. The current and past political climate remains hostile toward any complete movement to inclusivity of teachers' coming out to their students (Bower-Phipps, 2017). Bower-Phipps suggested that the imposed closeting of teachers must be addressed before any progress can be made for acceptance and inclusion of students of diverse sexual orientations and gender identities.

In hostile school environments, teachers of diverse sexual orientations and identities often fear retaliation by firing or not being promoted (DePalma & Atkinson, 2010; Rudoe, 2010). This is enabled by the default heteronormative context where heterosexual teachers are immune and exempt from any and all decisions about disclosure of sexual orientation (Bower-Phipps, 2017). This othering of sexuality and gender indirectly others students of other-than-heterosexual orientation by preventing teachers from acting as role models and softening the experience of coming out among peer groups (Ferfolja, 2010).

In Bower-Phipps's (2017) study of 20 LGBTQQA+ K–12 teachers, issues of safety, diversity, and sexuality and gender as public knowledge emerged. By queering issues of safety, we are able to confront notions of "non-normative as unsafe" (Bower-Phipps, 2017, p. 34). By queering issues of sexuality and gender identity as "publicly held knowledge contribute [sic] to the disruption of heteronormative assumptions, rejecting the assumption that everyone is heterosexual" (p. 34), we are able to disrupt traditional, incorrect notions that sexuality and gender are a simple binary.

The Modern Classroom

Historically, as well as currently, there has been a huge fear of including the queer in the classroom. School cultures of suppression and oppression are fostered, queer voices are stifled, and the LGBTQQA+ are further closeted (Greteman, 2017). Research offers some suggestions on how to create LGBTQQA+ inclusive and inviting classrooms, rich and diverse in curriculum.

Issues of sexuality and gender identity can and should be introduced into the everyday K–12 classroom in various contexts (Connell & Elliott, 2009). Connell and Elliott explored the roles schools, peers, and parents play in students' sexuality education. Even though there appears to be a trend toward increasing acceptance of sexual expression in the U.S., there is still violence toward individuals of other-than-heterosexual identities (Connell & Elliott, 2009; Seidman, 2002).

Dodge (2018) provided a framework wherein classroom culture included more than just learning *about* others of diverse backgrounds, including diverse sexualities and gender identities. Teachers need to interrogate "current pedagogical, instructional, and curricular norms to determine changes that can be made to be inclusive of and build on the strengths of diverse learners" (p. 137). Dodge recommended simply including and conceptualizing LGBTQQA+ texts into the already-existing curriculum.

Greteman (2017) challenged status quo teaching practices in his effort to incorporate queer theory in art education. By disrupting silences regarding gender identity and sexuality in art education, beyond issues of crisis and safety that narrow the focus to queer victimization, teachers can enrich their curricular offerings by redirecting the dialogue to how queers still manage to flourish in oppressive heteronormative environments. Greteman argued that knowledge about sexual differences between individuals is critical. Similarly, Palkki (2017) brought to the forefront the issue of voice parts and gender identity in the choral classroom while Larsson, Fagrell, and Re-delius (2009) discussed hostility in physical education classes.

More broadly, K–12 classroom teachers need to be aware of gender and sexual fluidity (Connell & Elliott, 2009; Dodge, 2018; Schieble, 2012). Gender can no longer be—and should never have been—thought of as bifur-cated: It is—and always has been—on a spectrum, just like sexuality (Bow-er-Phipps, 2017; Matsuno & Budge, 2017). It is all too easy and convenient to classify students as male or female. One cannot know another's gender unless said person reveals it to you (Bonfatto & Crasnow, 2018; Glasser & Smith, 2008). It is important to note the difference between "assigned gender," which indicates what parents (or otherwise) indicate the gender is, versus "identified gender," which is reflective of the individual's own iden-tification of gender.

In the classroom, teachers should be aware of, sensitive to, and respect-ful of students of all genders and sexualities. In pedagogical practices in training elementary classroom teachers, Schieble (2012) used texts featuring LGBTQQA+ characters. Via "'queering' of a supposed heteronormative ac-ademic context" (Rothmann, 2018, p. 1), such practices early on in educa-tion contexts can help queer individuals flourish in their self-identification and grow into resilience (Grace, 2017). By actively queering their classrooms, teachers have the ability and potential to influence their students to seize and embrace their sexual identities early on in life (Connell & Elliott, 2009).

In this way, the effects of sexuality as a primary means of organizing inequality will be at least somewhat tempered by adequate and proper sexu-ality education (Connell & Elliott, 2009). As it stands, schools are culpable in "reproducing the taken-for-granted notions of sexuality that maintain systems of inequality" (Connell & Elliott, 2009, p. 88). Such heterosexist attitudes are buried deeply within school culture and usual approaches to sex education classrooms in particular and K–12 classrooms in general in what Friend (1993) labeled "layers of silencing" (p. 211).

Queer Inclusion in K–12 School Culture

Disparaging bifurcation of sexuality and gender commonly occurs during sexual education courses, where the heteronormative model is used to ex-plain and illustrate sexual behavior (Connell & Elliott, 2009). This nor-mative model is often used out of fear, not necessarily from ignorance (MacNamara, 2017). Research has demonstrated that elementary and high schools are critical learning sites for sexual and gender identity development and sexual socialization (Connell & Elliott, 2009). Thorne and Luria (1986) discovered that business-as-usual gender practices in elementary schools teach children to view sex from a heterosexual and homophobic standpoint.

By freely and openly discussing these issues in an open forum in K–12 classrooms, students will be exposed to identities they did not know existed and will be able to further solidify understanding of their own genders and sexualities (Bower-Phipps, 2017; Connell & Elliott, 2009).

Teachers always need to assume they have students in their classrooms representing an array of sexual orientations and gender identities. Never (or rarely) will a room full of individuals possess *only* heterosexual males and females. Teachers must realize the extensive diversity within their class-rooms, whether visible or not, if only for the sake of their students' safety. Improper, ill-conceived, and/or inadequate gender and sexuality education leads to improperly "embodying gender and sexuality" (Connell & Elliott, 2009, p. 83). Those opposing proper sexuality and gender education argue that the well-being of children is on the line, but in extreme circumstances, such poor education has led to the murder of those who vary from gender and sexuality "norms" (Connell & Elliott, 2009).

The issue of childhood sexual innocence intersects with issues of race and class—social constructionism presumes that children are "innocent" when it comes to sexuality. However, the literature indicates exceptions occur when race and class enter the picture: When children are not White and at least middle-class, privileges seem to disappear (Pascoe, 2007). African American children have been classified as "hypersexual, dangerous, and a corrupting influence on those 'innocent' children" (Connell & Elliott, 2009, p. 87).

QUEER CRIT: NEXT STEPS

There continues to be a divide between the queer and the heterosexual. Teacher education programs and schools by and large continue to other queer teachers and students, thereby promoting and furthering heterosexual norms. By queering the teacher's role, the classroom and curriculum, and overall school culture, we can move toward a more inclusive society, as heteronormative and hegemonic male practices will be stymied early on in students' lives (Sedgwick, 1990; Seidman, 1996).

Queering the Teacher

First and foremost, queer teachers need to be supported and encouraged to be open about their gender identities and sexualities. Without this step, an open and honest school climate cannot be fostered, queer students will con-tinue to be marginalized, and the queer voice will continue to be stifled. The literature is clear that change begins with the teacher (Bower-Phipps, 2017; Connell & Elliott, 2009; Greteman, 2017).

By keeping teachers of diverse sexualities and gender identities in the margins, we also keep students of those same sexualities and gender iden-tities in the margins. This maintenance of the status quo inhibits students from engaging in a rich and diverse curriculum. By perpetuating the White, heterosexual male agenda, we are perpetrating a fraud upon our students; diversity will be frowned upon, inclusivity will be damned, and social justice efforts will only crawl forward.

Queering the Classroom and Curriculum

K–12 classroom praxis in the United States must become more inclusive and accommodating of a diverse spectrum of gender identities and sexual orientations (Simonsson & Angervall, 2016). Persistent old-fashioned applications of bifurcated and categorical understandings of gender and sexuality are false, misleading, and damaging (Seidman, 2002). Understandings of gender identity and sexual expression continue to develop over time (Savin-Williams, 2017; Ward, 2015). Yet, in the classroom, other genders and sexualities continue to be suppressed by lack of appropriate curriculum expansions, which acts to further oppress those of nonheterosexual identity and to perpetuate heteronormativity (Lundin, 2014).

Teacher education, through critical transformative pedagogy, must provide teachers with tools to adapt and thrive in the constantly evolving landscape of queer identities (Zacko-Smith & Smith, 2010). If prepared with a transformative pedagogy, prospective teachers will be "interpreting human sexuality politically, socially, and culturally" (Drazenovich, 2015, p. 5). A queer pedagogy can be transformative to students' understandings of gender and sexuality issues, and teachers will be able to facilitate discussions that will aid in "unmasking and undermining disguised and evident forms of domination that are embedded in scientific knowledge" (p. 15).

Queering School Culture

Within the heteronormative dominant school culture in the U.S., binary oppositions play an important role in how students and teachers view themselves and others. For example, bifurcations of male/female and straight/gay operate in a way that emphasizes one being better than the other, producing misunderstandings of gender and sexuality (Simonsson & Angervall, 2016). School can be seen as an institution that actually "produces gender and sexuality" (Simonsson & Angervall, 2016, p. 38). Through an inclusive culture, we can begin the process of disavowing exclusion.

Through school-wide inclusive sexuality and gender practices, students and teachers will not have to guard their identities so vehemently, donning personas and trying to "pass" for straight or otherwise (Friend, 1993). Schools ought to strive to be oases of diversity and inclusion. This can be accomplished through a rich and diverse curriculum, along with well-trained teachers. These practices can begin the process of valuing the other and not othering the other.

Schools as institutions are difficult places for many LGBTQQA+ individuals to thrive—issues of safety, inauthenticity to oneself, and marginalization are rife. If this sort of school culture is left unchecked, unexamined, and uninterrogated, student and teacher voices alike will be further silenced. Critical exchanges must occur early on in K–12 classrooms and continue through high school in order for students to be fully immersed in and understand diverse cultures of which they are—often unknowingly—a part. We must directly call into question those wielding the power, those who promote the heterosexual agenda, and those who act to constantly stifle social progress of LGBTQQA+ individuals—this fight and disavowing of the hegemonic, heterosexual model starts in the K–12 classroom.

REFERENCES

Barber, S. M., & Clark, D. L. (2002). *Regarding Sedgwick: Essays on queer culture and critical theory.* New York, NY: Routledge.

Bonfatto, M., & Crasnow, E. (2018). Gender/ed identities: An overview of our current work as child psychotherapists in the gender identity development service. *Journal of Child Psychotherapy, 44*(1), 29–46.

Bower-Phipps, L. (2017). Discourses governing lesbian, gay, bisexual, transgender, queer, intersex, and asexual teachers' disclosure of sexual orientation and gender history. *Issues in Teacher Education, 26*(3), 23–37.

Callis, A. S. (2009). Playing with Butler and Foucault: Bisexuality and queer theory. *Journal of Bisexuality, 9*(3–4), 213–233.

Chauncey, G. (1994). *Gay New York: Gender, urban culture, and the makings of the gay male world, 1890–1940.* New York, NY: Basic Books.

Connell, C., & Elliott, S. (2009). Beyond the birds and the bees: Learning inequality through sexuality education. *American Journal of Sexuality Education, 4*(2), 83–102. DOI: 10.1080/15546120903001332

DePalma, R., & Atkinson, E. (2010). The nature of institutional heteronormativity in primary schools and practice-based responses. *Teaching and Teacher Education, 26*(8), 1669–1676.

Dodge, A. M. (2018). Reading toward equity: Creating LGBTQ+ inclusive classrooms through literary and literacy practices. In E. Ortlieb & E. H. Cheek (Eds.), *Addressing diversity in literacy instruction* (pp. 135–154). Bingley, UK: Emerald.

Drazenovich, G. (2015). Queer pedagogy in sex education. *Canadian Journal of Education, 38*(2), 1–22.

Ferfolja, T. (2010). Lesbian teachers, harassment and the workplace. *Teaching and Teacher Education, 26*(3), 408–414.

Ferfolja, T., & Hopkins, L. (2013). The complexities of workplace experience for lesbian and gay teachers. *Critical Studies in Education, 54*(3), 311–324. DOI: 10.1080/17508487.2013.794743

Friend, R. A. (1993). Choices, not closets: Heterosexism and homophobia in schools. In L. Weis & M. Find (Eds.), *Beyond silenced voices: Class, race, and gender in U.S. schools* (pp. 209–235). New York, NY: State University of New York Press.

Glasser, H. M., & Smith, J. P., III. (2008). On the vague meaning of "gender" in education research: The problem, its sources, and recommendations for practice. *Educational Researcher, 37*(6), 343–350.

Goldberg, A. E., & Allen, K. R. (2018). Teaching undergraduates about LGBTQ identities, families, and intersectionality. *Family Relations, 67*(1), 176–191. DOI: 10.1111/fare.12224

Grace, A. P. (2017). *Growing into resilience: Sexual and gender minority youth in Canada.* Toronto, ON: University of Toronto Press.

Green, M. W., Jr. (2017). Same-sex sex and immutable traits: Why Obergefell v. Hodges clears a path to protecting gay and lesbian employees from workplace discrimination under Title VII. *Journal of Gender, Race and Justice, 20*(1), 1–52.

Greteman, A. J. (2017). Helping kids turn out queer: Queer theory in art education. *Studies in Art Education, 58*(3), 195–205.

Hartman, E. (2017). The queer utility of narrative case studies for clinical social work research and practice. *Clinical Social Work Journal, 45*(3), 227–237. DOI: 10.1007/s10615–017–0622–9

Hermann-Wilmarth, J. M., & Bills, P. (2010). Identity shifts: Queering teacher education research. *The Teacher Educator, 45*(4), 257–272. DOI: 10.1080/08878730.2010.508324

Ingraham, C. (1996). The heterosexual imaginary: Feminist sociology and theories of gender. In S. Seidman (Ed.), *Queer theory/sociology* (pp. 168–193). Cambridge, MA: Blackwell.

Larsson, H., Fagrell, B., & Redelius, K. (2009, 1–17). Queering physical education: Between benevolence toward girls and a tribute to masculinity. *Physical Education and Sport Pedagogy, 14*(1).

Lundin, M. (2014). Inviting queer ideas into the science classroom: Studying sexuality education from a queer perspective. *Cultural Studies of Science Education, 9*(2), 377–391. DOI: 10.1007/s11422–013–9564-x

MacNamara, J. (2017). Experiencing misgendered pronouns: A classroom activity to encourage empathy. *Teaching Sociology, 45*(3), 269–278. DOI: 10.1177/0092055X17708603

Marinucci, M. (2016). *Feminism is queer: The intimate connection between queer and feminist theory.* London, UK: Zed Books.

Matsuno, E., & Budge, S. L. (2017). Non-binary/genderqueer identities: A critical review of the literature. *Current Sexual Health Reports, 9*(3), 116–120. DOI: 10.1007/s11930–017–0111–8

McCormack, M., Anderson, E., & Adams, A. (2014). Cohort effect on coming out experiences of bisexual men. *Sociology, 48*(6), 1207–1223. DOI: 10.1177/0038038513518851

McIntosh, M. (1996). The homosexual role. In S. Seidman (Ed.), *Queer theory/ sociology* (pp. 33–40). Cambridge, MA: Blackwell.

McNair, R. P. (2017). Multiple identities and their intersections with queer health and wellbeing. *Journal of Intercultural Studies, 38*(4), 443–452. DOI: 10.1080/07256868.2017.1341398

Mucciaroni, G., & Killian, M. L. (2008). Immutability, science and legislative debate over gay, lesbian and bisexual rights. *Journal of Homosexuality, 47*(1), 53–77. DOI: 10.1300/J082v47n01_04

Ozturk, M. B. (2014). Gay male academics in UK business and management schools: Negotiating heteronormativities in everyday work life. *British Journal of Management, 25*(3), 503–517.

Palkki, J. (2017). Inclusivity in action: Transgender students in the choral classroom. *Choral Journal, 57*(11), 20–34.

Pascoe, C. (2007). *Dude, you're a fag: Masculinity and sexuality in high school.* Berkeley, CA: University of California Press.

Pfeffer, C. A. (2012). Normative resistance and inventive pragmatism: Negotiating structure and agency in transgender families. *Gender & Society, 26*(4), 574–602.

Rothmann, J. (2018). A social constructionist approach to resilience for lesbian, gay, bisexual, transgender, intersex, queer and/or questioning academics and students in South African universities. *Transformation in Higher Education, 3,* a34. DOI: 10.4102/the.v3i0.34

Rudoe, N. (2010). Lesbian teachers' identity, power and the public/private boundary. *Sex Education, 10*(1), 23–36. DOI: 10.1080/14681810903491347

Rumens, N. (2012). Queering men and masculinities in construction: Towards a research agenda. *Construction Management and Economics, 31*(8), 802–815. DOI: 10.1080/01446193.2013.765021

Savin-Williams, R. C. (2017). *Mostly straight: Sexual fluidity among men.* Cambridge, MA: Harvard University Press.

Schieble, M. (2012). A critical discourse analysis of teachers' views on LGBT literature. *Discourse: Studies in the Cultural Politics of Education, 33*(2), 207–222. d

Sedgwick, E. K. (1990). *Epistemology of the closet.* Berkeley, CA: University of California Press.

Seidman, S. (1996). *Queer theory sociology.* Cambridge, MA: Blackwell.

Seidman, S. (2002). *Beyond the closet? The transformation of gay and lesbian life.* New York, NY: Routledge.

Shahani, P. (2008). *Gay Bombay: Globalization, love and (be)longing in contemporary India.* Thousand Oaks, CA: SAGE Publications.

Simonsson, A., & Angervall, P. (2016). Gay as classroom practice: A study on sexuality in a secondary language classroom. *Confero, 4*(1), 37–70. DOI: 10.9976/confero.2001–4562.160622

Teman, E. D. (2016). Hands on my hips: Politics of a subversive fish. *Qualitative Inquiry, 22*(4), 274–279. DOI: 10.1177/1077800415615601

Teman, E. D. (2018). Stifled [queer] voices. *Cultural Studies, 18*(2), 133–139. DOI: 10.1177/1532708616655819

Teman, E. D., & Lahman, M. K. E. (2012). Broom closet or fish bowl? Using educational ethnography to explore the culture of a university queer youth center. *Qualitative Inquiry, 18*(4), 341–354. DOI: 10.1177/1077800411433548

Thorne, B., & Luria, Z. (1986). Sexuality and gender in children's daily worlds. *Social Problems, 33*(3), 176–190.

Ward, J. (2015). *Not gay: Sex between straight white men.* New York, NY: New York University Press.

Weeks, J. (1996). The construction of homosexuality. In S. Seidman (Ed.), *Queer theory/sociology* (pp. 41–63). Cambridge, MA: Blackwell.

Wilkinson, L., & Pearson, J. (2009). School culture and the well-being of same-sex attracted youth. *Gender & Society, 23*(4), 542–568. DOI: 10.1177/0891243209339913

Williams, F. (2016). Critical thinking in social policy: The challenges of past, present and future. *Social Policy & Administration, 50*(6), 628–647. DOI: 10.1111/spol.12253

Yoshino, K. (2002). Covering. *The Yale Law Journal, 111*(4), 769–939.

CHAPTER 10

The Normalization of Anti-Blackness in Teacher Education
A Call for Critical Race Frameworks

Andrew B. Torres and *Lamar L. Johnson*

Anti-Blackness is a plague infecting generations of all ethnic groups who co-exist in the institutions we navigate daily. Through anti-Blackness, marginalization of Black bodies continues to be an everyday reality that is often argued to be nonexistent. The normalization of anti-Blackness is a global reality—apartheid in South Africa, *blancimiento* in Central and South America, the current migrant slave trade in Libya. Through understanding the historical origins of anti-Blackness as rooted in settler colonialism and how certain institutions have shaped, informed, and perpetuated anti-Blackness, we continue the process of finding pathways by which we may take individual and collective action to enact change.

Considering the Black Lives Matter movement as a beacon, there has been a shift toward Black bodies and voices no longer being passive about their racialized lived realities. The Black Lives Matter movement is not inseparable from the racial injustices and the anti-Black racism deeply entrenched in academic spaces. As Black educators, we have to ask ourselves: How are our Black bodies and lives mattering in higher educational spaces?

Predominantly White Institutions (PWIs) have fostered a culture of anti-Blackness that has become normalized. With the re-emergence of scholarship around BlackCrit and Critical Race Theory (CRT), there are more calls to action. Moreover, those able to transcend these boundaries and work within these institutions still find themselves isolated and their voices stifled (Cole, McGowan, & Zerquera, 2017). This chapter aims to examine the marginalization of Black bodies in the academy through the lens of anti-Blackness.

Beginning with a description of BlackCrit Theory and anti-Blackness, this chapter frames the necessity of BlackCrit Theory in relation to CRT as a pivotal access point into theorizing how we can move toward action-oriented strategies to disrupt and challenge anti-Blackness. Subsequently, we provide evidence of anti-Blackness in the academy through racial storytelling

(Johnson, 2017). We conclude with a vision statement of how the academy may be shifted as steps are taken to address anti-Blackness.

Definition of labels: To work against injustices, we intentionally capital-ize *Black* to engender a sense of pride in Blackness, love for Blackness, and liberation of Blackness. We view Black as beautiful and complex in order to convey the message that our racialized realities are not damaged. The exceptions to this distinction are all mentions of anti-Blackness, which rep-resent epistemologies and ontologies that conflict with our understanding of Blackness. The intention behind this exception is to denote the inherent prejudices against Blackness that anti-Blackness embodies, which we refuse to celebrate.

CALL IT BY ITS NAME: FOUNDATIONS OF ANTI-BLACKNESS

Anti-blackness infiltrates U.S. society and is interwoven throughout curricu-lum and pedagogical practices. Educators miseducate students about Black-ness by feeding them deficit ideologies and specious claims with a disdain for Blackness: "The thought of the inferiority of the Negro is drilled into him in almost every class he enters and in almost every book he studies" (Woodson, 1933/2006, p. 2). If students are constantly indoctrinated with concepts of Black culture and humanity as inferior, then it is counterintui-tive to assume that schooling, as it has been and is currently structured, is conducive to the advancement of Black people.

Anderson (1988) described universal education as preparing newly freed Black people to enter the urban workforce, which mirrors current standardization trends in education as a means of preparing students for college and career readiness. What is often neglected is that these students often go on to attend PWIs where they have been "equipped to begin the life of an Americanized or Europeanized white man" (Woodson, 1933/2006, p. 5). Students are trained for careers that advance and maintain White supremacy under the guise that the knowledge and skills they gain are uni-versal and benefit their individual progress.

Historically, this trend can be traced to settler colonialism, whose Euro-pean perpetrators primarily focused on the stealing of Native land through violent and dehumanizing means (Tuck & Yang, 2012). The ontological and epistemological grounding of settler colonialism became the basis for which the stealing, objectifying, and murdering of Native and Black bodies was justified and rationalized.

BlackCrit

In examining students of color in teacher education, Haddix (2016) acknowl-edged that CRT and other critical race frameworks have gained attention in teacher education programs; however, Haddix enumerated two critiques: "(1) critical race theories' failure to provide evidence of a distinctive voice of color and (2) critical race theories' reliance on storytelling as a valid form of making truth claims" (p. 103). For this chapter, we focus on how CRT fails to explicitly address the Black experience and the racial subjugation of Black people (Dumas & Ross, 2016; Johnson, 2017). Dumas and Ross (2016) argued CRT is often confounded with Black Critical Theory (BlackCrit), but it is rooted in theorizing race in general and racism specifically. BlackCrit, on the other hand, helps "address how antiblackness—which is something different than White supremacy—informs and facilitates racist ideology and institutional practice," by providing a means to "explain precisely how Black bodies become marginalized, disregarded, and disdained, even in their highly visible place within celebratory discourses on race and diversity" (p. 417). Within higher education, it has become increasingly evident that the educational praxis offered by Woodson (1933/2006) is salient to the progress of Black people within these institutions.

Understanding that ideological underpinnings of education in the West are predicated on a history centering Whiteness while at the same time erasing and distorting Black lived realities is central to developing points of access and action to effect change within higher education institutions. Putting this educational praxis in conversation with Freire's (2000) understanding of praxis offers a way to push what Patel (2016) described as *pedagogies of survivance* that highlight the inherent modes of resistance within the lived realities of people who have been marginalized: "places of formal schooling present an almost constant mixture of promise and heartbreak" (p. 397). This promise often ties to the idea that going to a place of formal schooling will lead to success, but in fact, and heartbreakingly, this outcome is insufficiently realized by Black people who attend college.

Complicating this notion of formal education for Black students is the reality that we embody multiple identities. Tatum (1997) described at least seven categories of otherness and described how "the salience of particular aspects of our identity varies at different moments in our lives. The process of integrating the component parts of our self-definition is indeed a lifelong journey" (p. 20). Through our multiple identities we can begin to paint a picture of the complexity that defines Black lived realities.

TEACHING WHILE BLACK: RACIAL STORYTELLING FROM INSIDE THE ACADEMY

Stories generate from a source, something that inspires the teller to share but also informs the formulation of the story. While one may be tempted to assume that stories of Black lived realities are inherently in opposition to Whiteness, we invite readers to consider how racial stories reflect that our experiences and who we are as people of Color are not always in relation to or with white people. That is, racial storytelling does not have to be utilized to counter dominant narratives. . . . However, this does not mean counter-stories cannot transpire from racial storytelling. (Johnson, 2017, p. 8)

Through *racial storytelling* we examine how our past, present, and future intersect and interact with one another.

We begin to address our *racial hauntings* as a means of self-actualization that prompts self-love, individual and collective action, and humanizing Black lived experiences that have historically been and continue to be marginalized. In other words, "If we do not confront our racial ghosts, then it is an act of repressed and symbolic violence against y(our)self that ultimately continues the narcissism of whiteness and white supremacy" (Johnson, 2017, p. 5; see also Matias, 2016). In confronting racial hauntings, ghosts, we disrupt acts of symbolic violence perpetrated against us by allowing our voice to flourish and our lived realities to be exercised in ways that promote collective and individual healing.

Applying these concepts to the Black experience may be one way to address anti-Blackness in higher education, but more importantly would address the pervasiveness of isolation and imposter syndrome that often permeates the experiences of Black women, men, and individuals whose identities do not align with a gender binary. Below, we engage in racial stories to illustrate the anti-Black racism we encounter as Black educators in PWIs and to show that our stories are not always in opposition to Whiteness.

Andrew's Racial Story: From Home to the Academy

Attending predominantly White universities has served as a process of racial discovery for me. Coming from the Bronx, I have always been surrounded by those who look like me (and some who don't), but with a shared geographical history the differences almost never outweighed our similarities. Understanding that anti-Blackness exists within the Puerto Rican community, I began to self-identify as Afro-Boricua to address the inherent forms of anti-Blackness that I witnessed and became compliant with within my community throughout my upbringing.

With the birth of my daughter, I knew I wanted to disrupt and challenge this pattern of anti-Blackness within my family community. This identification has become more central to my scholarship as a parent-scholar; I've experienced anti-Blackness now as a doctoral student at a large PWI. WestU (pseudonym) as a whole has been criticized for not supporting Black students on campus, and the program that I am currently in has a reputation for failing to retain Black students. To my knowledge, three students, one female and two males, who identify as Black left the program because they didn't feel supported. Although these three were able to transfer to different departments and programs within the university, many who endure this isolation drop out.

In an effort to address the lack of support for Black students, the program's higher-ups took initiative to bring in more Black professors to support Black students. Despite these changes within the program, tensions for Black students and faculty still exist and the Black students currently within the program still feel unsupported in many contexts. As is typical of predominantly White-serving institutions, Black students are only seen as valuable if they participate on an athletic team that represents the school.

Tensions Rising. Everything on campus changed when Trump won the presidency. When Trump was elected to office, my cohort colleague, Mary (pseudonym), told me about a protest that she was helping plan: We would march to the center of campus.

Many of us on campus, who knew that our safety was even more at risk now, believed the administration of the university did nothing to address our concerns. This was echoed in the stories shared with all of us when the march reached its destination, the administrative building. Following the protests WestU began a campaign entitled "Hate Has No Home" to address the increase of racist acts against people of the global majority on the university's campus as well as to address the concerns for safety that students of the global majority felt. The increased confidence that racist White people found with one of their own back in office, forced the university to take initiative rather than consider the needs of Black, Latinx, South Asian, African, Native, and Asian students. Anti-Blackness is as blatant as ever on college campuses and there is no shame in those who perpetuate this ideology.

The Space(s) We Need. During the spring 2018 semester, I was working as a teaching assistant for an undergraduate course on social diversity in education. There were a group of Black students who felt that they were constantly speaking on their experiences as Black students while their White counterparts spectated and acted as an audience to their stories without fully comprehending the complexities of Black lived experience. The professor, a Black woman, decided to take the Black students to dinner at the end of semester after they expressed their feeling that the classroom space was not being held for them. She attempted to provide a safe and brave space, as she termed it, for students to candidly voice ways that the class could be structured to better support Black students. While I was not invited to this outing, I believe that it was a step toward understanding and an act of praxis that White professors would not have willingly undertaken. More important, I do not suspect that Black students would have voiced their frustrations to any professor of an ethnic and racial background that didn't align with their own.

Lamar's Racial Story: This Is America

It was Fall 2016, the morning after Trump was elected as the president of the United States. I remember waking up and wishing it was a bad dream, only to realize that this nightmare was my actual reality. Anguish and pain lingered through my body, and several thoughts ran through my mind. First, I contemplated canceling my classes for that day because I didn't feel like taking my body through the racial violence that the academy, White faculty and staff, and White students tend to inflict upon Black people's bodies. I wanted to cancel class and just take a sick day.

My second thought was that this is America and I shouldn't be surprised by this country's actions. I could see the writing on the walls. Historically and in the present moment, Black children and youth, men, and women have all been the prime targets of White supremacy and anti-Black racism. With all of these thoughts swirling through my mind, I decided to go teach.

When I arrived at my class, a still, ominous feeling permeated the room. *This will be an interesting class,* I thought to myself. There were 17 students in this course; out of the 17, I had only one biracial Black female. While setting up my technology for class, I could hear the students chatter about the previous night's election. As the students discussed the outcome of the election, one White female, Amanda (pseudonym), began to tear up during her conversation with some of her peers. Openly, she explained her frustration and agitation about the election.

Please don't ask me my thoughts about the election . . . in this moment, I don't want to discuss the election with people who don't look like me. This is not my "safe" space. But, of course, they want to know my thoughts, especially as we have been tackling the intersections of literacy, language, education, race, anti-Blackness, and racial violence. With tears in her eyes, "Dr. J., how are you feeling?" Amanda asked. I can't remember the first part of my response to Amanda; however, I remember saying, "If you are feeling hurt, angry, and broken inside, imagine how people of color feel in this moment."

Make America "White" Again. It was still the day after Trump had been elected. That morning, I had to deal with Amanda's tears. In conjunction with White tears, I was reminded of the racial violence and anti-Black racism by the anti-Black rhetoric that was tagged on the grounds and walls across campus. Hours later, while walking to my second class, from a distance, I spotted a White male faculty member on his hands and knees with a bucket filled with soap and water. As I approached the White male, I stopped to see exactly what he was trying to remove. It was "Make America Great Again" rhetoric that was tagged in red and blue spray paint on the cement. As I looked at the anti-Black and anti-Brown rhetoric, I responded, "I guess this is a nice gesture, but you are going to be scrubbing for days seeing that racial epithets are tagged throughout this campus."

Leading up to the election, institutions throughout the U.S. reminded us (Black faculty and staff and students) of the ways in which race and anti-Black racism operate in higher educational spaces. The anti-Black racism that plagued the streets also plagued our academic streets. Similarly, I am also reminded of the symbolic and racial violence that plagued pre-K–12 contexts. On Wednesday, November 9, 2016, in Royal Oak, Michigan, at Royal Oak Middle School just a day after Donald Trump was elected president, a video of White students screaming, "Build that wall!" went viral on social media. On that same day, in Wellsville, NY, a dugout at Island Park was marked with the words "Make America White Again," along with a large swastika symbol. One common thread that runs through all of these incidents is the devaluing of Black lives and the erasure of Black people.

All Lives Matter. That was at the beginning of Trump's term. Fast-forward to the present moment: anti-Black racism and the anti-Black rhetoric that we have witnessed is connected to the anti-Blackness that exists in the academy. Recently, in my course on Black language, during a conversation about the interconnectedness among language, literacy, racial violence, and anti-Blackness, a White female exclaimed, "I don't think police officers are only killing Black and Brown people—they are equally killing White people, too."

As the White female explained her argument, I tried to remain calm, cool, and collected. But this was a prime example of racial and symbolic violence at its finest. While I tried to gather my thoughts, the White female proceeded to say, "Also, I understand why it is important to say their names, but I believe we need to do a further investigation about the person and why they were killed. One of the names that are on the Black Lives Matter website, I decided to go find out what happened and come to find out, the Black guy resisted arrest and he was on PCP. . . .That easily could have been a White person."

Immediately, a student of color interrupted, "I disagree with your statements. Where are the receipts? You can't compare the racial violence and police brutality that people of color encounter to White people. You can turn on the TV or go to social media and see the racial violence that Black and Brown children and youth face in communities and within classrooms."

NEXT STEPS: RACIAL JUSTICE COURSES IN TEACHER EDUCATION

King (2017) argued that since the 2016 presidential campaign and election, Trump's White supremacist patriarchal discourse and ideologies reflect the ideologies and perceptions that many White teachers and schools hold about Black youth and their communities. Trump's political message and *dog whistle* politics of "Make America great again" represent a racially coded message that many people understood as *Make America White again*. As mentioned above, many schools and teachers inflict anti-Black racial violence upon Black children and youth without understanding how the curricula, their pedagogical practices, and their lack of criticality and awareness can symbolically kill Black students' spirits.

It is no surprise that many preservice teachers are not prepared to have conversations about race, racism, and Whiteness when teacher educators are not well versed in critical race- and justice-oriented frameworks and methodologies (Johnson & Bryan, 2016). Further, teacher education must begin to center the Black experience (Dumas & Ross, 2016) within curricula and pedagogical practices. Teacher education needs to focus more openly on how Black people construct and conceptualize knowledge and how Black knowledge is valued or devalued.

Considering the thematic sequencing of coursework for students, there is rarely a requirement for courses that center race or ethnicity. In talking about White "highly educated" people, Woodson (1933/2006) said, "These things [race] did not figure in the courses which they pursued, and why should they" (p. 7). If required to take such a course from the onset, what value would education hold for students of the global majority? Additionally, how would White students react to such demands from a university? We believe that through such restructuring of thematic sequencing of courses, there would be a shift in the ways students from various ethnic and racial backgrounds interact across lines of difference.

For instance, social justice–oriented courses are a hot commodity across universities, especially given the chaos that has resulted from the current sociopolitical climate, but are they truly pursuing justice for the students who are enrolled? Could there be courses that specifically consider racial justice? Within a social justice framework, race is reduced to a topic covered over 1 or 2 weeks and, even through an intersectional lens, we find race getting confounded with other identity categories. Within a classroom context, this can take the discussion away from race, further isolating those who center race within their lived realities, and continue the cycle of anti-Blackness by the marginalization of Black bodies and voices.

Another area that requires some development for most, if not all, students is coursework on critical literacy with regard to racialized discourse (Lee & Slaughter-Defoe, 1995). It is pivotal that students pursue coursework that allows them to disseminate racial discourse in productive and constructive ways. Within these types of courses, racial storytelling that "allows us to confront our racial hauntings and to work against our own miseducation while moving toward liberation and self-actualization" (Johnson, 2017, p. 4) might function in a plurality of ways.

First, it might be a pedagogical tool through which we educate and are educated about racialized lived realities within academic and educational contexts. Second, as a theoretical framing, racial storytelling might allow for more nuanced forms of theorizing and humanizing the ways in which Black people navigate PWIs while also delineating how life has shaped and continues to shape multiple identities. Most important, as a research methodology, racial storytelling might provide a structure through which we simultaneously collect and analyze data through a lens of racial narrative inquiry.

The reality of anti-Blackness is one that cannot be unlived for Black people. These initiatives are meant to show possible pathways of action toward shifting racial incompetence and indifference toward racial consciousness. We offer these modes of action because we feel all too often there is a greater tendency to complain about issues than to create ways to change these circumstances. Even those who can enact change through action-oriented means tend to face opposition that is stifling and limiting. Our suggestions are in no way the only means by which we can begin to shift anti-Blackness, but we believe they are keenly grounded in modalities and practices of humanization and decolonization to counteract the roots of anti-Blackness as situated in settler colonialism and acts of dehumanization.

CODA

The marginalization of Black bodies continues to act as tangible evidence of the ongoing reality of anti-Blackness. We use the word *reality* to emphasize that this is real for Black women, men, and individuals who identify as gender fluid. Though there is a laundry list of complaints providing a scope of how treacherous this reality is, we argue that there must be more moves toward reformation and restructuring within higher education.

Through educational *praxis* (Freire, 2000; Woodson, 1933/2006), and with *racial storytelling* (Johnson, 2017) at the core of these changes, we may begin to develop *racial consciousness* through reflection and action to transform our *limit situations*. We must reconsider the finality of being *woke*, and move toward an understanding of racial consciousness not as a finish line that we cross but rather as an ongoing marathon that we run for the rest of our lives. Black is beautiful, Black is human, and we must continue the work of our ancestors to ensure that their sacrifice is not erased from the history of this nation.

REFERENCES

Anderson, J. D. (1988). *The education of Blacks in the South, 1860–1935.* Chapel Hill, NC: University of North Carolina Press.

Cole, E. R., McGowan, B. L., & Zerquera, D. D. (2017). First-year faculty of color: Narratives about entering the academy. *Equity & Excellence in Education, 50*(1), 1–12.

Dumas, M. J., & Ross, K. M. (2016). "Be real Black for me": Imagining BlackCrit in education. *Urban Education*, *51*(4), 415–442.

Freire, P. (2000). *Pedagogy of the oppressed: With an introduction by Donaldo Macedo*. New York, NY: Continuum.

Haddix, M. (2016). *Cultivating racial and linguistic diversity in literacy teacher education: Teachers like me*. New York, NY: Routledge.

Johnson, L. L. (2017). The racial hauntings of one Black male professor and the disturbance of the self (ves): Self-actualization and racial storytelling as pedagogical practices. *Journal of Literacy Research*, *49*(4), 476–502.

Johnson, L. L., & Bryan, N. (2016). Using our voices, losing our bodies: Michael Brown, Trayvon Martin, and the spirit murders of Black male professors in the academy. *Race Ethnicity and Education*, *20*(2), 163–177.

King, J. E. (2017) Who will make America great again? 'Black people, of course . . .'. *International Journal of Qualitative Studies in Education*, *30*(10), 946–956. DOI:10.1080/09518398.2017.1312605

Lee, C. D., & Slaughter-Defoe, D. T. (1995). Historical and sociocultural influences on African American education. In J. A. Banks & C. A. M. Banks (Eds.), *Handbook of research on multicultural education* (pp. 348–371). New York, NY: Macmillan.

Matias, C. E. (2016). *Feeling White: Whiteness, emotionality, and education*. Boston, MA: Sense Publishers.

Patel, L. (2016). Pedagogies of resistance and survivance: Learning as marronage. *Equity & Excellence in Education*, *49*(4), 397–401.

Tatum, B. D. (1997). "*Why are all the Black kids sitting together in the cafeteria?*" *And other conversations about race*. New York, NY: Basic Books.

Tuck, E., & Yang, K. W. (2012). Decolonization is not a metaphor. *Decolonization: Indigeneity, Education & Society*, *1*(1), 1–40.

Woodson, C. G. (1933/1990). *The mis-education of the Negro*. Trenton, NJ: Africa World Press.

Part III

BEYOND CRT

CHAPTER 11

Ghanaian Epistemology in Teacher Education

Adeline Borti

Ghanaian epistemology comprises historically and culturally conditioned practices and principles of knowing dependent on collectively generated information (Adjei 2007; Dei & Simmons, 2011; Manu, Osei-Bonsu, & Atta, 2015). This collectively generated knowledge is constructed as knowledge "for us by us" (Oppong, 2013). Thus, the practices and thoughts of the Ghanaian people are communal (Oppong, 2013; Sitoe, 2006).

This communal knowledge generation regards the knowledge of individuals, especially persons in authority and the elderly, as valuable (Osman, 2009; Tempels, Rubbens, & King, 1959). The Ghanaian Indigenous knowledge system (GIKS), an embodiment of Ghanaian epistemology, existed through proverbs, folklore, riddles, family stories, myths, rituals, folk songs, moral values, beliefs, customs, music, art symbols, and traditional institutions before the arrival of colonialists (Ani, 2013; Dei & Simmons, 2011; Gyekye, 1987; Jimoh, 2017; Nsamenang & Tchombé, 2011; Oppong, 2013). Prior to 1957, communal knowledge and ways of knowing were located in oral tradition (Jimoh, 2017).

Concerning the central tenets of Ghanaian epistemology, the first is communal knowledge, communal knowledge construction, and collectivist culture (Manu et al., 2015; Oppong, 2013; Sitoe, 2006). This tenet represents beliefs, principles, and practices of Indigenous Ghanaians, especially before colonialism (Adjei 2007; Dei & Simmons, 2011; Ramoupi, 2012; Wiredu, 1997). As per Manu et al. (2015), "Among the different tribal groups in Ghana, there are shared cultural beliefs that are important to the people," (p. 140), confirming the collectivist culture embedded in the GIKS.

The second tenet, omniscient authority and the hierarchy of the knowledgeable (Manu et al., 2015; Ntim, 2017; Sitoe, 2006; Tempels et al., 1959), refers to elders, leaders, ancestors, or authorities whose knowledge and wisdom cannot be critiqued or questioned, especially by young people. The GIKS perpetuates these practices; however, colonialism also encouraged dominance and abusive use of omniscient authority and the hierarchy of the knowledgeable.

The third tenet is spirituality (Adjei, 2007; Ani, 2013; Jimoh, 2017). The value of spirituality in the GIKS and African Indigenous knowledge system leads Jimoh (2017) to assert, "For the African, there is more to reality than what is within the realm of empirical inquiry" (p. 122), validating indigenous Ghanaians' belief in the seen and unseen worlds.

The final tenet of the Ghanaian epistemology is situated and contextualized knowledge (Akyeampong & Stephens, 2002; Dei & Simmons, 2011; Manu et al., 2015; Ntim, 2017; Oppong, 2013; Osman, 2009). This tenet acknowledges learning and knowing as a result of practice and engagement in authentic actual life activities and situations. By practice one gets experiential knowledge that enhances a person's understanding. The four tenets represent the multidimensionality of Ghanaian epistemological beliefs and practices.

HISTORY OF THE GHANAIAN EPISTEMOLOGY

The existence of the Ghanaian epistemology in Ghana (formerly the Gold Coast) can be traced to long before the arrival of the first colonialists (the Portuguese) in 1471 (Hilliard, 1957; McWilliam & Kwamena-Poh, 1975). Before the colonialists, the Ghanaian Indigenous knowledge system was valued, used, and reproduced by the Ghanaian ancestors. The rest of this section is organized according to the development of Ghanaian epistemology before the arrival of the colonialists, during the reign of the colonialists, and after independence in 1957.

Ghanaian Epistemology Before Colonialists

The Ghanaian epistemology emanated from the culture and the tradition of Indigenous Ghanaians (Ani, 2013; Dei & Simmons, 2011; Gyekye, 1987). Indigenous knowledge was represented, presented, constructed, and disseminated by traditional heads of families, communities, and societies. Elders and Indigenous people in authority also played crucial roles in knowledge construction and transmission.

Until the establishment of colonial schools, Indigenous Ghanaians had their own form of education in which they trained the younger generation through transmission of the communal and collective knowledge that was validated by the various members of the communities concerned (Hilliard, 1957; Jimoh, 2017; Oppong, 2013). Knowledge dissemination included equipping the learner with the knowledge and skills that influenced the individual's emotional, relational, environmental, spiritual, political, leadership, sociocultural, geopolitical, and economic aspects of life.

For example, through proverbs, young learners were taught how to be respectful and hardworking in order not to incur the wrath of God, the gods, the ancestors, and the elders. The principal means and modes of transmission of Ghanaian epistemology were through oral traditions and oral Ghanaian languages.

Ghanaian Epistemology During Colonialism

The colonial era was characterized by disapproval of the Ghanaian epistemology (Agbenyega & Klibthong, 2011; Oppong, 2013; Ramoupi, 2012). The Indigenous nature of knowledge was considered counterdevelopmental, primitive, and not empirical. This unfair attitude toward a people on their own land stifled the presentation, representation, validation, use, construction, and dissemination of Ghanaian Indigenous knowledge, especially at the official level.

For example, Ramoupi (2012) indicated that through the colonialists and Ghanaian elites, Indigenous Ghanaian knowledge was "silenced" even at the then-colonial university in Ghana. Additionally, Adjei (2007) confirms that the dominance of colonial control perpetuated Western knowledge and ways of knowing in order to produce human capital fit for the needs of the colonialists. Relegating the Ghanaian epistemology to the background resulted in stifling its growth.

Ghanaian Epistemology After Independence in 1957

After independence, the first president of Ghana, Osagyefo Dr. Kwame Nkrumah, campaigned for the promotion and use of Ghanaian Indigenous knowledge for the development of the country. Nkrumah did not limit his crusade for the validation of Indigenous knowledge to Ghana. As a Pan-Africanist, he extended his campaign to the continent of Africa, encouraging the rest of Africa to value, use, develop, and disseminate African epistemology for the development of the continent (Oppong, 2013; Ramoupi, 2012):

> We must seek an African view to the problems of Africa. This does not mean that western techniques and methods are not applicable to Africa. It does mean, however, that in Ghana we must look at every problem from the African point of view. . . . Our whole educational system must be geared to producing a scientifically-technically minded people. (McWilliam & Kwamena-Poh, 1975, p. 94)

Unfortunately, subsequent political leaders have not taken Nkrumah's philosophy about the essence of Ghanaian epistemology seriously, although Ghanaian epistemology is passed on from older generations to younger generations in informal settings. Further, the Ghanaian epistemology still competes for survival and the Ghanaian educational system has not done much to de-colonialize formal educational settings in Ghana (Dei & Simmons, 2011).

Nevertheless, with the establishment of Westernized schools coupled with the spread of writing, the tenets of the Ghanaian epistemology have been documented. Consequently, they are no longer transmitted by oral tradition and oral languages only. Despite the progress made, there is room for improvement as far as the inclusion of Ghanaian epistemology in the Ghanaian educational system, and in all aspects of Ghanaians' lives, is concerned.

GHANAIAN EPISTEMOLOGY'S APPROACH TO TEACHER EDUCATION

Teacher education in Ghana has two official trajectories for initial teacher preparation. First, the teacher training colleges of education (TTCE) are 3-year diploma-awarding postsecondary institutions. They are supervised by two public universities that also train teachers in Ghana (University of Education Winneba, University of Cape Coast). Currently, in Ghana, there are 50 teacher preparation colleges. The programs offered at the TTCE consist of 2 years of coursework and a 1-year teaching internship in the public elementary schools in Ghana. The two public universities run diploma, postdiploma, degree, and graduate programs.

The paradox of the Ghanaian teacher education program is in the implementation of a Westernized teacher preparation program that denies full recognition and validation of the Ghanaian epistemology. Ghanaian epistemology and Western epistemology in teacher education together are unable to produce "graduates who are well-grounded in those aspects of African [Ghanaian] technology, arts, culture, history, and heritage needed for the sustained development of the continent [country]" (Ramoupi, 2012, p. 7). This defeats Dr. Nkrumah's agenda for Ghana and Africa. Ramoupi therefore argued for an African-centered curriculum in the arts and human sciences.

I extend this argument to contend for Ghanaian-centered curricula in teacher education if our peculiar and global developmental issues are to be addressed appropriately. Indeed, implementation of Ghanaian-centered curricula requires significant commitment from Ghanaian leaders, scholars, and citizens. In addressing the manner in which the Ghanaian epistemology has been approached in the preparation of the teachers in Ghana, I organize the following sections according to how Ghanaian epistemological tenets affect teacher preparation.

Communal Knowledge, Ways of Knowing, and Collectivist Culture

The communal knowledge, ways of knowing, and collectivist culture of the Indigenous Ghanaians represent sociocultural values, beliefs, and practices, and transcend tribes and cultures. This communal worldview facilitates and promotes dialogue and discursive practices that are common in Indigenous communities. The communal principle is that one mind cannot produce beneficial ideas and solutions in a society. Ways of knowing manifested by various sources and people are beneficially multifaceted. Additionally, communal knowledge and ways of knowing produce wisdom, the companion of knowledge (Gyekye, 1987; Osman, 2009). Indigenous Ghanaians regard knowledge as incomplete without wisdom because their combination enhances the progress of a society and an individual (Gyekye, 1987; Osman, 2009).

Unfortunately, teacher preparation does not incorporate communal knowledge, communal ways of knowing, and collectivist culture in teacher preparation curriculum and practices. If not by design, then by default, the lack of collaboration and of communal knowledge construction have silenced the voices of many preservice teachers and nurtured fearful teachers who are likely to struggle with confidence as professionals. Teachers are unlikely to be reflective enough to make useful professional judgments that could enhance students' learning and achievement. Agbenyega and Deku (2011) noted that instructor-centered practices coupled with minimal interaction among teacher educators, teachers, and preservice teachers promote knowledge transmission that perpetuates cultural norms and colonial supremacy.

According to Agbenyega and Deku (2011), preservice teachers complained, "The issue is the lack of support systems for pre-service teachers in training colleges or universities. . . . The moment you enter [college] you are on your own" (p. 13). Ghanaian epistemology is not being valued and practiced by teacher educators and preservice teachers. If education is a social process and the Ghanaian epistemology upholds communal knowledge and collective knowledge construction, then it is ironic that the teacher education program and the Ghanaian school system reflect otherwise.

In the aftermath of colonialism and current Western influence on Ghanaian epistemology in teacher education, collective and communal knowledge are weakened and the distorted identities that result are detrimental to national, societal, and individual dignity and respect for what and who the Ghanaians are. Finally, the disconnect between the communal lifestyle of the Indigenous Ghanaians and the individualistic lifestyle without communal support system being promoted in teacher training colleges of education calls for a critical look at teacher education policies and their implementation.

Omniscient Authority and the Hierarchy of the Knowledgeable

This tenet projects the elders, leaders, authorities, and the ancestors as omniscient sources of unquestionable authority, wisdom, and knowledge (Dei & Simmons, 2011; Ntim, 2017; Sitoe, 2006; Tempels, Rubbens, & King,

1959). Sitoe (2006) bemoaned the fact that the omniscient authority presents elderly people and sages as "endowed with knowledge and wisdom that transcended that of the community in general" (p. 36). The idea of omniscient authority also leads to hierarchical presentation of the knowledgeable person or the elder as one whose knowledge and wisdom cannot be questioned. This results in nurturing passive teachers who consider it rebellion to question the status quo.

This Ghanaian epistemological tenet is similar to the authoritarian system of colonial masters where their knowledge, principles, and practices could not be critiqued or questioned. Schommer (1990) indicated that college students regarded omniscient knowledge as accessible only to authorities. Uncritical reverence of omniscient authority has negative developmental and educational implications.

Ntim (2017) revealed how omniscient authority creates "teachers [who] could rarely raise objections even if they disagree with content and structure of the curricula for teacher education" (p. 161). Additionally, "the teacher educator can hardly question state authority and mandate" (p. 161). Likewise, Manu et al. (2015) noted that as a result of promoting omniscient authority, "Ghanaian student teachers are more likely to believe that only experts and authorities have the true knowledge" (p. 147).

Furthermore, Oppong (2013) lamented that omniscient authority and hierarchy of knowledge stifle creativity and collaboration. There is a lack of freedom of expression in teacher-centered classrooms compared to learner-centered classroom (Akyeampong, 2017; Oppong, 2013). Oppong argued for critical pedagogy if the purpose of education and teacher education is social transformation. Critical pedagogy would nurture democratic teachers who would, in turn, raise democratic students and citizens who could advance the course of a nation.

In conclusion, there is a need for some order and respect in teacher education; however, the general perpetuation of the Ghanaian epistemology that emphasizes omniscient authority and the hierarchy of the knowledgeable to the detriment of progress needs to be interrogated and addressed soon.

Spirituality

The tenet of spirituality in GIKS and other African Indigenous knowledge systems led Jimoh (2017) to assert that "for the African, there is more to reality than what is within the realm of empirical inquiry" (p. 122). Jimoh's claim validates Indigenous Ghanaians' belief in the seen and unseen worlds. Adopting Western science and Western epistemology in their entirety in Ghanaian society and education creates dissonance because our spiritual beliefs and claims cannot be subjected to empirical validations (Osman, 2009) and "to standards of justification other than the culture in which they are found" (Jimoh, 2017, p. 133). Thus, secularism is foreign to Indigenous Ghanaian culture.

Adjei (2007) believes that spirituality and equity need to be addressed in Ghanaian education. Even as teacher educators teach about love, commitment, transformation, humility, compassion, dedication, and openness, it behooves them to demonstrate these virtues. Spirituality is evident in Ghanaian schools; however, there is still more to be done. Adjei indicated that Hindman (2002) "challenges educators to work towards the spiritual development of their students and inspire them to dedicate their lives towards the struggle against social injustices, inequity, and unfairness that affect every member of society" (p. 1054).

The spirituality demonstrated in Ghana's current teacher education program does not adequately reflect love toward the students, commitment to students' learning and students' achievement, transformation of unjust practices, humility of teacher educators, compassion for students' diverse needs, and openness of teacher educators. Consequently, a serious evaluation of what is conceptualized as spirituality in the Ghanaian education system is necessary.

Situated and Contextualized Knowledge

Appreciable progress has been made to situate and contextualize knowledge construction, use, and dissemination in teacher education in Ghana. However, there is still a reliance on foreign knowledge. This is not to say that only knowledge about the Ghanaian situation should be privileged but priority should be given to knowledge relevant to Ghanaian teacher preparation.

Ghanaian epistemology thrives on experiential knowledge. According to Sitoe (2006), African epistemology is built on the assumption that the practice of knowing does not occur in isolation or detached from the reality in which the actual knowledge is to be found; "African epistemology is based on the principle that one learns and comes to know by actually doing, in real life circumstances" (p. 188).

Sitoe indicated that communities should train younger generations by letting them acquire knowledge and skills through practice in the communities. Because knowledge and the ways of knowing must be relevant to the knowledge constructed and its users, situated and contextualized knowledge is what each society needs for authentic and meaningful advancement.

Dei and Simmons (2011) questioned the amount of local cultural resource knowledge that students are exposed to in schools. They highlighted the fact that "contemporary education is mired in the reproduction of colonial hierarchies of power and knowledge" (p. 97). Unfortunately, the repercussions of Westernized and colonized education and knowledge in Ghana is the "increasing number of unemployed graduates in Ghana, whose expertise generally fails to match the demands of the Ghanaian labour market" (Ntim, 2017, p. 150). This finding is not surprising because research shows (see Dei & Simmons, 2011; Manu et al., 2015; Ntim, 2017; Ramoupi, 2012) that contemporary Ghanaian education rarely helps use, produce, and advance the situated and contextualized knowledge needed to address Ghana's educational, cultural, social, economic, political, and geopolitical needs.

Adjei (2007) lamented how Indigenous knowledge and knowledge about our own environment are ignored and preference is given to knowledge from outside Ghana. Despite his observation, more Indigenous textbooks, storybooks, and other learning resources are being introduced in teacher education. The hope is for this positive trajectory to continue in order to train teachers who are not aliens in their own culture.

NEXT STEPS

There can be no quality development in a nation without efficient teacher education programs. In any modern society, teachers train a nation's human capital. Therefore, in order to develop as a nation, attention should be paid to teacher education (Akyeampong, 2017). Social justice and compassion are important to raising democratic teachers. Based on the discussion in the preceding sections, it is evident that tenets of Ghanaian epistemology are useful in advancing teacher education when they are employed with a critical approach.

The engagement and validation of communal knowledge, communal knowledge construction, and collectivist culture in teacher education would address the silencing of voices of vulnerable preservice teachers. The support of the social constructivist paradigm in the Ghanaian epistemology should be incorporated in the teacher education program in order to change the teacher-centered instructional approach. In addition, the gap between informal settings where communal knowledge, communal knowledge construction, and collectivist culture are valued and formal settings where this epistemological tenet is not valued and promoted should be closed.

Further, formal recognition of Indigenous knowledge raises questions as to why teacher education in Ghana has not taken the opportunity to value and validate Ghanaian epistemology to the betterment of the nation and the continent, as Ghana was the first country to gain independence and lead the way in sub-Saharan Africa. An overreliance on foreign epistemologies has resulted in overwhelming materialism. There is a need to disrupt and question the perpetuation of Western hegemony. A system that promotes social justice and compassion is swiftly disappearing and a frantic effort to restore and improve it could enhance teacher education.

An adherence to omniscient authority and a hierarchy of the knowledgeable should be tempered with caution in order to promote critical pedagogy. There should be order and respect in teacher education; however, abuse of power is unnecessary. Preservice teachers should learn and grow in an atmosphere of love, peace, engagement, and critical exploration instead of an atmosphere of fear and intimidation.

Teachers' and teacher educators' understanding of the fact that "no cultural group is 'better' in any absolute sense" (Browaeys & Price, 2008, p. 10) and their acceptance of the fact that "every culture has the right to conceive the world in its own image" (Wiredu, 1980, p. 60) would be a starting point to reorient Ghanaian teachers and teacher educators to value, respect, present, use, validate, and grow Ghanaian epistemology in teacher education. This approach will build the confidence lost through colonialism. Self-respect and acceptance of one's own epistemology first, with respect and acceptance of other epistemologies in order to position oneself holistically to be relevant in the local, national, and global context, are achievable.

Further, a rigorous training to orient teacher educators to promote knowledge "by us, for us" is urgently needed. When teacher educators value and reflect upon the benefits of the Ghanaian epistemological tenets, they nurture their own practices, beliefs, and positive convictions. These convictions can enable teacher educators to promote the need for a more transformed teacher education in Ghana. Without a more reflective and reflexive approach to teacher education in Ghana, less compassion and social justice will be realized.

In conclusion, some educational gains have been made in teacher education in Ghana and the government continues to explore ways to improve teacher education and education in general. However, another look at the objectives of teacher education in Ghana is vital for any educational endeavor to become fully realized. According to Charles Aheto-Tsegah, acting executive secretary for the National Council for Curriculum and Assessment, the vision for current teacher education in Ghana includes the raising of well-trained, empowered, professionally qualified, motivated, creative teachers who possess the fundamental skills of literacy and numeracy, and problem solving, and are analytical and mature in the use of their cognitive, interpersonal, and social skills. Teachers who have ethical values and attitudes would be able to make informed decisions in response to local and global challenges (Section 9 of the Incheon Declaration, May 2015).

Based on these excellent intentions, teacher educators and teachers do not only need content knowledge, pedagogical content knowledge, and curriculum knowledge in order to be effective. To better prepare these professionals, they need to understand and engage humanizing pedagogy, where human beings, as sociocultural beings, are creative enough to engage in and with their environment in order to question and resist oppression and to advance respect, compassion, care, diversity, and equity for the betterment of the society and Ghana's teacher education.

REFERENCES

Adjei, P. B. (2007). Decolonising knowledge production: The pedagogic relevance of Gandhian Satyagraha to schooling and education in Ghana. *Canadian Journal of Education, 30*, 1046–1067.

Agbenyega, J. S., & Deku, P. K. (2011). Building new identities in teacher preparation for inclusive education in Ghana. *Current Issues in Education, 14*(1), 1–37.

Agbenyega, J. S., & Klibthong, S. (2011). Early childhood inclusion: A postcolonial analysis of pre-service teachers' professional development and pedagogy in Ghana. *Contemporary Issues in Early Childhood, 12*, 403–414.

Akyeampong, K. (2017). Teacher educators' practice and vision of good teaching in teacher education reform context in Ghana. *Educational Researcher, 46*, 194–203.

Akyeampong, K., & Stephens, D. (2002). Exploring the backgrounds and shaping of beginning student teachers in Ghana: Toward greater contextualisation of teacher education. *International Journal of Educational Development, 22*, 261–274.

Ani, N. C. (2013). Appraisal of African epistemology in the global system. *Alternation, 20*, 295–320.

Browaeys, M. J., & Price, R. (2008). *Understanding cross-cultural management*. Harlow, UK: Pearson Education.

Dei, G. J. S., & Simmons, M. (2011). Indigenous knowledge and the challenge for rethinking conventional educational philosophy: A Ghanaian case study. *Counterpoints, 352*, 97–111.

Gyekye, K. (1987). *An essay on African philosophical thought: The Akan conceptual scheme*. Cambridge, UK: Cambridge University Press

Hilliard, F. H. (1957). *A short history of education in Ghana*. London, UK: Longmans Green & Sons Co. Ltd.

Hindman, D. M. (2002). From splintered lives to whole persons: Facilitating spiritual development in college students. *Religious Education, 97*, 165–182.

Incheon declaration and framework for action for the implementation of sustainable development goal 4: Ensure inclusive and equitable quality education and promote lifelong learning opportunities for all. (2015). *UNESCO*. Retrieved from uis.unesco.org/sites/default/files/documents/education-2030-incheon-framework-for-action-implementation-of-sdg4-2016-en_2.pdf

Jimoh, A. K. (2017). An African theory of knowledge. In I. E. Ukpokolo (Ed.), *Themes, Issues and Problems in African Philosophy* (pp. 121–136). London, UK: Palgrave Macmillan.

Manu, J., Bonsu, R. O., & Atta, G. P. (2015). Epistemic beliefs and their instructional practice: Perspective of a private university in Ghana. *International Journal of Innovative Research and Development, 4*, 139–151.

McWilliam, H. O. A., & Kwamena-Poh, M.A. (1975). *The development of education in Ghana*. London, UK: Longman.

Nsamenang, A. B., & Tshombé, T. M. S. (Eds.). (2011). *Handbook of African educational theories and practices: A generative teacher education curriculum.* Bamenda, Cameroon: Human Development Resource Centre.

Oppong, S. (2013). Indigenizing knowledge for development: Epistemological and pedagogical approaches. *Africanus, 43*(2), 34–50.

Osman, A. (2009, November). *Indigenous knowledge in Africa: Challenges and opportunities.* An inaugural lecture presented at University of the Free State, South Africa.

Ramoupi, N. L. L. (2012). Deconstructing eurocentric education: A comparative study of teaching Africa-centred curriculum at the University of Cape Town and the University of Ghana, Legon. *Postamble, 7*(2), 1–36.

Schommer, M. (1990). The effects of beliefs about the nature of knowledge on comprehension. *Journal of Educational Psychology, 58*, 498–504.

Sitoe, A. (2006). Epistemological beliefs and perceptions of education in Africa: An explorative study with high school students in Mozambique. Retrieved from www.rug.nl/research/portal/publications/epistemological-beliefs-and-perceptions-of-education-in-africa(faab423f-3b1a-4bb8-8ab9-62c5f8a9dd39).html

Tempels, P., Rubbens, A., & King, C. (1959). *Bantu philosophy.* Paris, France: Présence Africaine. Retrieved from www.congoforum.be/upldocs/Tempels%20BantuPhil%20English%201959.pdf

Wiredu, J. E. (1997). How not to compare African traditional thought with Western thought. *Transition, 75*, 320–327.

CHAPTER 12

Working Within a Contact Zone to Explore Indigenous Fijian Epistemology

Cynthia Brock, Pauline Harris, and *Ufemia Camaitoga*

In her classic transcultural work,[1] *Imperial Eyes*, Mary Louise Pratt (2008) defined *contact zones* as shifts in centers of gravity and points of view from European expansionist perspectives to "space[s] and time[s] where subjects previously separated by geography and history are co-present, the point at which their trajectories now intersect" (p. 8). Moreover, Pratt emphasized how subjects and subject positions are co-constructed between people from social, cultural, and historical backgrounds that are often disparate; these multifaceted transactional encounters are often fraught with complex power dynamics and differentials.

Pratt's (2008) work provides a provocative conceptual lens for us (Pauline, Ufemia, and Cynthia) as we contemplate the manner in which we entered into a contact zone approximately 5 years ago. We experienced diverse transactional encounters with different agendas and purposes throughout our collaboration. For the purposes of this chapter, we foreground our shared experiences with, and developing understandings of, Fijian epistemology.

We begin with personal background information and information about the project that brought us together. We introduce key features of Fijian epistemology and discuss the history of our evolving understandings of Fijian epistemology. Then we consider implications of our understandings of Fijian epistemology for our work as teacher educators. Finally, we reflect on implications for our work with teachers as agents of social justice and compassion.

ENTERING THE CONTACT ZONE AND INDIGENOUS FIJIAN EPISTEMOLOGY

Pauline is a White Australian woman, Ufemia is an Indigenous Fijian woman, and Cynthia is a White American woman. We mutually recognize, respect, and honor one another's backgrounds and expertise. We are all academics in our respective countries. We came together to collaborate (with a host of other scholars) on a 3-year federal grant funded by the Australian government[2] to work with in-country Fijian partners to develop and explore a collaborative community approach supporting preschoolers' vernacular and English language and literacy development in communities without access to early childhood services. Critical to this undertaking was striving to develop a deep understanding of Fijian epistemology. For this chapter, we draw examples from one community, Duavata (pseudonym), to explore Fijian epistemology and its potential role in teacher education.

Two Central Features of Indigenous Fijian Epistemology

Indigenous scholars in the Pacific region (e.g., Nabobo-Baba, 2006; Thaman, 2009) argue that thoughtful and appropriate teaching and research in the Pacific Islands must take into account indigenous epistemologies. *Vanua* and *talanoa* are two central aspects of Fijian epistemology that Pauline and Cynthia are learning from Ufemia and other Fijian colleagues and scholars.

Vanua refers to cultural norms or ways of being Fijian (Thaman, 2009). Vanua research "takes into account indigenous Fijian values, protocols of relationships, knowledge and ways of knowing" (Nabobo-Baba, 2006, p. 24). Attending to vanua means affording deep honor and respect to people of a community (Nabobo-Baba, 2006). As Ratuva (2007) described, educators and researchers using a vanua framework acknowledge three levels of knowledge in indigenous Fijian settings: (1) *kila ni vuravura*, knowledge about the empirical world; (2) *kila ni bula vakaveiwekeni kei na itovo*, knowledge about social order and sociocultural relationships; and (3) *kila ni bulavakayalo*, knowledge about the cosmos.

Talanoa refers to "the process in which two or more people talk together, or in which one person tells a story to an audience of people who are largely listeners. . . . Talanoa is guided by rules of relationship and kinship, shared ways of knowing and knowledge, and worldviews" (Nabobo-Baba, 2006, p. 27). "[I]t is the context of the particular talanoa that determines the appropriate behaviors and values for it" (Johansson Fua, 2014, p. 56). Used as a culturally appropriate Pacific research tool with de-colonizing underpinnings (Nabobo-Baba, 2006; Vaioleti, 2006), talanoa operates from a perspective whereby knowledge is socially constructed through dialogue governed by Fijian norms and worldviews (Johansson Fua, 2014).

Western Epistemology and Indigenous Fijian Epistemology

Table 12.1 provides a comparison between Western epistemological norms and Fijian vanua epistemological norms on three different criteria. While there are many other criteria we might consider, these provide examples of

differences meriting attention when engaging our scholarly work. Notice
the different conceptions of time, authority, and ownership of knowledge.

ENGAGING IN THE CONTACT ZONE:
INDIGENOUS FIJIAN EPISTEMOLOGY AND HISTORY

We further unpack key tenets of Fijian epistemology by introducing the
community of Duavata to illustrate the central role that local conceptions
of epistemology must play in cross-cultural scholarly work (see also Harris,
Brock, Diamond, McInnes, Neill, Camaitoga, & Krishna, 2018). Finally, we
situate this example in the broader history of Fiji.

Indigenous Fijian Epistemology in Duavata

Duavata is a small village on the main island of Viti Levu. Fifty-eight
families (345 people) live there. Duavata's people are Indigenous Fijian
and their first and primary language is iTaukei. Young children speak
iTaukei, which is used for all interactions in the village. Most adults and
older children who have been to school also speak some English. English
is one of Fiji's three official languages, along with iTaukei and Fiji Hindi
(sometimes called Hindustani). English is a primary language used in Fiji's schools and businesses. Some individuals in Duavata are employed in
government positions and as white-collar workers in various businesses.
Many adults work in blue-collar jobs as day laborers or babysitters. There
is one church in Duavata, a Methodist church, and most families in Duavata are Methodist.

In the following, we explore an epistemological tension that arose
in our cross-cultural research, illustrating (1) the complexity of striving
to learn and attend to cross-cultural epistemological norms, and (2) the
importance of employing research frameworks that allow for mutual
collaboration and learning during collaborative unfolding of research in
cross-cultural contexts.

Epistemological Tensions in Our Work. Whereas our Duavata community mentor was exceptional as the project's mentor in guiding and di-
recting the fieldwork in Duavata, Cynthia's initial lack of understanding
of the vanua, Fiji's cultural norms, negatively affected our first attempts at
using ongoing data collection and analysis to begin to build sustainability
into our work. During Cynthia's first in-country visit, she was invited to
attend a Duavata Methodist Youth Fellowship (MYF) Group meeting. At
the meeting, she learned that members of this MYF group were encouraged
to engage in community service. Cynthia asked the group leader if any of
the members wanted to help with the research project. Four members of the

Table 12.1: Epistemological comparisons between the Western Academy and
   Fijian *Vanua* Research (from Nabobo-Baba, 2006)

Western Academy	Fijian *Vanua* Research
Time The academy works on strict scheduling of activities and events.	*Time* In the *vanua*, there are stories to be exchanged and the "respectful presentations" to be made before interviews can begin. The flow of events does not follow a strict time schedule.
Authority/Consent The University IRB has the final say on research ethics.	*Authority/Consent* During a *sevusevu*, the ceremonial presenter talks in depth about the purpose of the research and asks the chief for consent for the research to go ahead. The chief's consent makes the research viable, not the consent forms from the university.
Ownership of Knowledge The scholarly work completed at the university, or in the name of the university, belongs to the university. The student must satisfy university criteria to earn a degree and be recognized by the field.	*Ownership of Knowledge* One belongs to a clan for life unless one has been banished. What a clan member owns, does, and achieves is seen to reflect the clan.

youth group agreed and worked with Cynthia and the Duavata community
mentor throughout the remainder of the project.

One objective of the project was to maintain project work between vis-
its. Cynthia worked with the MYF volunteers to develop a plan to continue
work between Cynthia's first in-country visit and her second. Upon arrival
at Duavata for her second visit, Cynthia learned the volunteers had not enacted the work plan. During a talanoa, a talking session, with the Duavata
community leader and Ufemia, Cynthia learned that this initial sustainability plan failed because she had overlooked the role of vanua in developing
and enacting the plan.

There are specific cultural protocols for developing and enacting plans
in Duavata. Inhabitants of Duavata are there by permission of the chief. The
chief and his relatives are considered the original landowners and are recognized as leaders. For a sustainability plan to work, it must be developed and

enacted with at least one of the recognized community leaders. The MYF volunteers could help carry out the plan, but it had to be codeveloped with one of the community leaders and the community leader must play a central role in the enactment of the plan. Once Cynthia understood and heeded this important cultural norm, it was possible to create sustainability plans that could continue after the project's end.

As this research project was designed according to a critical participatory action framework (Kemmis, McTaggart, & Nixon, 2014), the project design provided a vehicle to address such tensions during data collection and analysis. Consequently, as researchers interacted to collect and analyze data during and after Cynthia's second visit to Fiji, there was space to change course and adhere to vanua research norms (Nabobo-Baba, 2006).

Situating Indigenous Fijian Epistemology in History

Fiji's history is long and complex; we do not attempt to address the intricate nuances of this history here. However, we identify a few highlights and speculate about the role of vanua and talanoa in the historical context.

Prior to contact with the West in the 1600s, Fijians lived in various clans spread across many of the 300-plus islands that make up the country (Campbell, 1989). Fijians have a history of strong clan affiliations and loyalties within clans headed by *ratus*, or chiefs (Singh, 2012). While dialects and cultural norms varied (and do vary) across clans, protocols surrounding vanua and talanoa date back centuries before the arrival of Westerners.

Beginning in the 1600s, and increasingly through the 1800s, settlers from Great Britain, Australia, and the United States came to Fiji (Campbell, 1989). On October 10, 1874, Fijian chiefs ceded Fiji to Great Britain. The reasons given by scholars for this vary; possible reasons include, but are not limited to (a) one powerful chief (Ratu Seru Cakobau) felt Fiji might fall into undesirable hands, and (b) important ratus felt that British rule could mitigate internal rivalries among them (Singh, 2012). Whatever the reason(s), the choice to cede Fiji to Great Britain was made by Fijian ratus themselves and honored by the Fijian people. For our purposes, what was most significant is that cession happened absent a war. It is reasonable to assume that protocols surrounding vanua and talanoa played a role in the choice to cede and the peaceful manner in which it occurred.

The onset of British rule in Fiji caused a significant shift in Fijian society (Campbell, 1989). Great Britain brought many workers from India to Fiji as indentured laborers to work in the sugarcane fields shortly after assuming control of Fiji in 1874. Across the decades that followed, people of Indian descent (called Indo-Fijians) became a substantial percentage of the Fijian population. Today, Indo-Fijians make up over one-third of the total population of Fiji, which is just under a million people. Not surprisingly, peoples of Indian descent brought different cultural, linguistic, religious, and spiritual beliefs and norms to Fiji. There have been tensions between indigenous Fijians and Indo-Fijians, but significant strides have been made—especially in recent decades—to unite all Fijians as equal citizens under Fijian law (Singh, 2012).

Just as Fijians themselves opted to cede their country to Great Britain in 1874, in 1970 Fijians sought and amicably obtained independence from Great Britain (Campbell, 1989). Although he died 12 years before Fijian independence, many attribute Fiji's successful bid for independence to important groundwork laid by the renowned and beloved statesman Ratu Sukuna (Ratuva, 2007). Born the son of a prominent Fijian chief, Ratu Sukuna was an Oxford-educated scholar. Because Ratu Sukuna understood both Fijian and British cultural norms, his insights into both worlds allowed him to navigate both worlds successfully and to provide invaluable insights while the independence process was negotiated between Fiji and Great Britain.

As a brief, but important, aside, when Fiji gained independence from Great Britain, the Fijian legislative council went to Marlborough House in England to finalize the terms for Fiji's independence. Ufemia's father was one of the members of the legislative council representing Fiji in Great Britain. Like her father before her, Ufemia's role in the vanua is that of *matanivanua*, which is translated as "heraldsman" in English. Matanivanua are considered the eyes and ears of the vanua and are afforded the right and the responsibility to disseminate information and mediate between clan members.

SHAPING AND REFINING THE CONTACT ZONE: IMPLICATIONS FOR TEACHER EDUCATION

Through the process of talanoa, situated within our evolving shared understandings of vanua, we sought to understand Indigenous Fijian epistemology as the basis on which to collaboratively develop strategies for fostering children's literacy in and within a Fijian community. In the remainder of this subsection, we delve more deeply into the implications of our work for teacher education.

Teacher Education and Our Collaborative Work in Fiji

Ufemia, our Duavata community mentor, and other Fijian friends and colleagues taught Pauline and Cynthia, through apprenticeship, the power of understanding and respecting the vanua in order to develop sustainable language and literacy learning progress with families in Duavata. This concrete example of learning about vanua through apprenticeship revealed unseen epistemological tensions that needed to be mitigated in order to move forward. Our collaboration worked in large part, we believe, because we all shared a common goal: promoting the language and literacy learning of children in Duavata by honoring and building upon their backgrounds and experiences. Moreover, we were all open to learning from, and listening to, one another.

While our collaborative endeavor to mitigate epistemological tensions worked, there exist intricate and nuanced epistemological tensions in Fijian teacher education more broadly that are much more complex to navigate. Largely as a result of British rule, English is the medium of interaction in Fiji's official government, business, and education sectors. Moreover, Western epistemologies have shaped not only the language used in education in Fiji but the educational structures themselves in terms of curricula, pedagogy, and materials. Fijian scholars (e.g., Camaitoga, 2008; Taufaga, 2007) are working tirelessly to shift education in Fiji to reflect Pacific epistemological norms, pedagogy, curriculum, and materials.

However, this important epistemological undertaking in teacher education is fraught with complexity on many levels; we share but two here. First, we used the term *Pacific* above rather than *Fijian* because over a third of the population in Fiji is Indo-Fijian. Inclusive education in Fiji must take into account epistemological norms that matter to iTauki (Indigenous Fijians) and to Indo-Fijian peoples. The impressive Fiji national early childhood curriculum Na Noda Mataniciva (NNM) serves as one concrete example of how language and literacy curriculum development work might be enacted at all levels, including teacher education. NNM was collaboratively developed and written in Fiji's three official languages (iTaukei, Fiji Hindi, and English) by indigenous Fijians, Indo-Fijians, and Westerners, taking into account authentic cultural and linguistic best practices in early childhood education.

Second, there exists a mismatch between the epistemologies that undergird everyday interactions in Fiji and Western epistemology. Because Indigenous Fijians—who make up the majority of the population in Fiji—are socialized into vanua, there is a tendency to accept protocols and cultural norms instituted by broader structures of which Indigenous Fijians are a part (Taufaga, 2007). Taufaga (2007) argued convincingly that Fijians "cannot be on the sideline and allow others [i.e., Westerners] to decide how our ball game is going to be played" (p. 30). Moreover, in the process of reclaiming Pacific epistemological structures in education in Fiji, Taufaga (2007) stressed the need to build bridges between the current Western schooling frameworks and the Pacific epistemologies that undergird everyday life in Fiji.

Teacher Education in Australia and the United States

Pauline and Cynthia are White, English-speaking, middle-class scholars in Australia and the U.S., respectively. Pauline was born into working-class circumstances and socialized into Anglo-Celtic ways of knowing and styles of discourse that she found jarred when, as the first member in her family history, she entered university and struggled to appropriate epistemological norms privileged there. Cynthia was born into a working-class American family; she is the first member of her immediate or extended family to earn a doctorate.

Although both Pauline and Cynthia struggled to acquire the norms of academia, being born White in their respective countries did afford them racial privilege (Howard, 2016). Currently, they both live and work in institutions of higher education founded on White, middle-class, Western epistemological norms. We share important lessons from our work and learning in Fiji that Pauline and Cynthia take back to their respective national and institutional contexts.

First, just as Fiji is a complex cultural and linguistic context, so, too, are Australia and the U.S. Different epistemological norms are held by the various linguistic and cultural groups within each country. This means that the White, middle-class, Western epistemological norms privileged in Pauline's and Cynthia's institutions are not representative of all children and families served by educators. Thus, it is incumbent on educators who reflect the epistemological power structures in their respective countries and contexts to recognize and critique epistemological hegemony.

Second, we experienced firsthand in our Duavata work that epistemological norms are often invisible until we work with others who embody different epistemological norms and bump up against difference. We propose that it can be educative to purposefully put ourselves in different contexts where we are likely to engage with others whose epistemological norms differ. This can make visible to us our own epistemological norms as well as those of others. As a note of caution, unless we engage in deep self-reflection and critique when we interact within and across diverse contexts, we may reify hegemonic epistemological norms (Boyd & Brock, 2015; Brock et al., 2006; Pennington & Brock, 2011).

REFLECTIONS ON THE CONTACT ZONE: NEXT STEPS

David Foster Wallace (2009) begins *This Is Water* as follows:

> There are these two young fish swimming along and they happen to meet an older fish swimming the other way, who nods at them and says, "Morning boys. How's the water?" And the two young fish swim on for a bit, and then eventually one of them looks over at the other and goes, "What the hell is water?" (pp. 3–4)

In many ways, epistemology can be like the two young fish swimming in water. It (the water) is *there*, and we (the fish) are *there*, but we may not be consciously aware of *it* or being *there*. As teacher education scholars, we must attend carefully to our own and others' conceptions of epistemology. We do not argue that Western teacher educators should—or perhaps even *can*—adapt Indigenous Fijian ways of knowing. This would be impossible without being socialized into these ways of knowing. Rather, the issue is that Western teacher educators should seek to learn from and with the many families, students, educators, and researchers with whom they work from a wide variety of social, cultural, and linguistic backgrounds, realizing that underlying epistemological norms are often invisible and may conflict.

We offer three lessons learned from our own work that may be helpful to others seeking to promote equitable, socially just, and compassionate teacher education:

1. It is important to examine the epistemological stances that undergird our work as teachers and researchers. It is wise to self-question and self-critique, asking if our work within these epistemological stances is structured such that there is space for different ways of knowing, learning, and understanding.
2. It is valuable to work with, and learn from, others whose backgrounds, cultures, and languages are different from ours.
3. Our work as teacher educators is most generative and productive if we adopt an inquiry mindset that involves learning and deep and respectful listening. (McVee & Boyd, 2016)

As we reflect on our collaborative work across the past 5 years, we note that active and thoughtful listening to and with one another was, perhaps, the most powerful vehicle for collaborating across very different cultural, linguistic, and epistemological spaces.

NOTES

1. While acknowledging Pratt's (2008) powerful transcultural work, we use the term *cross-cultural. Transcultural* refers to features that transcend cultures (Brink, 1994; Pratt, 2008). Our work focuses on features of Fijian culture unique to Fiji and distinct from Australian or American culture.

2. This chapter is based on a research project led by Professor Pauline Harris, with Dr. Anne Glover, Dr. Elspeth McInnes, Dr. Jenni Carter, Alexandra Diamond, professor Cynthia Brock and Dr. Bec Neill. This research has been funded by the Australia Department for Foreign Affairs and Trading through the Category 1 AustralianAID Development Research Awards Scheme under an award titled Developing a community approach to supporting literacy for preschoolers in Fiji. The views expressed in this chapter are those of the authors and not necessarily those of the Commonwealth of Australia. The Commonwealth of Australia accepts no responsibility for loss, damage, or injury resulting from reliance on any of the information or views contained in this paper.

REFERENCES

Boyd, F. & Brock, C. H. (Eds.). (2015). *Social diversities within multiliteracies: complexity in teaching and learning.* New York, NY: Routledge.

Brink, P. J. (1994). Transcultural versus cross-cultural. *Western Journal of Nursing Research, 16*(4), 344-346.

Brock, C. H., Wallace, J., Poulsen, H., Herschbach, M., Nikolai, M., Johnson, C., Warren, K., & Raikes, B. (Spring 2006). Negotiating displacement spaces: Exploring teachers' stories about learning and diversity. *Curriculum Inquiry, 36*(1), 35–62.

Camaitoga, U. (2008). The way forward for ECCE in Pacific Island countries. In P. Q. Puamau & F. Pene (Eds.), *Early childhood care and education in the Pacific* (pp. 144–151). Suva, Fiji: Institute of Education, University of the South Pacific.

Campbell, I. (1989). *A history of the Pacific Islands.* Berkeley, CA: University of California Press.

Harris, P., Brock, C., Diamond, A., McInnes, E., Neill, B., Camaitoga, C., & Krishna, M. (2018). You, us and a bus: Exploring analysis as cross-cultural collaboration in Fiji. In S. Madrid-Akpovo, M. Moran, & R. Brookshire (Eds.), *Collaborative cross-cultural research methodologies in early childhood education* (pp. 169–186). New York, NY: Routledge.

Howard, G. (2016). *We can't teach what we don't know: White teachers, multiracial schools.* New York, NY: Teachers College Press.

Johansson Fua, S. (2014). *Look back to look forward: A reflective Pacific journey.* Suva, Fiji: University of the South Pacific Press.

Kemmis, S., McTaggart, R., & Nixon, R. (2014). *The action research planner: Doing critical participatory action research.* New York, NY: Springer.

McVee, M., & Boyd, F. (2016). *Exploring diversity through multimodality, narrative, and dialogue: A framework for teacher reflection.* New York, NY: Routledge.

Nabobo-Baba, U. (2006). *Knowing and learning: An indigenous Fijian approach.* Suva, Fiji: Institute of Pacific Studies, The University of the South Pacific.

Pennington, J. L., & Brock, C. H. (2011). Constructing critical autoethnographic self-studies with white educators. *International Journal of Qualitative Studies in Education, 25*(3), 225–250.

Pratt, M. L. (2008). *Imperial eyes: Travel writing and transculturation* (2nd ed). New York, NY: Routledge.

Ratuva, S. (2007). Man versus myth: The life and times of Ratu Sukuna. *Fijian Studies, 13*(1), 3–16.

Singh, T. (2012). Fiji's coup culture 1987–2006: A media perspective. *Pacific Journalism Review, 18*(2), 167–181.

Taufaga, L. (2007). Between two worlds: taking control of our destiny through relevant literacy. In P. Puamau & F. Pene (Eds.), *The basics of learning literacy and numeracy in the Pacific* (pp. 19–31). Lautoka, Fiji: The University of the South Pacific Press.

Thaman, K. H. (2009). Towards cultural democracy in teaching and learning with specific references to Pacific Island Nations (PINs). *International Journal for the Scholarship of Teaching and Learning,3*(2), 1–9.

Vaioleti, M. (2006). Talanoa research methodology: A developing position on Pacific research. *Waikato Journal of Education, 12,* 21–34.

Wallace, D. F. (2009). *This is water: Some thoughts, delivered on a significant occasion, about living a compassionate life.* New York, NY: Little, Brown & Company.

CHAPTER 13

Kenya's Education
An Eclectic Epistemological Collage

Lydiah Nganga and *John Kambutu*

For many African nations, colonialism and postcolonialism played a defining role in the creation of currently practiced epistemologies. As a result, Nyamnjoh (2012) noted, "The colonial conquest of Africans—body, mind, and soul—has led to real or attempted epistemicide—the decimation or near decimation or near killing and replacement of endogenous epistemologies with the epistemological paradigm of the conqueror" (p. 129). This reality holds true in the development of epistemologies in Kenya. Indeed, a well-thought-out hybrid of Western and indigenous epistemologies may be the best recipe for teacher education in Kenya.

Kenya is an East African country that is home to 42 different ethnic groups with a total population of roughly 45 million people. Prior to occupation and eventual colonization by Britain in the early 1800s, individual ethnic groups in Kenya lived in social groups where individualism and competition for personal gain was almost unknown; the welfare and survival of the whole ethnic group was paramount.

Before British colonization, different communities practiced traditional education or epistemologies of survival for millenia (Bukenya & Gachanja, 2004; Shillington, 1995). Indigenous Kenyans did not practice a single monolithic epistemology. Rather, each ethnic group enacted epistemologies that best met the survival needs and wants of the local people and developed essential survival knowledge and skills (Maeda, 2009).

During the colonial period (1820–1963), however, the British government enacted "African Education." The purpose of African Education was to neutralize African traditions and establish political and cultural spaces ideal for expansion of British colonial hegemony (Abreu, 1982; Mwiria, 1991; Ominde, 1964; Republic of Kenya, 1999). In addition to focusing on acculturating indigenous Kenyans into accepting and appreciating British cultural practices, competitive individualism instead of community gain was introduced (Gachathi, 1976).

Also prevalent were elevated poverty levels; without the mastery of skills and knowledge needed for white-collar jobs, many Indigenous Kenyans were employed in low-paying occupations, starting a culture of poverty still prominent. As a result, Kenyans developed a strong preference for academic success, seen as a solution to the high levels of poverty affecting them.

The newly formed Kenyan government at independence in 1963 introduced a "Kenyanization" program emphasizing the need for academic success as a solution to poverty (Nganga & Kambutu, 2012). The new government supported the use of high-stakes tests as measures of academic success. Additionally, it introduced new epistemologies to restore Indigenous cultural pride while providing local people with knowledge, skills, and dispositions essential for self-rule (Nganga & Kambutu, 2012; Wamahiu, 1996).

Clearly, then, Kenya has never had a single unifying epistemology. Instead, it has adopted a variety of epistemologies for national, social, economic, and political needs at different times. Yet postcolonial Kenya has a preference for academic success as measured by high-stakes tests. Consequently, children are socialized to take academic work seriously and to compete for success. To ensure academic achievement, parents will do everything within their power to support their children (Nganga, 2012).

KENYA'S EPISTEMOLOGIES: BACKGROUND

Before Great Britain colonized Kenya in the early 1800s, different ethnic groups embraced Indigenous epistemologies. Kenya is geographically diverse: from coastal regions, to wet highlands, to arid and semi-arid areas (Nganga & Kambutu, 2010). According to Maeda (2009), Indigenous epistemologies were regionally determined because their role was to ensure survival; each ethnic group developed epistemologies that best addressed their respective needs and wants.

For example, the Bantu group, who were predominantly agriculturalist, focused on animal and plant preservation. Conversely, the Nilotes generally focused on nomadism (except the Luo people who settled around Lake Victoria, and therefore lived mainly on fishing) because they inhabited arid and semi-arid regions of Kenya (Ominde, 1964).

Ethnic epistemologies were taught orally. While it was the responsibility of all community members to teach essential survival skills, grandparents and community elders played important roles in preserving critical cultural practices, traditional organizations, values, languages, beliefs, worship knowledge, and skills; they were highly regarded educators because they had lived experiences (Bogonko, 1992; Bukenya & Gachanja, 2004).

Upon arriving in Kenya in the 1800s, the priority for the British colonial government was to create cultural and political spaces to govern Indigenous people. The most practical way was to undermine local epistemologies. To do so, the colonial government introduced African Education, championing the acquisition of British cultural practices (Gachathi, 1976) and a culture of competition for personal gain.

To ensure quick adoption of British cultures by Indigenous people, the newly introduced African Education adopted an "Asomi" epistemology requiring local people to learn British cultural practices first before studying the "history, art, literature, theater and dances" of the indigenous people (Ngugi, 1981, p. 4). The main goal of this education was to acculturate the local people with various British cultural practices and transform them into more agreeable subjects of British colonial rule (Mwiria, 1991).

Thus, the colonial government prohibited Indigenous Kenyans from developing critical thinking, leadership skills, curiosity, independence, and problem solving. Learning that focused on leadership skills was reserved for people of European and Asian descent residing in Kenya or ethnic Kenyans who were sympathetic and agreeable to British colonial hegemony (Léglise & Migge, 2007). By contrast, the British colonial government punished noncollaborators, a majority of Kenyans, by limiting them to elementary education only (not higher than 4th grade) that taught basic reading, writing, and arithmetic. Equally forced was the study of Christianity, along with mechanical memorization of skills deemed necessary for colonized people (Abreu, 1982).

Reflecting on the effects of African Education, Ojiambo (2007) concluded that it transformed Indigenous people into dependable and effective workers in various British enterprises. Maeda (2009) bitterly criticized African Education, labeling it a destructive epistemology that not only acculturated Indigenous Kenyans into believing and accepting subordinate roles in colonial Kenya but also introduced capitalistic ideas to a people who previously lived in social community groupings that attended to the well-being of everyone. As a result of African Education, Kenya became an increasingly competitive society that also struggles with issues of cultural identity confusion.

By the time Kenya gained political independence in 1963, it had an abundance of Indigenous people who mimicked British cultural practices quite effectively but with limited understanding and appreciation of Indigenous cultures. Through African Education and British rule, many Indigenous people developed distorted cultural identities that "normalized" British cultural practices (Ngugi, 1977, 1980). They tended to lack essential skills for self-rule, like critical thinking and problem solving.

Thus, the newly formed government of Kenya, headed by Indigenous Kenyans, introduced a "Kenyanization" education program whose main goals were to enact new epistemologies that would restore cultural pride while developing in the local people knowledge, skills, and dispositions essential for self-rule (Nganga & Kambutu, 2012; Republic of Kenya, 1976; Wamahiu, 1996).

The task of restoring pride in Indigenous cultures as well as preparing Kenyans for self-governance was monumental considering that a majority of ethnic Kenyans had adopted and internalized British cultural practices. After experiencing prolonged cultural insults from the British colonizers, many indigenous people had accepted a constant craving for "external recognition," participating fully in activities that supported "self-delusion and self-belittlement" (Nyamnjoh, 2012, p. 134). As a result, the enacted Kenyanization programs could not succeed unless they borrowed and adopted aspects of British/European curricula.

While the charge for the 1964–1965 Ominde Commission was to design an education that would restore Indigenous cultural pride and prepare a highly qualified Indigenous workforce, it adopted British academic curricula that were designed in Britain for English people (Wamahiu, 1996). And because the British education system used high-stakes tests, the Ominde Commission recommended the use of similar assessments in postcolonial Kenya as measures of academic success. As a result, epistemologies in postcolonial education continued to mirror British values both in design and practice.

For example, although Kiswahili was declared a national language after independence, English is still the favored language of instruction and therefore testing. Léglise and Migge (2007) noted that many learners who fail to master the required standards in English language at primary and secondary levels as measured in high-stakes standardized examinations are not able to continue with their education:

> At the end of the 8th year . . . a large percentage of children get weeded out of the school system with notoriously low academic skills. As for those who proceed to secondary school, poor language skills continue to hamper their educational performance because educators have until recently failed to see any direct link between good language skills and the ability to do well in exams. (p. 2)

The emphasis on English language as a "normal and natural language" not only supports British cultural hegemony, but also communicates the superiority and inferiority of British and Kenyan ethnic cultures, respectively.

To help solve the conundrum of adopting foreign curricula with limited value for the needs and wants of Indigenous people, the government of Kenya established additional commissions, including the Gachathi in 1976, the MacKay in 1981, and the Kamunge in 1988. These commissions recommended the use of curricula that would restore a sense of pride, dignity, and self-rule in Indigenous cultures (Republic of Kenya, 1999).

Notwithstanding the value of the proposed curricula, many Kenyans participated, albeit reluctantly because they still preferred epistemologies with a British tilt. On the economic side, an education with a British slant was advantageous while seeking employment in coveted white-collar jobs (Abagi & Odipo, 1997). Equally problematic was the use of high-stakes tests as measures of academic success in all Kenyanization programs. Learning in order to pass "the test" continued to be the priority in postcolonial Kenya because succeeding in high-stakes tests was and is considered a sure way to escape poverty. A high unemployment rate is an omnipresent challenge in postcolonial Kenya. Thus, all postcolonial epistemologies in Kenya tended to have a special focus on ideal strategies to reduce poverty levels in the country.

Increased parental pressure on educators to teach to the test has dramatically shaped epistemological landscapes in postcolonial Kenya. As standardization of curricula for purposes of focusing on national examinations is the guiding beacon, instructional strategies that are teacher-centered are widely used in Kenyan classrooms. Perhaps because of increased focus on good performance in high-stakes tests, the nation slowly drifted away from its goal of implementing an education for national cultural and ethnic cohesion. For example, Kiswahili, the national language (which would be a unifying factor), continues to be marginalized in favor of English (the language of instruction and testing).

Perhaps as a result of the lack of a unifying language and competition derived from the existing system of education, there has been an increase in ethnic tensions, a fact that became obvious after the 2007 presidential election that resulted in the death of nearly 1,200 Kenyans. As a result, the government realized the need to reevaluate the existing education system yet again. Consequently, it formed the Educational Provisions of Kenya Vision 2030 group that was fairly representative in terms of ethnicity and other stakeholders. The charge for the group was to make recommendations for an education system that would change Kenya into a middle-income society. After collecting data from different stakeholders, the Vision 2030 group recommended an education that empowered people economically, socially, and politically (Republic of Kenya, 2007). To that end, the government announced the introduction of a new education system in 2017 that would be diverse in scope, structure, and implementation (Wanjohi, 2017).

TEACHER EDUCATION IN KENYA

Generally, there are two groups of educators in Kenya: formal and informal. Formal educators teach in typical schools that implement government-required curricula, informal educators are responsible for teaching Indigenous epistemologies. As stated earlier, teachers for Indigenous curricula are mainly grandparents and other community elders who orally teach epistemologies of survival (Bukenya & Gachanja, 2004). There are no formal training programs for these educators. Rather, the ethnic-based survival knowledge and skills they teach are acquired through experience. Community elders teach younger generations by way of folktales, proverbs, riddles, songs, and dances.

According to Bukenya and Gachanja (2004), community elders are invited to different community ceremonies like harvesting, marriage, and initiation (rite of passage) to inculcate the youth with the knowledge and skills they need to function productively in their respective communities. For example, during harvesting ceremonies, the lessons taught focus on crop management and food preservation. On the other hand, young people learn about the rules and regulations that holistically govern community relations during initiation and wedding activities.

Although community elders have always had the prerogative of determining the knowledge and skills that the youth needed to master, the government has increasingly infused epistemologies of survival in formal school curricula via forms of oral literature. As a result, certified teachers are now also involved in teaching Indigenous epistemologies of survival.

All certified teachers in Kenya are trained using government-provided academic standards. During the colonial period, teacher training programs focused primarily on preparing educators of Kenyan origin to teach basic literacy skills that were implemented by African Education. This reality changed in postcolonial Kenya because the country had need for Kenyans equipped with skills and knowledge for self-rule and self-reliance. As a result, postcolonial teacher training programs used recommendations from the 1964–1965 Ominde Commission to develop standards that mainly focused on teaching a highly qualified Indigenous workforce academic-oriented skills borrowed from British academic curricula (Wamahiu, 1996).

Teacher training standards in Kenya are revised regularly in order to comply with recommendations from various commissions (Republic of Kenya, 1999). Kenya has three tiers of educators: teachers for preprimary level (0–5 years), teachers for primary levels (grades 1–8), and teachers for secondary levels (grades 9–12). Also available is training for special, vocational, and technical educators. Because Kenya has different tiers of educators, a variety of epistemologies and teacher training programs exist. But regardless of tier, all teachers are trained to prepare learners to perform well on high-stakes tests. With this focus on testing, preparing teachers who can apply teacher-centered instructional approaches effectively in upper grades is rarely the focus.

Currently, Kenya's education system has 8 years of primary education and 4 years of secondary and college education, respectively. At the end of every stage (8-4-4), learners complete high-stakes national examinations that determine each learner's future career. It is the government's responsibility to set passing and failing scores on standardized high-stakes tests. While learners with passing scores progress to the next level in the academic spectrum, all others pursue various opportunities based on the scores received.

Training for primary school teachers requires 2 years of education at a teacher training college. A satisfactory performance on the Kenya Certificate of Secondary Education (KCSE) examination (a high-stakes test) is a requirement for admission. The government compels all primary-level educators to receive training in all academic subjects that are taught at the primary level of education. A broad content, paired with lack of teaching and learning resources necessitates that teacher training programs use teacher-centered instructional strategies, lectures especially (Nganga & Kambutu, 2017).

The government of Kenya requires all teacher candidates in secondary education to have a university education (or higher diploma) and to specialize in two academic subjects. Teacher candidates for secondary education are required to embrace teaching strategies that enhance successful performance in high-stakes tests for their future students. As a result, a focus on teacher-centered instructional approaches is high in all programs that prepare teachers for secondary education.

Given the government's interest and focus on education for national cohesion, it is necessary to rethink the training practices in use, not only in the colleges that prepare secondary education teachers, but in all teacher preparation programs as well. Although teacher-centered teaching approaches have value, they are not necessarily effective when teaching skills for national cohesion, yet this is a critical goal for the Kenyan government. Rather, the use of educational epistemologies that embrace learner-centered instructional processes and learning, coupled with the use of authentic assessment instead of competitive high-stake tests, might be the answer (Kambutu & Nganga, 2009).

PREPARING EDUCATORS FOR SOCIAL JUSTICE AND COMPASSION: NEXT STEPS

Kenya lacks a coherent epistemology because the current curricula tend to be the combined result of political, cultural, and economic realities. But as a whole, Kenya's education is a product of colonial ideologies and Western/European epistemologies. A continued use of colonial-based curricula in Kenya has created ideal spaces for sustained marginalization of ethnic possibilities while maintaining British neocolonial hegemony.

Modern globalization, with its heightened human interdependence and interconnection in terms of cultural, economic, and political practices (Krieger, 2005), necessitates epistemologies that empower everyone. An education for empowerment is unlikely to occur in learning environments that embrace educators as the source of knowledge. Rather, empowerment is likely to occur when learners are invited to participate fully in their own learning through collaboration, critical thinking, and problem-solving skills (Nganga & Kambutu, 2012). An education that empowers is fundamentally different because it embraces learners' ideas. Consequently, learners are free and able to generate their own understanding of global issues, and also strategies to establish a socially justice world.

One crucial strategy, for example, is respect for Indigenous knowledge, a reality that was embraced by the 1999 Koech commission in its visionary recommendations for a holistic education that addressed issues of democracy, equity, respect, and tolerance, social exclusion, and income inequality (Nafula, 2002). An education thus designed and practiced is an education for social justice.

Indigenous knowledge has value. Because it is based on community needs and wants, it enables learners to develop better understanding of local problems, cultural heritage, and pride, values, and beliefs. Essentially, then, Indigenous knowledge is a social justice matter. Consider, for example, that while exposing learners to Western perspectives only could cause them to adopt a one-dimensional perspective, using Indigenous knowledge as part of curricula could facilitate the development of multiple perspectives, thus validating other ways of knowing.

Being a multiethnic society, therefore, Kenya is well placed to teach for globalization and social justice by not only embracing different ethnic epistemologies but by also continuing to use relevant and meaningful Western/European epistemologies. Using a mixture of epistemologies is beneficial. Such practice could allow learners to acquire knowledge and skills needed for success in both local environments and global contexts.

Critics like Briggs and Sharp (2004) have considered the inherent danger in using Western/European curricula that are largely normalized as universal ways of knowing. Indeed, when applied inappropriately, Western/European epistemologies have been used to expand the political, cultural, and economic hegemonies of the dominant societies in the world to the detriment of Indigenous beliefs and traditions. Thus, we recommend increased application and use of Indigenous epistemologies in all contexts, particularly teacher education, because they are developed to address the needs and wants of local people and communities.

REFERENCES

Abagi, O., & Odipo, G. (1997). *Efficiency of primary education in Kenya: Situational analysis and implications for education reform*. Discussion paper No. DP 004/97, Institute of Policy Analysis and Research, University Way, Nairobi, Kenya.

Abreu, E. (1982). *The role of self-help in the development of education in Kenya, 1900 to 1973*. Nairobi, Kenya: Kenya Literature Bureau.

Bogonko, S.N. (1992). *A history of modern education in Kenya (1895–1991)*. Nairobi, Kenya: Evan Brothers.

Briggs, J., & Sharp, J. (2004). Indigenous knowledges and development: a postcolonial caution. *Third World Quarterly, 25*(4), 661–676.

Bukenya, A. S., & Gachanja, M. (2004). *Oral literature: A junior course*. Nairobi, Kenya: Longhorn Publishers.

Gacathi, P. J. (1976). *Report of the national committee on education objectives and policies.* Nairobi, Kenya: Government Printer.

Kambutu, J., & Nganga, L. (2009). Moving from a standalone/teach-alone model to integrated pedagogical practices in a teacher education program. In A. Selkirk & M. Tichenor (Eds.), *Teacher education: Policy, practice and research* (pp. 389–402). Hauppage, NY: Nova Science Publishers.

Kamunge, J. M. (1988). *Report of the presidential working party on education and manpower training for the next decade and beyond.* Presented to His Excellency Daniel T. Arap Moi, President and Commander-in-chief of the Armed Forces of the Republic of Kenya. Nairobi, Kenya: Government Printers.

Koech, D. K. (1999). *Totally integrated quality education and training—TIQET.* Report of the commission of inquiry into the education systems of Kenya. Nairobi, Kenya: Government Printer.

Krieger, J. (2005). *Globalization and state power.* New York, NY: Pearson/Longman.

Léglise, I., & Migge, B. (2007). Language and colonialism. Applied linguistics in the context of creole communities. In M. Hellinger & A. Pauwels (Eds.), *Language and communication: Diversity and change* (Handbooks of Applied Linguistics, Vol. 9, pp. 297–338). Berlin, Germany: De Gruyter Mouton.

MacKay, C. B. (1981). *Second university: Report of presidential working party* (Mackay Report). Nairobi, Kenya: Government Printer.

Maeda, M. (2009). Education and cultural hybridity: What cultural values should be imparted to students in Kenya? *Compare: A Journal of Comparative and International Education, 39*(3), 335–348.

Mwiria, K. (1991). Education for subordination: African education in colonial Kenya. *History of Education, 20,* 261–273.

Nafula, N. N. (2002). *Achieving sustainable universal primary education through debt relief.* Kenya Institute for Public Policy and Analysis, Nairobi, Kenya. World Institute for Development Economic Research Discussion Paper No. 2002/66, United Nations University.

Nganga, L. (2012). Children and cultural socialization across two nations (Kenya and the U.S.). In O. N. Ukpokodu & P. Ukpokodu (Eds.), *Voices from the margin: Perspectives of African-born teacher educators on African and American education* (pp. 109–129). Charlotte, NC: Information Age.

Nganga, L., & Kambutu, J. (2010). Education in Kenya: Primary and secondary school curriculum development since independence. In J. Kirylo & A. Nauman (Eds.), *Curriculum development: Perspectives from around the world* (pp. 182–193). Olney, MD: Association for Childhood Education International.

Nganga, L., & Kambutu, J. (2012). Perspectives on public education in Kenya and the U.S. In O. N. Ukpokodu & P. Ukpokodu (Eds.), *Voices from the margin: Perspectives of African-born teacher educators on African and American education* (pp. 169–196). Charlotte, NC: Information Age.

Nganga, L., & Kambutu, J. (2017). Preparing teachers for a globalized era: An examination of teaching practices in Kenya. *Journal of Education and Practice, 8*(6), 200–211.

Ngugi wa Thiong'o. (1977). *Petals of blood*. London, UK: Heinemann.

Ngugi wa Thiong'o. (1981). *Education for a national culture*. Harare, Zimbabwe: Zimbabwe Publishing House.

Ngugi wa Thiong'o, & Ngugi wa Mirii. (1980). *Ngaahika ndeenda: Ithaako ria ngerekano (I will marry when I want)*. Nairobi, Kenya: Heinemann Educational Books.

Nyamnjoh, F. B. (2012). Potted plants in greenhouses: A critical reflection on the resilience of colonial education in Africa. *Journal of Asian and African Studies*, 47(2), 129–154.

Ojiambo, P. C. O. (2007). Quality of education as tool for development: A case study of Kenya's educational reforms. *The African Symposium*, 7(2), 113–119.

Ominde, S. H. (1964). *Kenya education commission report, Part 1*. Nairobi, Kenya: The Commission.

Republic of Kenya. (1976). *Report of the national committee on educational objectives and policies*: Nairobi, Kenya: Government Printer.

Republic of Kenya. (1999). *Totally integrated quality education and training (TIQET)*. Report to the Commission of Inquiry into the Education of Kenya. Presented to His Excellency, Hon. Daniel, T. arap Moi, CCH, MP. President and Commander-in-Chief of the Armed Forces of the Republic of Kenya. Nairobi, Kenya.

Republic of Kenya. (2007). *Vision 2030*. Nairobi, Kenya: Government Printer.

Shillington, K. (1995). *History of Africa*. New York, NY: St. Martin's Press.

Wamahiu, S. (1996). The pedagogy of difference: An African perspective. In P. Murphy & C. Gipps (Eds.), *Equity in the classroom: Towards effective pedagogy for girls and* boys (pp. 46–58). London, UK: Falmer Press.

Wanjohi, A. M. (2017). *New education system in Kenya: An excerpt from basic education curriculum framework*. Retrieved from schoolsnetkenya.com/downloads/new-education-system-in-kenya-an-excerpt-frombasic-education-curriculum-framework.pdf

CHAPTER 14

Confucian Epistemology and Its Implications for Teacher Education

Qi Sun and *Reed Scull*

This chapter presents Confucian epistemology and its importance for teacher education in the globalized world with calls for more social inclusiveness, global-mindedness, and cultural equality. First, we address the need to educate global learners and develop culturally sustaining pedagogy by learning from non-Western perspectives. Second, we introduce Confucian philosophy, epistemology, core teaching principles, and learning principles. Finally, we offer recommendations and implications for teacher education and K–12 practice in our multiethnic and multilingual society, which may expand the Western paradigm and deepen social inclusiveness through openings to non-Western perspectives.

CONTEXT

Increasing globalization and internationalization of higher education "has destabilized the normalizing and ordering cultures of modernity by bringing the binaries between self and the Other, between natives and non-natives, into a new kind of spatial relation" (Kostogriz & Doecke, 2006, p. 2); teacher education is no exception. In the West, with the global mobility of finance, goods, services, people, and their ideas, education must keep up with and proactively play a role in serving increasingly diverse learners and needs from different social, cultural, and ethnic backgrounds.

Given that we live in an increasingly interconnected world, teacher education needs more knowledge of other cultures to better human relations in our diverse society and to foster global citizenship (Aktas, Pitts, Richards, & Silova, 2017; Jorgenson & Shultz, 2012). Global-minded learners can grow through non-Western ways of learning and knowing (Merriam & Associates, 2007; Reagan, 2018) under culturally responsive teachers (Brown, 2007) and work toward cultural pluralism and cultural equality (Paris, 2012).

Culture plays a foundational role in constructing the education, teaching, and learning of a society (Chan, 2008; Tan & Chua, 2015). Teacher education and its K–12 practice has been facing increasingly diverse student populations who come from a multiplicity of cultural backgrounds (Nguyen, Terlouw, & Pilot, 2006). According to the National Center of Education Statistics (2017), in the United States 4.6 million public school students were English language learners (ELLs) during the academic year 2014–2015, 9.4% of the total. Among the 11 most commonly reported home languages of ELL students, 4.6% represented nationalities influenced by Confucian Heritage Culture (CHC).

Evidently, there is a critical need for preservice teachers and teaching professionals to gain knowledge and develop skills working with students from different racial, ethic, and cultural backgrounds (Cochran-Smith & Villegas, 2015), as "there is a pressing need for students to develop, from an early age, the ability to communicate with and relate to others from various racial, cultural, linguistic or national backgrounds" (Keengwe, 2010, p. 197). Introducing non-Western epistemologies to Western teacher education may help develop cultural pluralism and cultural equality (Paris, 2012).

Along with diverse learner populations are coupled issues of growing inequality resulting from globalized demographic and geopolitical changes, new immigration patterns, institutionalized racism, and the impoverishment of minority families. Yet classroom teachers are overwhelmingly White and not adequately trained to teach students who are culturally, economically, and linguistically different from themselves (Cochran-Smith & Villegas, 2015). The ability to understand one's own presence and context, and in turn interpret another's context, requires critical development and transformation in an individual's mindset (Sun & Roumell, 2017).

As professionals requiring continuing education and lifelong learning, teachers are obligated to learn from and appreciate non-Western perspectives, such as CHC, so as to broaden their cultural competency (Ball & Forzani, 2009), recognize other available cultures as "capital" (Bourdieu, 1977, 1986), improve engagement with nondominant languages, and bring updated knowledge and skills to the classroom. CHC still has profound influence on Asian people's education, teaching, and learning, even for those who have moved to and reside in Western countries, such as the United States (Cheung & Chan, 2010).

Students from a CHC hold distinctive ways of understanding the goal of education and the role of teachers, and show different learning preferences in and outside of the classroom compared with learners from other cultural backgrounds. These students also bring lived knowledges that are invaluable sources for mutual learning among different cultural, ethnic, and linguistic backgrounds. It is within this context that we introduce Confucian epistemology and discuss its value to teacher education in the West.

CONFUCIUS AND CONFUCIAN EDUCATIONAL PHILOSOPHY

Confucius (孔子; 551 B.C.E.–479 B.C.E.) was a Chinese educator, philosopher, and politician who considered himself primarily a scholar, teacher, and a transmitter of culture (Lin, 1938; Tu, 1985). Confucian teaching practice has profoundly influenced Chinese culture and education for centuries. Confucius helped model the role of the private teacher in the history of China, accomplish the idea and practice of lifelong learning, design educational contents and instructional principles and methods, and execute the broad application of liberal arts learning and the acceptance of students of all social backgrounds (Sun, 2011). Because of his historical influence on education, Confucius has been entitled the Centuries Exemplar Educator (万世师表) by the Chinese.

There are several concepts to mention before introducing Confucian epistemology:

- *Ren* (仁), generally translated as "humanity, morality, and righteousness," is the core value and serves as the theoretical pillar of Confucian education philosophy;
- *Li* (礼) functions as the practical pillar manifesting *Ren*; the true nature of human beings refers to properly expressing ritual and socially accepted human behavior through daily interactions with people and routines of life;
- *Yi* (义), justice, and *Xiao* (孝), filial piety, are essences of virtue, social order, and harmony that guide people's way of life through lifelong learning and practice (Chuang, 2012); and
- *Jun Zi* (君子), as the Confucian exemplar of the educated person and model of morality (Sun, 2008, 2012), is synonymous with a person of humanity characterized by outstanding knowledge, courage, and skills to access and practice humanity. A *Jun Zi* is not only able to establish him- or herself but also willing to enlighten others.

Confucian Epistemology

Confucian epistemology rests upon an educational philosophy that holds rich meanings about humanity and righteousness and the integration of moral, social, and political dimensions. From an axiological or value-theory perspective, *Ren* (humanity and righteousness) is the utmost virtue of the universe. It is the totality of morals, the summation of ethics. From an epistemological perspective, *Ren* is the knowledge of morality and humanity. Central to Confucian learning is to realize the wholeness of the conscious being, to become a balanced moral and responsible person. Confucius believed everyone was able to gain knowledge through lifelong self-cultivation and practice. *Jun Zi* is the Confucian learning outcome (Sun, 2012).

The Confucian view of knowledge is "to know *Ren*," the core of humanity and morality. Confucius stated, "Knowledge, if apart from the main stream of humanity and morality, serves little purpose except as an adornment" (*Analects*, Book XII, 221)[1]. Tu (1985) precisely described Confucian knowledge as "not a cognitive grasp of a given structure of objective truths; nor is it an acquisition of internalized skills but rather essentially, an understanding and channel of one's mental state and one's inner feelings to be human" (p. 19). Confucius saw *Ren* as an end for knowledge acquisition and dissemination. Without a spirit of morality and humanity, people become empty and unscrupulous, which implies that the acquisition of knowledge without the acquisition of moral judgment is dangerous (XV, 32).

Similarly, learning *Li*, the code of conduct governing proper behaviors, facilitates the practice of a moral person by action. Confucius exhibited a concrete example, not only learning to gain knowledge and skills but also to apply these skills in life: "Courtesy and gravity in conduct of himself; loyalty and reverence in serving his prince; kindness and benevolence in nourishing the people; and morality and justice in ordering and employing the people" (V, 17). *Li* illustrates how the rectitude of human beings is morally oriented. Thus, moral development and moral practice become foundations of learning and applying knowledge (Sigurðsson, 2017). In other words, Confucian education is not merely for the sake of knowledge but connects to the social contexts that need moral understanding and how to use knowledge morally and justly.

To Confucius, human beings are moral, social, and political beings, and learning happens within social contexts. In social relationships and learning processes, the various and constant interactions among people not only enable learning from and exchanging ideas with one another, but also create opportunities for individual and collective co-construction of new knowledge. Confucius valued the creation of an open-minded character. At a higher level, Confucius reminded us that to realize a commitment to one's own culture, one must go beyond simple-minded cultural or national chauvinism. It is thus that learning helps us relate meaningfully to an ever-enlarging network of human relationships (Sun, 2012) that present great implications in our globalized world.

Learning for Holistic Development

Confucius stressed holistic education for complete development. Confucius applied the pre-Confucius *Six Arts* of rites (礼), music (乐), archery (射), driving (御), the Book of Documents (书), and math (数) (Sun, 2012), and also developed his own Confucianized six arts: poetry (诗), the Book of History (书), *Yi—I Ching* (易), rites (礼), music (乐), and *Chun quo zou zhuan*

(春秋) (Jia, Pan, & Tang, 2009; Zhang, 2009). Each content area facilitates learning of knowledge and skills of various kinds for human development.

For instance, when ritual (礼), poetry (诗), and music (乐) are integrated, rites express actions while artistic expression represents feelings. Ritual helps people identify one another. Music assists people to enjoy their commonalties.

History becomes significant as we relate to our past and enter into personal dialogue with generations who contributed to the culture that shapes us today. Confucius believed that human holistic development is essential to establish oneself, raise a family, perform citizen's and leadership roles, and govern the nation.

Confucius strongly emphasized learning from one's own culture, history, and social-political situation. He regarded human experience and human concerns in the culture as being crucial to the process of learning to become human. Thus, as Sun (2012) summarized, Confucian epistemology exhibits a holistic version of learning to be fully human via lifelong learning and practice: There is not only the poetic version, the ritual version, the historical version; there is also the political version and a cosmic version of being human.

All these signify that to become fully human, one must learn lifelong and life-wide, and one must transform through holistic approaches toward successfully living in and interacting with worlds of many kinds (Sun, 2008). Confucius believed that everyone can learn and become knowledgeable, which has critical implications for equal opportunity and access in our society.

Confucian Teaching Principles

There are three primary Confucian teaching principles:

Individualization. Confucius recognized individual differences and adjusted his teaching methods to the needs, circumstances, and backgrounds of his students. For instance, Confucius provided diverse answers to the same questions raised by different disciples regarding *Ren* and *Jun Zi* (II, 5–7). Disciples received diverse responses because each had their own background, situation, and level of personal development; thus, Confucius endeavored to individualize his teaching to best meet each learner's needs. This principle describes how teacher education should pay close attention when working with learners from different cultural, ethnic, social, and economic contexts.

Apperception. Apperception means cognition through relating new ideas to familiar ideas, the unknown to the known. Confucius extensively drew upon students' previous knowledge and frequently referenced well-known historical events and classic texts. He also made effective use of the symbols, metaphors, analogies, and parables with which students grew up. Confucius said, "one can gain new insight through re-search (learning), what one has been learned may serve as a teacher" (II, 11). This implies that teachers should use the resources that learners from different cultural backgrounds bring to effectively teach diverse students.

Motivation and Facilitation. Confucius paid attention to motivation yet did not push students when there was no engagement in learning: "If one is not eager to learn, I do not open up the truth, nor help push any one who is not anxious to explain himself or herself. When I have presented the corner of a subject to any one, and she or he cannot from it learn some other things, I do not repeat my lesson" (VII, 8). Confucius encouraged learners to open their minds, to think for themselves, reflect on issues, and develop their own understanding. Motivation and facilitation encourage students to make their own conclusions rather than be fed what a teacher believes is good or true. As indicated in *The Book of Rites*, a teacher should lead but not herd, resulting in harmony; motivate and not discourage, bringing ease; and initiate and not complete, facilitating reflection.

Confucian Learning Principles

There are three primary Confucian learning principles:

Study Extensively. Extensive study describes how learning is not only from books but also from life and experiences, which is clearly reflected in the old and new six arts. "*Jun Zi* should study extensively, stick to his or her aspirations and interests, eagerly ask about what is not understood, and constantly reflect on what is at hand" (XIX, 6). In addition, what one has already acquired, one should not forget. In fact, one must constantly review lessons, which leads to further inquiry. Thus, the more we seek, the more extensive the field becomes, and the more extensive the field, the greater subtlety our knowledge attains. Confucius guided his learners to learn holistically and from all kinds of sources.

Think Pensively. To Confucius, learning and thinking were constantly integrated: "Learning without thinking is labor in vain; thought without learning is perplexity" (II, 15). He deemed reflection essential to full comprehension. In the realm of knowledge, we must associate what we know with what we remember and deliberate on their mutual relationships. Only then can conception be formed and information may turn into knowledge. Leaving room and time for students to think and integrate what they have learned is critical for deep learning.

Practice Earnestly. Confucius recognized the importance of learning through doing. In fact, learning must be applied. He urged disciples to be doers and not listeners or learners just for the sake of learning. In the opening sentence of *Lun Yu*, this whole idea is brought out clearly: "Is it not pleasant to learn with a constant perseverance and application?" (I, 1). In fact, he frequently practiced the skills he had acquired and tried all his life to apply them. Application is the meaningful use of what one has learned. "What is the use of being able to recite the three hundred songs if one cannot perform the official duties given, or negotiate properly when sent to other states?" (XIII, 5). It is clear that one learns for the purposes of application in life.

NEXT STEPS

Confucian epistemology highlights moral development. Knowledge serves holistic development toward the greatest goal of being fully human. One must learn and do, study and think, reflect and act, connect and construct. Confucianism recognizes various purposes and the multidimensional nature of learning. Learning and teaching are one entity with two sides, and teachers and learners both need holistic development via lifelong and life wide learning and practice. Addressing teacher education in a globalized world, we contend Confucian education perspectives offer meaningful implications.

First, a general familiarity with Confucian epistemology may help serve as a reminder, or perhaps better an inspiration, for teacher educators. Moral development as a critical part of Confucian learning may remind us of other works on the moral dimensions of teaching (Fenstermacher, Osguthorpe, & Sanger, 2009). Although different cultures may have established different values systems, teacher educators and teaching professionals may revisit works like Goodlad et al.'s (1990) *The Moral Dimensions of Teaching*, Nodding's (1984, 2002, 2008) care ethics, Peterson's (2017) compassion concepts, and Sergiovanni's (1994, 2009) conception of a school as a community.

In each case, these concepts move far beyond the mere espousing of values and contain ideas on how to actualize these values for long-lasting moral character building and truly caring about learners' growth as democratic global citizens. Learners' moral development helps lay critical foundations that support the success of already succeeding students by not only gaining knowledge and skills but also making morally correct judgments on how to use knowledge and skills for the common good.

Second, with an increasingly internationalized, multicultural, and multilinguistic student population, social inclusiveness, global-mindedness, and cultural equality are necessary for teacher education (Cochran-Smith

& Villegas, 2015). Confucius's example of learning from all people is a model for the creation of an open-minded character, which implies that learning from one another helps by exchanging ideas for better understanding, and also reduces cultural confusion and ethnocentrism (Reagan, 2018). Besides, Confucian epistemology emphasizes how lifelong learners must go beyond simple-minded cultural or national chauvinism, which facilitates a move toward inclusiveness, global-mindedness, and cultural equality.

Third, several Confucian teaching and learning principles offer both theoretical understanding and practical strategies. *Individualization* may be a great teaching strategy for culturally diverse learners who can connect to each learner's culture background. *Thinking pensively* may lead to reflective and deep learning.

Further, Confucian epistemology has important implications for educational leaders and policymakers. Instead of thinking of what teacher education *must* be, perhaps we may move toward more transformational thinking of what *might* be; from seeing accountability and its emphasis on testing as a way to achieve good teaching, we move toward seeing inclusion, diversity, and globalism as indications of excellent practice.

In summary, prevailing clusters of research and studies in teacher education accurately portray accountability, teaching for knowledge, and teaching for diversity and inclusion as distinct endeavors (Cochran-Smith & Villegas, 2015; Cochran-Smith et al., 2015). We believe a transformative view is needed. With Confucian epistemology, we may understand accountability and test scores as less of a benchmark and more of a first step along a continuum of conceptualization of teacher education, with teaching for global awareness, diversity, and inclusion as a more advanced step toward achieving professional excellence.

NOTE

1. The *Analects of Confucius* (*Lun Yu*) are cited throughout as (Chapter, Verse).

REFERENCES

Aktas, F., Pitts, K., Richards, J. C., & Silova, I. (2017). Institutionalizing global citizenship: A critical analysis of higher education programs and curricula. *Journal of Studies in International Education. 21*(1), 65–80. DOI: 10.1177/1028315316669815

Ball, D. L., & Forzani, F. M. (2009). The work of teaching and the challenge for teacher education. *Journal of Teacher Education. 60*(5), 497–511.

Bourdieu, P. (1977). *Reproduction in education, society, culture.* Beverly Hills, CA: Sage Publishing.

Bourdieu, P. (1986). The forms of capital. In J. G. Richardson (Ed.), *Handbook of theory and research in the sociology of education* (pp. 241–258). New York, NY: Greenwood Press.

Brown, M. R. (2007). Educating all students: Creating culturally responsive teachers, classrooms, and schools. *Intervention in School and Clinic, 43*(1), 57–62. DOI: 10.1177/10534512070430010801

Chan, C. (2008). Pedagogical transformation and knowledge-building for the Chinese learner. *Evaluation & Research in Education, 21*(3), 235–251. DOI: 10.108-/09500790802485245

Cheung, H. Y., & Chan, A. W. H. (2010). Education and competitive economy: How do cultural dimensions fit in? *Higher Education. 59*, 525–541. DOI: 10.1007/s10734-009-9263-4

Chuang, S. (2012). Different instructional preferences between Western and far East Asian adult learners: A case study of graduate students in the USA. *Instructional Sciences. 40*, 477–492. DOI: 10.1007/s1 1251-011-9186-1.

Cochran-Smith, M., & Villegas, A. (2015). Framing teacher education research: An overview of the field, part I. *Journal of Teacher Education, 66*(1), 7–20.

Cochran-Smith, M., Villegas, A, Abrams, L., Chavez-Moreno, L., Mills, T., & Stern, R. (2015). Critiquing teacher preparation research: An overview of the field, part II. *Journal of Teacher Education, 66*(2), 109–121.

Confucius. *Lun Yu [The analects of Confucius].* (1992). Trans. into Modern Chinese by Bao Shixiang & Trans. into English by Lao An. Shangdong, Ji Nan: Shandong Friendship Press.

Fenstermacher, G., Osguthorpe, R., & Sanger, M. (2009). Teaching morally and teaching morality. *Teacher Education Quarterly, 36*(3), 7–19.

Goodlad, J., Soder, R., & Sirotnik, K. (Eds.). (1990). *The moral dimensions of teaching.* San Francisco, CA: Jossey-Bass.

ICE/NCES. (May, 2017). *English language learners in public school.* Retrieved from nces.ed.gov/programs/coe/indicator_cgf.asp

Jia, S., Pan, D., & Tang, P. (2009). 论语新编诠释。[*Reorganizing themes of the Analects with new interpretations*]. Chengdu, China: Si Chuan Publishing Group, Bashu Book Society.

Jorgenson, S., & Shultz, L. (2012). Global citizenship education (GCE) in postsecondary institutions: What is protected and what is hidden under the umbrella of GCE? *Journal of Global Citizenship & Equity Education, 2*(1), 1–22.

Keengwe, J. (2010). Fostering cross cultural competence in preservice teachers through multicultural education experiences. *Early Childhood Education Journal, 38*, 197–204.

Kostogriz, A., & Doecke, B. (2006). Encounters with strangers: Towards dialogical ethics in English education. Paper presented at The Natives are Restless: Shifting Boundaries of Language and Identity Conference, Monash University, Clayton, Australia, March 3, 2006.

Lin, Y. (1938). *The wisdom of Confucius.* New York, NY: Random House.

Merriam S. B., & Associates. (2007). *Non-western perspectives on learning and knowing.* Malabar, FL: Krieger.

Noddings, N. (1984). *Caring: A feminine approach to ethics and moral education.* Berkeley, CA: University of California Press.

Noddings, N. (2002). *Educating moral people: Essays on moral education.* New York, NY: Teachers College Press.

Noddings, N. (2008). Spirituality and religion in public schooling. *Teachers College Record, 110*(17), 185–195.

Nguyen, P., Terlouw, C., & Pilot, A. (2006). Culturally appropriate pedagogy: The case of group learning in a Confucian Heritage Culture context. *Intercultural Education, 17*(1), 1–19. DOI: 10.1080/14675980500502172

Paris, D. (2012). Culturally sustaining pedagogy: A needed change in stance, terminology, and practice. *Educational Researcher, 41*(3), 93–97. DOI: 10.3102/0013189X12441244

Peterson, A. (2017). *Compassion and education: Cultivating compassionate children, schools, and communities.* London, UK: Palgrave-Macmillan.

Reagan, T. (2018). *Non-Western educational traditions: Local approaches to thought and practice* (4th ed.). New York, NY: Routledge.

Sergiovanni, T. (1994). *Building community in schools.* San Francisco, CA: Jossey-Bass.

Sergiovanni, T. (2009). *The principalship: A reflective practice perspective.* Boston, MA: Pearson Publishers.

Sigurðsson, G. (2017). Transformative critique: What Confucianism can contribute to contemporary education. *Studies in Philosophy & Education, 36,* 131–146. DOI: 10.1007/s11217-015-9502-3.

Sun, Q. (2008). Confucian educational philosophy and its implication for lifelong learning and lifelong education. *International Journal of Lifelong Education, 27*(5), 559–578.

Sun, Q. (2011). *East meets West: Perennial wisdom for the ends/means issue of modern adult education.* Saarbrücken, Germany: VDM Verlag Publishing.

Sun, Q. (2012). The Confucian learning: Learning to become fully human. In P. Jarvis (Ed.), *The Routledge international handbook on lifelong learning* (pp. 475–485). New York, NY: Routledge.

Sun, Q., & Roumell, E. A. L. (2017). Interrupting the mindset of educational neocolonialism: Critical deliberations from East and West international adult educators. *Asia Pacific Education Review, 18*(2), 177–187. DOI: 10.1007/s12564-017-9482-9

Tan, C., & Chua, C. S. K. (2015) Education policy borrowing in China: has the West wind overpowered the East wind? *Compare, 45*(5), 686–704. DOI: 10.1080/03057925.2013.871397

Tu, W-M. (1985). *Confucian thoughts: Selfhood as creative transformation.* Albany, NY: State University of New York Press.

Zhang, X. (2009). 孔子的现象学阐释九讲：礼乐人生与哲学。[Review and nice lectures of interpretations of the phenomenon of Confucius: Ritual and music in life and philosophy]. Shanghai, China: China Eastern Normal University Publisher.

CHAPTER 15

Critical Race Theory and Teacher Education
Toward Compassionate Coalitions for the Future?

Andrew Peterson and *Robert Hattam*

The chapters in this book have drawn on a range of perspectives to examine the meaning, place, role, expression, and complexities of Critical Race Theory in teacher education. Asked by the editors of the collection to author a concluding chapter that both summarizes the contents of the book and highlights ways forward for future research and thinking, we seek here to say something about the ways in which compassion might act as a basis for building "coalitions for the future."

In our previous work, and drawing from different philosophical positions, we have each written separately of the importance of virtues and, in particular, the virtue of compassion (e.g., Hattam & Baker, 2015; Peterson, 2017). Our concern in this chapter is to offer some thoughts on compassion as a fruitful concept for framing cross-cultural dialogue that contests racism, and for working with preservice teachers to prepare them to teach in highly diverse classrooms. In advancing these thoughts, we wish to suggest that compassion is of value in understanding and challenging racism through education. We argue for a form of compassion that transforms power relationships in ways that respect human dignity and liberation and, on this basis, can play a role in delineating a "pedagogy, curriculum and research agenda that accounts for the role of race and racism" (Solórzano & Yosso, 2001, p. 3).

WHY COMPASSION?

Our interest stems from observing how compassion, appropriately framed and expressed, can serve to bring human beings into closer relation with one another. This need to learn to live together across cultural differences and avoid the perils of *interest convergence* (Bell, 1980) is a concern that runs through the chapters in this collection. Being mindful to avoid using the term in an overly generalized and ubiquitous way, we conceive compassion as a virtue:

> One which can be understood as a cognitive, emotional and volitional response to the suffering of others. Compassion is based on a recognition and appreciation of common humanity, including humanity's fragility. It requires empathic distress, care for others, and can inform and lead to actions in support of others. Compassion represents an expression of ourselves and our humanity, and relates to notions of the good life and human flourishing. (Peterson, 2017, p. 2)

An appropriate framing of compassion avoids a weak version that forgets that *self, I, me*; is constituted out of the ways that our countries and societies are governed; and hence renders compassion for others' suffering as purely psychological.

We are not speaking here of a "liberal, romanticized, or merely feel-good" (Darder, 2003, p. 497) version of compassion, nor the "long suffering or self-effacing variety" (p. 497) often invoked by religious dogma. A strong framing for compassion instead positions it as socially engaged. That is, as we understand it, compassion is a sensibility that can be cultivated, and which is felt in response to the systemic suffering of others. An example related to the struggle against racism is presented by Nelson Mandela (1994) who, in fighting the apartheid regime in South Africa, was very clear that the *system* of government, not individuals, was the problem, and on that basis he felt compassion even for his prison guards on Robben Island.

In a similar vein, Paulo Freire struggled against the suffering of those living in the favelas in Brazilian cities in the 1960s and beyond. Key to Freire's *pedagogy for the oppressed* was his insight that dehumanization was cultural and not natural, and hence arises out of social, political, and economic conditions. His response was often couched in terms of action on a *terrain of affect* (Hattam & Zembylas, 2010):

> I have the right to be angry and to express that anger, to hold it as my motivation to fight, just as I have the right to love and to express my love for the world, to hold it as my motivation to fight, because while I am a historical being, I live history as a time of possibility, not of predetermination. (Freire, 2004, p. 59)

For this chapter, the key tension is how critical educators can think past anger as "the first political emotion" (Critchley, 2007, p. 130) and work instead to cultivate a strong version of socially engaged compassion.

To engage with this tension we need, then, to consider what compassion requires of us in terms of engaging with others, recognizing the ingrained discrimination of others, and working in solidarity with others. A first step is to appreciate that—counter to its popular usage in public discourse—being disposed to compassion is not an altogether easy or straightforward task. As the Catholic theologian Henri Nouwen (2009) suggested, "Let us not underestimate how hard it is to be compassionate. . . . What we desire most is to do away with suffering by fleeing from it or finding a quick cure for it" (p. 18). In addition to facing the two challenges identified here by Nouwen, compassion also requires us to engage honestly (and, indeed, not without compassion) with our own self, including our histories, experiences, and actions—an engagement that requires a great deal of support and cultivation.

Compassion is difficult because it is shaped to a large extent by agent- and context-centered specificities. While we may have a general view of what compassion means, beyond this generality we need to appreciate and discern specifics if we are to exercise any meaningful judgment about what it is to be compassionate and what the compassionate thing to do is in a particular situation. From this viewpoint, it is more useful to consider how a given act or encounter is *more* or *less* compassionate than another possible action than it is to consider whether an act or encounter is compassionate or not in absolute terms. An adjunct to our contention here is that seeking to be compassionate is not a linear, developmental process; compassion is not automatic but involves ongoing cultivation involving honesty, courage, and reflexivity.

A second step is to recognize that a socially engaged compassion demands solidarity with oppressed and suffering others, with whom we have some sort of sympathetic fellow-feeling. Solidarity denotes the unity of common feeling and/or action between individuals and groups with shared interests. So far as solidarity is concerned, our thoughts and actions are framed to work *with* the other, and in this way solidarity embeds individuals within collectivities, providing and sustaining mutual care and support. On this reading, solidarity involves recognition of a shared fate among humans and an appreciation that the human condition can be, and often is, a fragile one.

For these reasons, solidarity brings people closer together, stemming from and building common interests, shared concerns, and mutual understanding. Moreover, solidarity involves a recognition of reciprocity, or what Nussbaum (2001) identified as a *eudaimonistic judgment*. Through this judgment, the suffering of others comes to be seen as inherently important to the life of the compassionate agent: "she must take that person's ill as affecting her own flourishing. In effect, she must make herself vulnerable in the person of another" (p. 319). In this way, solidarity brings the cause and interests of the suffering others into our own cause and interests. As Hattam and Baker (2015) contended, "compassion demands alleviating suffering and that includes one's own suffering, and the suffering of others, and hence the courage to transform 'one's own' mind-heart and those social conditions that sustain the suffering of 'others'" (p. 265).

COMPASSION, CRITICAL RACE THEORY,
AND TEACHER EDUCATION

Teacher education programs in many nations have become key targets for neoliberal and neoconservative forces. Through various means, these forces have acted to deprofessionalize the work of teacher educators (Cochran-Smith et al., 2018). Space does not permit us to elucidate this claim in full, but, for example, in 2013 the then–secretary of state for education in the United Kingdom, Michael Gove (2013), referred to academics who helped run university departments of education responsible for developing curricula and teacher training courses as "enemies of promise." According to Gove, these academics "seem more interested in valuing Marxism, revering jargon and fighting excellence."

Depicting debates about contemporary education and schooling as a "battle," Gove referred to "The Blob—the network of educational gurus in and around our universities who praised each other's research, sat on committees that drafted politically correct curricula, drew gifted young teachers away from their vocation and instead directed them towards ideologically driven theory." Writing in 2014, the now–minister of state for school standards, Nick Gibb, asked, "Who is to blame for our education system slipping down the international rankings? The answer is the academics in the education faculties of universities."

In place of serious and rigorous engagement with the discipline of education, politicians like Gove and Gibb say that beginning teachers should master decontextualized and uncritical forms of knowledge, curriculum, and teaching strategies. Yet, as each of the chapters herein reminds us, teacher education is concerned with much more than the acquisition of technical, mechanistic skills for the classroom.

A fundamental question raised by the authors in this book is whether teacher educators and their students wish to be part of a system that ingrains discrimination and oppression of various kinds—including racism—or whether they wish to work with others in compassionate ways to recognize (as a first step) and actively challenge (as a second step) discrimination, oppression, and suffering. In raising this question, we are mindful of the condition identified by Matias and Aldern (this volume): "An oft-invoked trope of preservice teachers is to 'help' or 'give back' to urban schools, communities of color, or students of color. CRT and critical Whiteness studies urge us to be sceptical of such readily accepted pageantries."

A further criticism common across chapters in this collection is that teacher education in Western democracies all too often focuses on Whiteness and the needs of White teachers, even when notions of social justice are invoked. In their chapter, Graham, Alvarez, Heck, Rand, and Milner define Whiteness as embodying "a complex synergy between racial identity and agency (Jupp, Berry, & Lensmire, 2016), while functioning as a property benefit related to power and privilege (Han et al., 2018; Harris, 1993)." Taking this critique seriously and working with compassion requires engagement with hard and sensitive questions about our own knowledges and positionality; that is, compassion necessitates that we are aware of the ways in which Whiteness is constructed and experienced in our own lives.

In turn, and as a necessary corollary, working with compassion requires that we understand how Whiteness can, and does, subjugate others as a feature of their everyday lived experiences. As Brock, Harris, and Camaitoga suggest in their contribution, "it is incumbent on educators who reflect the epistemological power structures in their respective countries and contexts to recognize and critique epistemological hegemony." Doing so, these authors remind us, provides opportunities to examine and reflect on "epistemological norms [that] are often invisible until we work with others who embody different epistemological norms." This said, in engaging with difference we must also be aware of the possibility that our understandings and (re)constructions of others may well be fallible. In other words, we must be cognizant of an empathic gap between ourselves and others.

Part of the weight compassion places on us is to be constantly mindful of this gap, and to continually work to ensure that, through various communicative and dialogical encounters, we actively work against misrepresentation and misrecognition. A core feature of CRT is the emphasis it places on hearing and valuing the experiences of people of color through their stories, texts, and testimonies. Beginning teachers need to encounter how structural forms of race and racism have shaped and continue to shape educational experiences, and how they do so through intersecting with other demographic realities (Milner & Laughter, 2015). In particular, through Critical Race Theory (Delgado et al., 2012; Gillborn & Ladson-Billings, 2010), we grapple with the following key tenets:

- Racism is endemic in our societies and sits at the center of exclusion and oppression of minority groups.
- Racism permeates policy thought and practice in education and in turn distorts all of our lives.
- We require a lens of *intersectionality* (Crenshaw, 2009) to discern and contest the ways that racism, sexism, and class are interconnected and work together to disenfranchise less powerful groups in multiple ways.
- *Counterstory telling* (Duncan, 2005) is one powerful way to interrupt the archive that perpetuates racism.
- We must reject (arrogant, whitewashed) monologic pedagogies and experiment with dialogic, improvisational pedagogies capable of sustaining a dialectical encounter across cultural difference.

We cannot take on all these themes here, but we want to argue that compassion can be enacted through practicing dialogic pedagogies. Rather than monologic approaches, variously referred to by metaphors such as banking, or transmission involving "lock-step teaching sequences" (Boomer et al., 1992, p. 5) experienced as "an almost self-perpetuating chain of subjections" (p. 5), we are advocating for dialogues that "consider the affective and sociocultural needs and identities of all learners" (New London Group, 1996, p. 85).

Dialogue here demands pedagogies of listening and a rejection of speaking for others. As Alcoff (1991–1992) argued, "The practice of privileged persons speaking for, or on behalf of less privileged persons has actually resulted (in many cases) in increasing or reinforcing the oppression of the group spoken for" (p. 7). Getting past *discursive imperialism* involves avoiding being part of a "conversation of 'us' with 'us' about 'them'" (Minh-Ha, 1989, p. 65). This involves tangling with a politics of representation; not only is speaking for or about others representing "who they are" (Alcoff, 1991–1992, p. 9), but it is also participating in the constitution of their subjectivity.

What is at issue here is that representation (negative, stereotypical, racialized, colonial) has material effects; it shapes attitudes and directly affects policy, employment, the labor market, and the political economy. Of special concern are long-term negative representations that become hegemonic, manufactured, and reinforced in literature, media, and the social sciences. A politics of representation then involves getting access to the means of cultural production and hence to engage in constituting what counts as common sense. In which case, we argue for pedagogies that enable our students to produce their own knowledge about "lifeworld problems that matter" (Zipin, 2017, p. 67).

Alcoff raised the ethical problem of whether it is "ever valid to speak for others who are unlike me or who are less privileged than me" (p. 7). Such concerns need to avoid erring toward those positions that obviate responsibility and to assume that "the oppressed can transparently represent their own true interests" (p. 22). Spivak (1988) took up this critique in response to Foucault and Deleuze's promotion of "listening to" as opposed to "speaking for." For Spivak, the problem is not speaking for or even listening to the subaltern, but learning how "to speak to the historically muted subject" (p. 295).

Spivak (1988) is often read as "an expression of terminal epistemological and political pessimism rather than . . . a challenge to articulate the discursive space in which we can meet finally the subaltern on her own terms" (Winant, 1990, p. 83). What is being proposed is a politics for dialogic encounters, for dialogic spaces, for dialogic pedagogy. The problematic of dialogic pedagogy is a significant theme in the contemporary educational literature, which Burbules (2000) summarized in his critiques of the fetishization of dialogue (p. 252)—that is, claims for dialogue that are caught between "the hope for the possibility of open, respectful, critical engagements"

(p. 252) and those exaggerated claims made on behalf of a certain kind of dialogue as inherently liberatory. The claims for dialogue are most fraught in contexts of cultural diversity, contexts in which dialogue struggles against the tendency to domesticate difference (Burbules, 2005).

As many contributors to this edition have suggested, intersubjective communication and dialogue make up a necessary process through which we as teacher educators can work with our students to recognize others. Indeed, recognition represents a crucial component of closing the empathic gap. Recognition on this account forms a fundamental basis of social justice (e.g., Fraser, 2005). As Taylor (1992, emphasis in original), reminded us:

> Our identity is partly shaped by recognition or its absence, often by the *mis*recognition of others, and so a person or group of people can suffer real damage, real distortion, if the people of a society around them mirror back a confining or demeaning or contemptible picture of themselves. Non recognition or misrecognition can inflict harm, can be a form of oppression, imprisoning some in a false, distorted, and reduced mode of being. (pp. 25–26)

NEXT STEPS

By way of concluding this chapter, and to provide a basis for identifying next steps, two further reflections are important. First, as a virtue that involves solidarity and eudaimonistic judgement, compassion recognizes the agency of sufferers, engaging with them as "capable and active, not as passive victims" (Hayes, Juarez, & Escoffery-Runnels, 2014). In the words often attributed to Aboriginal elder, activist, and educator Lilla Watson, "If you have come here to help me, you are wasting your time. But if you have come because your liberation is bound up with mine, then let us work together."

Second, Critical Race Theory engages compassion in identifying the problem of *false empathy*. Focusing on the importance of ally-ship with others, in their explication of false empathy, Warren and Hotchkins (2015) argued that "becoming an ally begins with an assessment of the nature of the oppression from the perspective of the individual(s) experiencing the oppression" (p. 270). Likewise, "it is likely that empathy becomes false empathy when left unexamined through a critical race lens" (p. 267). We contend that empathy alone is insufficient to bring about the sort of understanding and perspective-taking necessary for working with others to challenge and overcome oppression and suffering. Conceiving of compassion (which involves, but extends beyond, empathy) as a virtue manifests the centrality of critical dispositions through which the compassionate agent discerns the morally salient features of a given situation—including the experiences and interests of those oppressed and suffering—and deliberates about the appropriate course of action in response.

It is precisely these critical dispositions and the need to engage with the experiences and interests of those oppressed and suffering that we need to know more about. The chapters in this collection have done a fine job of elucidating both the challenges and possibilities involved in such work within teacher education and preparation programs. Yet there is a clear and compelling need for further research exploring how experiences and understandings of race and racism are framed and en/countered within teacher education programs in different countries.

A profitable focus for this research, continuing the aim of this collection, will be to examine and elucidate important specificities within given contexts while also seeking to identify commonalities and shared concerns that cut across contexts (including the intersectionality of demographic realities). Accepting that such work is neither easy nor straightforward, it is only through working in compassionate ways (ways that prioritize solidarity, reflexivity, and mutual shared concern) that meaningful coalitions between educators can be enacted and sustained.

REFERENCES

Alcoff, L. (1991–1992). The problem of speaking for others. *Cultural Critique, 20* (Winter 1991–1992), 5–32.

Bell, D. A. (1980). *Brown v. Board of Education* and the interest-convergence dilemma. *Harvard Law Review, 93*, 518–533.

Boomer, G., Lester, N., Onore, C., & Cook, J. (Eds.) (1992). *Negotiating the curriculum: Educating for the 21st century.* London, UK: Falmer.

Burbules, N. (2000). The limits of dialogue as a critical pedagogy. In P. Trefonis (Ed.), *Revolutionary pedagogies: Cultural politics, instituting education, and the discourse of theory* (pp. 251–273). New York, NY: RoutledgeFalmer.

Burbules, N. (2005). Dialogue and critical pedagogy. In Gur-Ze'ev I (Ed.), *Critical Theory and critical education today: Toward a new critical language in education* (pp. 193–206). Haifa, Israel: University of Haifa.

Cochran-Smith, M., Cummings, M., Stringer Keefe, E., Burton, S., . . . Baker, M. (2018). *Reclaiming accountability in teacher education.* New York, NY: Teachers College Press.

Crenshaw, K. (2009). Mapping the margins: Intersectionality, identity politics, and violence against women of colour. In E. Taylor (Ed.), *Foundations of Critical Race Theory in education* (pp. 213–246). New York, NY: Routledge.

Critchley, S. (2007). *Infinitely demanding: Ethics of commitment, politics of resistance.* London, UK: Verso.

Darder, A. (2003). Teaching as an act of love: Reflections on Paulo Freire and his contributions to our lives and our work. In A. Darder, M. Baltodano, & R. D. Torres (Eds.), *The critical pedagogy reader* (pp. 497–510). New York, NY: Routledge.

Delgado, R., Stefancic, J., & Liedno, E. (2012). *Critical Race Theory: An introduction* (2nd ed.). New York, NY: New York University Press.

Duncan, G. (2005). Critical race ethnography in education: Narrative, inequality and the problem of epistemology. *Race Ethnicity and Education, 8*(1), 93–114.

Fraser, N. (2005). Reframing justice in a globalizing world. *New Left Review, 36* (Nov/Dec), 1–19.

Freire, P. (2004). *Pedagogy of Indignation.* Boulder, CO & London, UK: Paradigm Press.

Gillborn, D., & Ladson-Billings, G. (2010). Education and critical race theory. In M. Apple, S. Ball, & L. Gandin (Eds.), *The Routledge international handbook of the sociology of education* (pp. 37–48). London, UK: Routledge International Handbooks.

Gibb, N. (2014, April 23). Teaching Unions aren't the problem—Universities are. *The Guardian.* Retrieved from www.theguardian.com/commentisfree/2014/apr/23/teaching-unions-arent-problem-universities-schools-minister

Gove, M. (2013, March 23). I refuse to surrender to the Marxist teachers hell-bent on destroying our schools: Education Secretary berates "the new enemies of promise" for opposing his plans. *Daily Mail.* Retrieved from www.dailymail.co.uk/debate/article-2298146/I-refuse-surrender-Marxist-teachers-hell-bent-destroying-schools-Education-Secretary-berates-new-enemies-promise-opposing-plans.html

Han, K. T., Scull, W. R., Nganga, L., & Kambutu, J. (2018). Voices from the red states: challenging racial positioning in some of the most conservative communities in America. *Race Ethnicity and Education, 14*(1), 1–5. DOI:10.1080/13613324.2018.1468751

Harris, C. (1993). Whiteness as property. *Harvard Law Review, 106,* 1709–1791.

Hattam, R., & Baker, B. (2015). Technologies of the self and the cultivation of virtues. *Journal of Philosophy of Education, 49,* 255–273.

Hattam, R., & Zembylas, M. (2010). What's anger got to do with it? Towards a post-indignation pedagogy for communities in conflict. *Social Identities, 16*(1), 23–40.

Hayes, C., Juarez, B., & Escoffery-Runnels, V. (2014). We were there too: Learning from Black male teachers in Mississippi about successful teaching of Black students. *Democracy & Education, 22*(1), 1–11.

Jupp, J. C., Berry, T. R., and Lensmire, T. J. (2016). Second-wave White teacher identity studies: A review of White teacher identity literatures from 2004 through 2014. *Review of Educational Research, 86,* 1151–1191.

Mandela, N. (1994). *Long walk to freedom: The autobiography of Nelson Mandela.* London, UK: Abacus Books.

Milner, H. R., & Laughter, J. C. (2015). But good intentions are not enough: Preparing teachers to center race and poverty. *Urban Review, 47,* 341–363.

Minh-Ha, T. T. (1989). *Woman, Native, other: Writing postcoloniality and feminism.* Bloomington, IN: Indiana University Press.

New London Group. (1996). A pedagogy of multiliteracies: Designing social futures. *Harvard Educational Review, 66,* 60–92.

Nouwen, H. (2009). *The way of the heart: The spirituality of the desert fathers and mothers*. San Francisco, CA: Harper.

Nussbaum, M. C. (2001). *Upheavals of thought: The intelligence of the emotions*. Cambridge, UK: Cambridge University Press.

Peterson, A. (2017). *Education and compassion: Educating compassionate children, schools and communities*. Basingstoke, UK: Palgrave.

Solorzano, D. G., & Yosso, T. J. (2001). From racial stereotyping and deficit discourse toward a critical race theory in teacher education. *Multicultural Education, 9*(1), 2–8.

Spivak, G. (1988). Can the subaltern speak? In L. Grossberg & C. Nelson (Eds.), *Marxism and the interpretation of culture* (pp. 271–316). Urbana, IL: University of Illinois Press.

Taylor, C. (1992). *The ethics of authenticity*. Cambridge, MA: Harvard University Press.

Warren, C. A., & Hotchkins, B. K. (2015). Teacher education and the enduring significance of "false empathy." *Urban Review, 47*, 266–292.

Winant, H. (1990). Gayatri Spivak on the politics of the subaltern: Interview with Howard Winant. *Socialist Review, 20*(3), 81–97.

Zipin, L. (2017). Pursuing a problematic-based curriculum approach for the sake of social justice. *Journal of Education, 69*, 67–92.

About the Contributors

Jared J. Aldern is a father and a PhD student at the University of Colorado–Denver. His scholarship is focused on racial identity development of Black children of White-identifying parents, and the deconstruction of Whiteness within family, government, and nonprofit systems.

Adam J. Alvarez is an assistant professor of urban education at Rowan University. His research investigates issues related to urban education and sociological factors that influence inequity as he focuses on supporting both preservice and in-service educators.

Ashlee Anderson is a clinical assistant professor at the University of Tennessee–Knoxville. Her primary research interests are foundations of education, sociology of education, equity and social justice, and cultural studies in education.

Brittany Aronson is an assistant professor of educational leadership at Miami University. Her research interests include critical teacher preparation, social justice education, Critical Race Theory, critical Whiteness studies, and educational policy.

Adeline Borti is a PhD student in curriculum and instruction at the University of Wyoming. Her teaching and research interests are in the areas of English as a second language, literacy education, and literacy teacher education.

Cynthia Brock is a professor at the University of Wyoming, where she holds the Wyoming Excellence in Higher Education Endowed Chair in Literacy Education. Brock's scholarly research agenda explores the literacy learning opportunities of elementary children from diverse cultural, linguistic, and economic backgrounds.

Ufemia Camaitoga is a highly respected early childhood expert in Fiji and the South Pacific. She is national president of the Fiji Early Childhood Teachers' Association, and she is a curriculum developer and writer in Fiji and the South Pacific.

DaVonna L. Graham is a doctoral student at the University of Pittsburgh. Her research interests include learning from Black teachers their perspectives on race talk with students, particularly regarding positive racial identity development.

Keonghee Tao Han is an associate professor at the University of Wyoming. Her research focuses on social justice in teacher education, counternarratives of faculty of color, and racial literacy in predominantly White university and elementary classrooms in rural settings.

Pauline Harris holds the de Lissa Chair, Early Childhood (Research) at the University of South Australia. Pauline has expertise in children's language, literacy, and literature; children's voices, participation, and citizenship; and matters related to the nexus of early childhood and literacy research, policy, and practice.

Robert Hattam is professor for educational justice in the School of Education and the co-director of the Centre for Research in Educational and Social Inclusion at the University of South Australia. His research has focused on teachers' work, critical and reconciliation pedagogies, refugees, and socially just school reform.

Derric I. Heck is a graduate research and teaching associate at the University of Pittsburgh. His research interests include identity development, race talk, and the role physical space can play as a facilitator of dialogue and learning.

Angela M. Jaime is director of Native American and Indigenous Studies at the University of Wyoming. Her expertise is in social justice, multicultural, and diversity education. Angela specializes in Native American and Indigenous education and the study of Native women and their experiences in higher education. Most importantly, she is a mother of two amazing boys.

Lamar L. Johnson is an assistant professor of language and literacy for linguistic and racial diversity at Michigan State University. He explores the complex intersections of anti-Black racism, race, language, literacy, and education.

John Kambutu is professor of education at the University of Wyoming. His research work is in cultural diversity, rural education, transformative learning and globalization/ internationalization efforts.

Judson Laughter is an associate professor of English education at the University of Tennessee, Knoxville. He specializes in Critical Race Theory, culturally relevant education, and teacher preparation for the diverse classroom.

Cheryl E. Matias is an associate professor at the University of Colorado Denver. Her research focuses on deconstructing the emotionality of Whiteness in urban teacher education, motherscholarship, and supporting women of color and motherscholars in the academy.

Gwendolyn Thompson McMillon is a professor of literacy at Oakland University. Her research examines the literacy experiences of African American children in their classrooms at school, and in out-of-school learning environments (especially the African American Church), to develop specific ways to improve academic achievement and ability to negotiate cultural border-crossing.

H. Richard Milner IV is Cornelius Vanderbilt Endowed Chair of Education and professor of education at Peabody College of Vanderbilt University. His research, teaching, and policy interests concern urban education, teacher education, African American literature, and the social context of education.

Lydiah Nganga is an associate professor of education at the University of Wyoming. Her research focuses on global education, multicultural education and transformative learning, contextually appropriate practice, curriculum studies, antibias education, and social justice.

Andrew Peterson is professor of character and citizenship education at the Jubilee Centre for Character & Virtues, University of Birmingham, UK. His research focuses on the connections between character and citizenship education, including civic virtues.

Jawanza K. Rand is a PhD student and dean's fellow at the University of Pittsburgh. Jawanza's primary focus is on identifying sustainable approaches to cultivating more critical, ethical, and equitable educational environments for public school students in urban areas.

Rebecca Rogers is a professor of literacy studies at the University of Missouri–St. Louis. Her research examines how educators and students work collectively to create the conditions for deep and meaningful literacy learning.

Caskey Russell is an enrolled member of the Tlingit tribe of Alaska. He is an associate professor in English and Indigenous and Native American studies at the University of Wyoming. He is the author of numerous articles and the coauthor of *Critical Race Theory Matters: Education and Ideology*.

Rachel Salas is an assistant professor of literacy at the University of Nevada, Reno. Her research focuses on the academic literacy needs of ELLs and the preparation of teachers to meet the needs of an increasingly culturally and linguistically diverse student population.

Reed Scull is the associate dean of the Outreach School at the University of Wyoming, leading distance education and outreach efforts. He was recently appointed associate professor in the College of Education's Higher Education Administration graduate program. He teaches courses in adult learning theory, continuing and professional education, and workforce training.

Qi Sun is an associate professor and program coordinator for the Adult Learning PhD Program at the University of Tennessee, Knoxville. Her research focuses include Confucian and Eastern philosophies on education, international and comparative education, non-Western perspectives on teaching and learning, and transformative learning in cross-cultural contexts.

Eric D. Teman is an assistant professor of educational research at the University of Wyoming. He specializes in arts-based qualitative inquiry, and his research interests include ethical and methodological appropriateness when studying queer individuals.

Andrew B. Torres is an Afro-Boricua father, partner/husband, poet, educator, and scholar, born and raised in the Bronx, who over the last 6 years has worked as a teacher, tutor, and workshop facilitator. Currently, Andrew is a doctoral candidate in social justice education.

Index